VOID

Library of
Davidson College

MARXISM and
INDIVIDUALISM

D. F. B. TUCKER

MARXISM and INDIVIDUALISM

St. Martin's Press · New York

© D. F. B. Tucker 1980

All rights reserved. For information, write:
St. Martin's Press, Inc.
175 Fifth Avenue
New York, NY 10010
Printed in Great Britain.
First published in the United States of America in 1980.

ISBN 0-312-51839-0.

Library of Congress Catalog No: 80-18389

To the memory of
Daantjie Oosthuizen

Contents

Acknowledgements
General Introduction … 1

PART I: MARXISM RECONSIDERED
Introduction … 11
1 Marx, Holism and Methodological Individualism … 13
   Individualism and Holism in Sociology
   Marxism and Individualism
   Marx's Response to Hegel
   Marx's Methodological Individualism

2 Historical Materialism and Consciousness … 35
   Lukács's Contribution
   The Base/Superstructure Distinction
   Marx and the Historicist Fallacy
   The Pluralist Challenge

3 Marx's Ethical Individualism and his Conception of Democracy … 57
   Ethical Individualism
   Marx's Critique of Hegel's Notion of the Autonomous Bourgeois State
   Marx, the Extreme Democrat
   Problems and Perspectives Relating to Marx's Democratic Assumptions

4	Marxism and Utopia: Macpherson's Contribution The Poverty of Radical Idealism Idealism and Utopia Marxist Utopian Theory	85
5	Problems with Marxism as an Ethical Theory Criticisms of the Marxist Approach The Marxist Concept of Freedom	106

PART II: RADICAL INDIVIDUALISM

Introduction		123
6	The Point of the Rights Thesis Possessive Individualism Utilitarian Individualism Radical Individualism	128
7	Rawls's Conception of Justice Rawls's Use of the Contract Device The Gambling Problem	146
8	Rawls and his Critics Robert Nozick's Response to Rawls Problems with Nozick's Conception of Justice The Place of Intuition in Moral Argument	161
9	Approaches to Democratic Theory Nozick's Theory of Democracy Rawls and Democratic Theory Radical Perspectives and Rawls's Liberalism Class and Political Power in Liberal Society	180
10	A Radical Conception of Law Authority Radical and Liberal Conceptions of Law	198
11	Disobedience and the Rule of Law Obligation and Civility – the Liberal View A Radical Conception of Civil Disobedience	212
Notes		230
Index		251

Acknowledgements

Some sections of this work have been presented at various times to conferences and seminars and I have enjoyed these opportunities to formulate my views and to benefit from criticism. Early versions of chapters 3 and 8 have appeared in the journal *Politics* and parts of chapter 4 in the *Melbourne Journal of Politics*. Part of the material was written while I was preparing a course of lectures at Melbourne University for the Interdepartmental Programme, *Classical Social Theory*. I should like to thank those whose criticisms and stimulation made the work seem worthwhile. Horst Imberger, who collaborated in running this course, was especially helpful and I learnt a good deal from the many discussions we enjoyed together.

Among my colleagues in the *Political Science Department* I owe a special debt to Adrian Nye whose suggestions were always well-taken and whose careful reading of the manuscript proved invaluable; I would also like to thank Alan Davies and Jean Holmes for their encouragement.

David Scolyer and David Wood helped with the reading of the proofs and Bonnie Doyle typed part of the manuscript. I should also like to acknowledge the help I received from those of my friends, particularly Michael Moynihan, Chris Ballenden, Michaela Kronemann and Ruan Maud, who read the manuscript at various stages.

My greatest debt is acknowledged in the dedication.

David Tucker
Melbourne University, April 1980

General Introduction

My purpose in the discussions which follow is to distinguish liberal from radical arguments within what has come to be known as individualist political theory. I hope to show, by reviewing a range of debate on topics currently of interest to political and legal philosophers, that many of those who are committed to defending 'left-wing' political positions need to rethink their attitudes towards individualist theory.

The work can be read as a commentary on some currently fashionable authors. I have chosen two works in particular as being worthy of extended consideration: I refer here to Robert Nozick's *Anarchy, State and Utopia* and John Rawls's *A Theory of Justice*.[1]* Despite the fact that these books have been deservedly acclaimed and that each has generated a growing secondary literature, there remains a need for the perspectives of both authors to be systematically assessed in the light of radical, and especially Marxist, political theory. I take C. B. Macpherson as an exponent of a Marxist view and Ronald Dworkin as typical of what I call a radical individualist.[2] A comparative approach, as I show, displays weaknesses in some of the arguments presented by even the most sophisticated liberal theorists.

I should state at the outset that the work is not intended to be about Marxism. I focus principally on Marx's own contribution and, where a contemporary statement is required, on Macpherson. The latter has provided a useful focus, partly because I have taken the idea of

---

* All notes are to be found at the end of the book, pp. 228–48

2 GENERAL INTRODUCTION

distinguishing 'possessive individualism'[3] from him; also, he is one of the few radical writers who have made an effort to deal with liberal theory on its own terms. Macpherson's interests are similar to my own, for his concern is to find what common ground there might be between liberal and Marxist political perspectives. He addresses liberals in an effort to persuade them that there is a great deal in Marxism worth taking seriously; my concern is to try to persuade Marxists that there is something to be learned from liberal writers. Thus, although it is hoped that this work will be of general interest to contemporary political theorists, the arguments and the exegesis of Marx are directed primarily at those who have taken Marx's criticisms of possessive individualism as a reason for rejecting all the good sense which careful analysis shows is to be found within the individualist tradition.

Marx's criticism of possessive individualism is well captured in the following statement:

> The further back we go into history, the more the individual, and, therefore, the producing individual, seems to depend on and constitute a part of a larger whole: at first it is, quite naturally, the family and clan, which is but an enlarged family; later on it is the community growing up in its different forms out of the clash and amalgamation of clans. It is but in the eighteenth century, in 'bourgeois society', that the different forms of social union confront the individual as a mere means to his private ends, as an outward necessity. But the period in which this view of the isolated individual becomes prevalent, is the very one in which the interrelations of society (general from this point of view) have reached the highest state of development. Man is in the most literal sense of the word a *zoon politikon*, not only a social animal, but an animal which can develop into an individual only in society. Production by isolated individuals outside of society — something which might happen as an exception to a civilized man who by accident got into the wilderness and already dynamically possessed within himself the forces of society — is as great an absurdity as the idea of development of language without individuals living together and talking to one another.[4]

We should also note the scepticism with which both Marx and Engels regard the notion of natural rights:

> We know today that this kingdom of reason was nothing more than the idealized kingdom of the bourgeoisie; that this eternal Right found its realization in bourgeois justice; that this equality reduced itself to our bourgeois equality before the law; that bourgeois property was proclaimed as one of the essential rights of man; and that the government of reason, the Contrat Social of Rousseau, came into being, and only could come into being, as a democratic bourgeois republic. The great thinkers of the eighteenth century could, no more than their predecessors, go beyond the limits imposed upon them by their epoch.[5]

I am fully in sympathy with the thrust of these sentiments — there is very little to be said in favour of an individualism which takes its orientation from a conception of the individual as essentially 'the proprietor of his own person, for which he owes nothing to society'.[6] So long as philosophers conceive of society as a device for the maintenance of an orderly relation of exchange between individuals relating to each other as proprietors of their own capacities and of what they have acquired by exercising them, they will continue to function as apologists for the many injustices engendered by capitalism. Marx's arguments are, however, directed only at this one extreme position, and not all individualists can be classified as 'possessive individualists'. We should note in particular that some writers, although clearly individualists, make no assumptions about proprietorship's being an essential prerequisite for the development of the human character; that it is possible to endorse a conception of rights which is primarily egalitarian; and that individualists do not deny that we are, in a real sense, creatures of culture and, as such, totally dependent on community with others for the development of our human capacities.

Once we realize that the radical critique of individualism has come to be a caricature, so that what is attacked is a straw man, it becomes significant to ask whether perhaps something is not lost to the 'left' because of the unremitting hostility towards individualism which is so characteristic of the popular polemic, as also of the more serious contributions made by radical writers. I will show that this is very much the case and to this end will argue:
(a) that, despite evidence of the kind illustrated in the quotations provided above, Marx and especially Engels ought to be classified as methodological individualists;
(b) that Marx and Engels were humanists who should be regarded as ethical individualists;
(c) that a 'radical individualist' position (which I distinguish by reviewing the work of Rawls and Dworkin) can be identified;
(d) that Marxism proposes an inadequate approach to ethics and to jurisprudence — I want to suggest that modern radicals can no longer afford to ignore political philosophy, and that they should be responsive to Dworkin's plea that we take rights seriously;
(e) that a radical approach to policy issues is the most reasonable (I shall do this by reviewing a wide range of arguments on topics of current interest to legal and political philosophers).

One method of analysis that I use throughout these various discussions is the distinctively individualist approach which has come to be described as game theory (more accurately, strategy analysis or situational logic). I assume that it is important, both for purposes of justification and in order to explain social phenomena, that we make an effort to demarcate how we would expect rational, self-interested agents to behave in various circumstances. The concept of 'rationality' which we need to employ here is, however, a very weak one. For example, let us take as our paradigm the three requirements listed by G. W. Mortimore:

1. The beliefs on which the agent acts are rational ones. It is plainly true that one way in which a man can fall short of rationality is by acting on irrationally held beliefs....
2. The end for the sake of which the agent acts is one which it is rational to pursue....
3. Finally, the agent believes that his action is better than any of the alternatives open to him, given his ends.[7]

We should note that a programme of situational analysis may often proceed even though requirements 1 and 2 are not satisfied. This is because theorists who adopt the method of strategy analysis employ a notion of rationality which, for the most part, takes beliefs and ends as given; they are concerned to imagine persons in circumstances where they can be clearly seen to have determinate wants and objectives and where there are often only a limited number of means by which they can achieve them. In such circumstances the theorist adopts a strategy of rational reconstruction and offers a conjectured explanation by showing that the action is objectively appropriate; that is, that a person or persons so situated, given even an outline of their particular aims and beliefs (which might be deduced from what knowledge we have about psychological variables such as wishes, memories and associations) would, if rational (in the sense that the agent is prepared to adopt the strategy which he or she believes to be the best available for realizing his or her goals), act in the way suggested. In this way the sociologist or historian can avoid many of the more difficult philosophical problems associated with the concept of rationality, for he has no need to define criteria in terms of which we may determine whether a person's goals are rational; nor need he set out reasons for claiming that some beliefs are rationally held while others are not.

Karl Popper, who has done as much as anyone to defend and articulate such an approach, describes the method in the following way:

admittedly I have different aims and I hold different theories (from, say, Charlemagne): but had I been placed in his situation thus analysed — where the situation includes goals and knowledge — then I, and presumably you too, would have acted in a similar way to him...The explanations of situational logic...are rational, theoretical reconstructions. They are oversimplified and overschematized and consequently in general false....Above all however, situational analysis is rational, empirically criticizable, and capable of improvement.[8]

For the most part, the method of strategy analysis is applied in a much cruder way in sociology than it is in history; this is because in modelling processes of social interaction one is usually forced to make certain simplifying postulates regarding the specific motives, beliefs and interests of agents. The sociologist may, for example, base an analysis on an assumption about goals and interests which, although accurate for most people in a given set of circumstances, are false in some instances; an economist, for instance, may assume that consumers wish to purchase goods at the cheapest price and that they will go to some trouble to achieve this goal, even though many consumers do not trouble to compare prices, and some may even want to impress by paying more for goods despite their poor quality. Examples here are businessmen who go to restaurants which are licensed to serve liquor rather than to those which allow customers to bring their own, even if the food is inferior, and those who purchase expensive perfume rather than equally sweet-smelling herbal mixtures in unimpressive packages.[9] Such an approach may be perfectly adequate where what is significant is the attempt to predict the most likely choices of a large number of similarly situated agents. What the sociologist tries to expose, using the method of strategy analysis, is not an explanation of one specific agent's action (as the historian might in reviewing the life of Charlemagne), but the likely interaction between different persons adopting strategies to realize their goals in structured circumstances.[10]

In political philosophy too a strategy approach is, I believe, a useful one. What we would hope to demarcate are the institutional arrangements which it would be rational for self-interested individuals to agree to, given certain assumptions about the human predicament. This approach has a long tradition, going back through Kant, Rousseau and Locke to Hobbes; it has also recently been revived by Rawls and Nozick, whose work I make the focus of my discussion.

Marx, as I show, was reluctant to take strategy analysis seriously in its application to normative problems. This was because, as he understood the so-called Contract approach, the method relies on postulating an account of an initial state-of-nature situation; but as Marx argues, the assumption of an individual squatting outside society is an absurdity, for persons can never be conceived of in the abstract. This same complaint is echoed by Macpherson and by many other radical critics. The former makes an additional claim, however, for he argues that the assumptions built into the state-of-nature accounts which can be found in the philosophical literature simply reflect the prejudices of the theorist responsible for constructing the abstract model.

There is, I believe, some force to these criticisms in so far as they are directed against specific writers, for example, Hobbes and Locke. As a general claim for the possible use of situational logic as a tool of normative philosophy, however, these radical objections are misconceived. This is because it is perfectly possible for writers to be self-reflective, so that they expose their own assumptions to rational scrutiny. We are, after all, free to make whatever assumptions we choose in constructing a state-of-nature model. Thus, Rawls attempts to justify all the psychological and sociological assumptions which he makes in discussing what he calls the 'original position'. Socialists are free to take issue with Rawls over his judgement and they may suggest alternative models, but they would be wrong simply to dismiss a strategy approach on the grounds that some assumptions have to be made. Marx himself, as I show, was prepared to work with an abstract model of the accumulation process under capitalist relations of production, and I suggest that if the problem of abstraction can be successfully coped with in the context of sociological analysis and economics, then it should be possible to apply a similar method to political philosophy.

I have divided the work into two parts: 'Marxism Reconsidered' and 'Radical Individualism'. In the first part I discuss the relationship between Marxism and individualism. In Chapters 1 and 2 I am concerned with Marx's methodology and provide an account of 'historical materialism', which I suggest can be defended on the grounds that it is based on the technique of strategy analysis; in Chapters 3, 4 and 5 I review Marx's contribution to ethical and political philosophy, and I comment also on the work of Macpherson, who has developed some of Marx's ideas in a fruitful way. In the second part of the book I discuss and identify a position in political philosophy which I call radical individualism. In Chapters 6, 7 and 8 I review the work of Rawls and Dworkin, whom I take to be exponents of such a position. I defend their conception of justice against some of the criticisms which have been directed at it. In the last few chapters of the work I demonstrate, by reviewing a wide range of topics of contemporary interest, that a radical individualist approach to political issues is the most reasonable.

In Chapter 9 I look at approaches to the problem of assessing political institutions and distinguish competing conceptions of the democratic commitment; in Chapter 10 I discuss competing conceptions of law; and in Chapter 11 I discuss the problem of civil disobedience, distinguishing liberal from radical approaches to the phenomenon.

PART I
MARXISM RECONSIDERED

Introduction

In Part I I am concerned to show that Marx, despite his criticism of abstract individualism and the anti-humanist polemic which can be found in much of his mature work, should be regarded as both an ethical and a methodological individualist.[1] I argue that Marx's criticisms of individualism are directed at those Utopian writers who fail adequately to face up to sociological realities and at the position which Macpherson has called 'possessive individualism'. They are not directed at the method of strategy analysis, typically used by the classical utilitarian economists (whom Marx admired for their method); nor are they directed at the Kantian notion that what distinguishes the human essence is that persons are rational agents with distinctive purposes and goals of their own. As the French scholar Louis Althusser has persuasively argued,[2] there is a shift of emphasis which makes it important to distinguish Marx's early humanism and rationalism from the work of his mature period. We can agree also that what is distinctive about mature Marxism is the development of a sociological theory, 'historical materialism', and the rejection of approaches to political questions which offer as a solution the hope of moral persuasion. In opposition to Althusser, I would, however, suggest that there is nothing about Marx's materialism which sets it apart from other scientific approaches in sociology or economics. Indeed, Marx's methodology is characteristically individualist; this is so because the motor mechanisms that provide the connecting links between the important structural features of each historical period (that is, the relations of production and the means of production) and thus underpin his account of social change are the choices which rational individuals would make if they were intent on protecting and enhancing their individual interests. I shall suggest, further, that if we read Marx in the way suggested many of the usual criticisms which have been directed at historical materialism can be adequately answered; we can show why he rejects Feuerbachian humanism as Utopian; and we can appreciate the relationship between Marx's own humanism and his materialism.

Althusser thinks that because Marx developed a sociological sophistication which made him question the assertive humanism of Feuerbach, his own humanism – his Promethean ethic, as it has been called – was simply abandoned.[3] But this is not so. I shall argue that Marx retains his humanist values, but that he disciplines his commitment by trying to comprehend the social circumstances in which the rational choices of individuals would coincide with their species (or collective) interests as social beings. It is precisely because Marx's sociology is individualist that there is no sharp break between his humanist period and the work which followed the development of 'historical materialism' – Marx attempts to explain why humanity is alienated by offering a strategy analysis of the human predicament.

1

Marx, Holism and Methodological Individualism

As my purpose is to distinguish a radical position within what has come to be known as individualist political theory, it may be useful if I explain first what I mean by individualism. This is especially necessary in view of the fact that this topic has generated a great deal of confusion and controversy.

Briefly, I use the term individualism to stand for a way of looking at the relations between the individual and society. At the level of social analysis it involves, primarily, an attempt to model the relations between people in terms of strategy and conflict; alternatively, individualists attempt to base explanations on reduction, by postulating certain presumptive psychological generalizations about the human character. Individualism also embraces certain ethical commitments, such as the principle of the supreme and intrinsic worth of the individual human being and the ideal of self-determination.[1]

In this chapter and Chapter 2 I will be concerned with individualism as an approach in social theory; I shall be concerned to show the sense in which Marx should be regarded as a methodological individualist. In the chapters which follow I will consider ethical individualism; my purpose will be to explore Marx's ethical assumptions and to show how these are developed in to a theory of democracy. Although it will be clear that I regard Marx as both an ethical and a methodological individualist, I should state at the outset that there is no necessary connection between the two, so that it is possible (and is often the case) that a writer may be an ethical individualist but not a methodological individualist. Most commentators concede that Marx is an ethical individualist; many argue, however, that he is not a methodological individualist.

Individualism and Holism in Sociology

Methodological individualists make certain clearly discernible assumptions, by means of which they can be identified.[2] Most accept, for example, the idea that human nature and reason are much the same throughout history and, consequently, that we can understand different historical periods in terms of how we would expect individuals to behave, given our understanding of persons in general. I do not wish to imply here that individualist writers ignore the obvious differences in personality, temperament, attitudes, values and beliefs which are characteristic within and between various cultures. What individualists assert is that these differences reflect the varied circumstances in which people are situated, and are, in this sense, very much dependent variables. Individualists aim at establishing a science of society which is universal, and they believe that this is possible because human responses, as ways of adapting which are general and not specific to particular cultural periods may come to be known.

The individualist methodological approach provides a sharp contrast to other, more sociological (holistic or collectivist) orientations[3] in a number of ways. First, individualists assume that the study of human behaviour can be conducted in a scientific way, and do not regard the fact that human agents have a conscious awareness of what they do as an insuperable barrier to this endeavour. It is, then, never by way of a reference to consciousness or even to the peculiarities of particular cultures that individualists require us to formulate explanations, but instead by way of some specification of the resources and material circumstances which give rise to social behaviour: they are, in this sense, materialists.[4]

Second, individualists are sceptical of all explanations which attribute to social entities purposes apart from the concerns of the persons who function within them. Thus, they deny that history has any special goal and resist any temptation to explain social institutions using the assumption that society has needs which can be distinguished from those of the individuals who form it.

George Homans, for example, distinguishes certain forms of functional argument as a species of what he regards as unacceptable holism. He tells us that any attempt to explain a given institution (or set of institutions) by reference to some *social* goal (such as structural continuity) constitutes a misleading anthropomorphism. He traces this kind of functional argument specifically to Durkheim, to Lévi-Strauss and to his colleague at Harvard University, Talcott Parsons. What vitiates each of their positions, according to Homans, is their claim that we can leave individuals out of sociological explanations and need only refer to institutions and their relations.[5]

The two individualist assumptions mentioned above have guided the aspiration of many writers to develop a science of society. Even some of those most hostile to reductionism acknowledge that this aspiration has been of great significance in the history of social thought. Parsons, for example, who is amongst the foremost of these critics, suggests that individualism was a necessary stage in the history of social thought. He argues that we can trace a progression from the social atomism of Hobbes and Spencer towards an ever greater sophistication, which for him goes hand in hand with an appreciation of the limitations of reductionism, until, in modern times, theorists have abandoned their earlier preoccupation with the individual actor and now conceive of society in organic terms. The more successful theorists, Parsons tells us, have learned to focus on the way that social relations are co-ordinated within systems and are no longer directly interested in the acting individual.[6]

Parsons is mistaken in thinking that social theory has reached its culmination after a long progression from individualism towards holism; nevertheless his analysis of the stages of this development does correspond to the main theoretical positions within sociology today. Furthermore, his basic insight that theorists can be categorized by the extent to which they trace the determinants of human behaviour to the acting individuals, or ground explanations in some understanding of the system of relations from which individuals take their orientation, attributing some sort of autonomy to the social system itself, is extremely helpful.

It is worth noting the main points of dispute between holists and individualists, as these are stated by Parsons. He tells us that individualists have an ahistorical and asocial conception of the human personality; they do not adequately comprehend how much of our nature is a reflection of our social selves. He also argues that a crucial weakness of the individualist approach is the failure to produce any adequate account of social order. Both these faults arise, in his view, because individualists fail hopelessly to comprehend the cultural dimension of life.

Individualists have responded to these charges by arguing that holistic theorists have been too ready to embrace an organic conception of social life. The organic analogy, it is suggested, does not allow for change, and because of this those who adopt a holistic approach fail to see that the historical dynamic emerges from the responses of individuals — their anger, frustrations, outrage and needs — which transcend the so-called values of the system. With regard to their psychological assumptions, individualists assert that they do not claim that people are the same in all societies, but only that the differences between them need to be accounted for as a response by individuals to their circumstances. Presumably, then, it makes sense to suppose that all individuals will be likely to respond in much the same way to the hazards and difficulties of their material and social lives. It is worth exploring these disputes more fully.

Taking first the arguments relating to the psychological assumptions of theorists, it is important to note that there is no disagreement over whether people are or are not constrained in diverse ways by the fact that they find themselves in social situations: all sociology is concerned with the social determinants of behaviour. The rival theoretical positions on the issue of whether reductionism is a viable method in sociology arise from different assumptions about personality development, and from conflicting judgements of the relevance of certain psychological claims about the way in which values are internalized. There is some irony here, of course, for holists are claiming that the psychological assumptions of individualist writers are too crude. Parsons, for example, argues that they fail to pay sufficient attention of the interrelationship between institutions, which constitute a way of life, and the psychological qualities and attitudes of individuals. More specifically, what distresses Parsons and many other critics about the individualist approach is that it does not seem to take account, in any theoretically adequate way, of the important fact that humans are creatures who have values and whose behaviour is constituted by purposeful deliberations in the light of these standards. Parsons's point is that behaviour should not be characterized as a simple response to an environment, but must be comprehended in the light of what we know of the intentions of the agents responsible.

There is a good deal of force to Parsons's claim; nevertheless, as I have already suggested, his arguments rest on an exaggeration. Individualists do not suppose that people are not changed by their values, but only that sociologists should not dispose of the individual entirely when providing social explanations. But this is what holists must do, for if they are to be convincing, they must show that the acting individual is merely a puppet whose goals and aspirations are provided by the social system. Once the rival perspectives are stated in this way, it is not at all clear that the holist has the more plausible assumptions.

It is significant to note that some individualists (following Popper's exposition of Marx) are prepared to argue that the debate about whether or not there are any important residual universal human characteristics — aspects of our nature which are not culture-specific — is to a large extent irrelevant when we are considering whether we should use strategy analysis: we can simply leave the psychological dimension out of some sociological explanations. In this regard Popper quotes Marx's famous statement: 'It is not the consciousness of man that determines his existence — rather, it is his social existence that determines his consciousness.' What Marx is suggesting, Popper tells us, is that sociology should be concerned to discover the less obvious dependencies in the social sphere, those which are not consciously intended because they do not result from planning or conspiracy but exist despite ourselves. The sociologist does not accomplish this by ignoring the choices which individuals make, however; rather, he or she must show how what is intended comes to be frustrated. The focus of sociology, according to this conception, must be the interaction between individuals; it must show why their likely strategies in given circumstances will come to produce contradictory results. Not all sociology, then, is concerned, as Parsons seems to suppose, with the psychological dimension (or, as Marxists like to put it, with the problem of consciousness).

THE PROBLEM OF ORDER

Parsons's objections to individualist ways of theorizing, because they are directed primarily at the psychological assumptions which he attributes to reductionists, do not comprehend the many writers in sociology and economics who adopt a strategy analysis approach. Nevertheless, it is worth exploring Parsons's critique in greater depth, for he presses his point about the importance of values in social life most forcefully when he discusses the explanations provided by theorists to account for the phenomenon of social order, and this is an issue of crucial importance for all individualist writers (and, as I show, especially for Marx).

Parsons tells us that if we hold to a view of human nature which is purely passive, in the sense that we conceive of actions as mechanistic responses to environmental stimuli in the way that Hobbes and Bentham tend to do, then we must reach by way of deduction the absurd conclusion that order, and hence social life itself, is impossible.[7] Hobbes is himself perfectly well aware that rational egoists could not be expected to co-operate unless some common interest provided the appropriate motive; given his assumptions, it is difficult to see how there could be co-operation in what he describes as the state of nature. Hobbes thinks he can show, nevertheless, that it is precisely because individuals can be made aware of the problem of order, and so perceive the threat of anarchy as a real one, that agreement between them is possible. Further, he argues that individuals who found themselves in a state of nature would agree to establish a sovereign, because this would be seen as being in the collective interests of all. Parsons suggests, quite correctly, that this solution is untenable and that Hobbes's contract account of order is incompatible with his psychological assumption of rational egoism.

It is interesting to observe that these objections were anticipated by the philosopher David Hume, who modified the Hobbesian notion that passions are natural (not shaped by social life) to provide an account which shows how behavioural dispositions can be internalized through habit.[8] In doing this, Hume provides a solution to the problem of order which, in its essential point (that individual values need to be diverted from purely egoistic responses), is not altogether different from that offered by Parsons. In Hume's view, people come to acquire civil dispositions and 'internalize' such features of social life as respect for property through a process of socialization. By offering this theory of psychological development Hume links his own utilitarian individualist approach with more organic views of social life, such as those of Edmund Burke, effectively undermining the critical rationalism which would be the significant characteristic of a more atomistic, reductionist approach.

Most individualists do not find it necessary to show how values come to be co-ordinated socially, and they are more cautious than Hume in their judgement of the extent to which individuals can be said to be shaped and moulded by life in community with others. Although they would admit that we acquire social dispositions, they resist the temptation to see social life in organic terms. Individualists argue that socialization does not produce such an extreme change in people that no general characteristics of human nature remain. They feel free, therefore, to refer to what they regard as universal human dispositions to react in particular ways in providing explanations of behaviour, and they oppose those theoretical approaches in which cultural factors loom as an overwhelming obstacle in the way of the development of a general science of society. In their view, we do not have to understand each specific culture in its own terms but should seek out what is common to all mankind. Hume's notion of 'internalized disposition', based as it is on his claims about the importance of habit as the mechanism by which we come to be socialized, has not seemed plausible to most modern writers attracted to a holistic approach, and there has been a tendency to turn to Freud for a more adequate account. Freud's model calls on a reconstruction of Darwin's views.[9] Man's most primitive association is said to be a horde formed purely through biological bonds and the fierce coercive domination of the father. The state of primitive, unbridled, patriarchal domination is conceived by Freud as a state of nature, for there are no cultural bonds between individuals at this stage in human development. Thus, there is no reason, Freud believes, for distinguishing a horde of this kind from the sorts of association that we find among beasts. A central feature of this form of patriarchal tyranny is said to be the monopolization of women — the father prevents his sons from obtaining access to women, and when he gets too old to assert his dominance one of the sons kills him and takes over the monopoly by excluding the brothers. In the Freudian myth, in terms of which the socialization process is modelled, this state of affairs is brought to an end by a traumatic event: the brothers and sons who have been excluded from access to the women in the horde and who have had to submit to the domination of the tyrant patriarch at some stage form an alliance (although how this comes about is not made clear) and eventually muster enough courage to attack the patriarch jointly; after killing him, they devour him in a cannibalistic orgy and divide the women amongst themselves. This event is said to be of central importance, for the communal act of patricide can only lead to the rule of the brothers (as opposed to the return of another patriarchy) if they are able to sustain much of the repression previously brutally imposed by the father. The patriarchal order has been maintained through coercion; the brothers who dare to challenge the dominance of the father face exile, castration and death. After the tyrant father is removed, however, the situation becomes one of potential anarchy as each of the brothers faces the others as possible successors. Freud explains that civilization begins when instead of fighting for the right to all, the brothers abandon naked coercion as the foundation of social life and come to accept taboos repressing their natural desires. This self-imposed repression, establishing the sharing rather than the monopolization of women, constitutes the first normative order. It is also this internalization of values which, according to Freud, provides a reason for distinguishing human associations from those of beasts. Freud uses his mythical account of the origins of social life to model the processes of socialization which, he tells us, can only be fully comprehended by means of psychoanalysis. He writes:

> [we need to suppose] ...that the tumultuous mob of brothers were filled with the same contradictory feelings which we can see at work in the ambivalent father-complexes of our children and of our neurotic patients. They hated their father, who presented such a formidable obstacle to their craving for power and their sexual desires; but they loved and admired him too. After they had got rid of him, and had satisfied their hatred and had put into effect their wish to identify with him, the affection which had all this time been pushed under was bound to make itself felt. It did so in the form of remorse. A sense of guilt made its appearance which in this instance coincided with the remorse felt by the whole group....[10]

Freud goes on to explain how, because of their remorse and a sense of guilt about the murder of the patriarch, the brothers are able to renounce the fruits of their deed by resigning their claim to the women. It is through this repression of their most basic desire that the brothers are able to establish order, even though there is no patriarch to dominate through naked coercion. Freud claims, then, that it is through the psychological mechanisms mobilized by the impact of incest taboos on the human psyche that we are able to internalize values.

It is important not to oversimplify Freud's model. Superficially, it would seem that there is nothing in his account which is in conflict with individualism; this is because, in terms of his model, the reactions and dispositions of individuals (the response of the infant child to the father) are such as to generate tensions and frustrations, leading to a sense of guilt and to fear, which in turn direct the individual away from purely natural responses towards cultural conformity and self-control. We are, Freudians tell us, creatures with a capacity for civilized life precisely because we are able to suppress our natural, egoistic drives and accept in their place socially appropriate dispositions. A consequence of this is that people's actions are always culturally determined in ways so fundamental that what we can expect them to do is a function of what society has made of them.

Two assumptions seem to characterize the holistic approach. These are, first, that the important human dispositions in terms of which behaviour must be understood result from social interaction and vary between cultures and, second, that social life is only possible where values co-ordinated within a culture are internalized as part of the personality of each individual. Eric Fromm clearly reflects this kind of approach when he writes:

> It is not as if we had on the one hand, an individual equipped by nature with certain drives and on the other, society as something apart from him, either satisfying or frustrating these innate propensities. Although there are certain needs such as hunger, thirst, sex which are common to man, those drives which make for the difference in men's characters, like love and hatred, the lust for power and the yearning for submission, the enjoyment of sensuous pleasure and the fear of it, are all products of the social process. The most beautiful and the most ugly inclinations of man are not part of a fixed and biologically given human nature, but result from the social process which creates man.[11]

Individualists, by contrast, are usually much more sceptical about the importance of the impact of culture on individuals and seek rather to explain social life by showing how institutions serve the needs and interests of individuals. The general principle in this orientation has been set out as follows:

> ...all social phenomena, and especially the functioning of all social institutions, should always be understood as resulting from the decisions, actions, attitudes, etc., of human individuals, and...we should never be satisfied by an explanation in terms of so-called 'collectives'.[12]

Thus, individualists are not prepared to view the origins of social life in Freudian terms, for they do not accept the idea that incest taboos can be explained by way of a reference to the social need for order (as opposed to the anarchy of rational egoism).

Freud has been criticized for assuming that the original act of patricide would give rise to feelings of remorse and guilt. Surely such responses are only intelligible in the light of values, for why would any of the brothers feel guilty unless each had come to accept that it was morally wrong to kill? Freud, then, seems to be importing values into his account of what will take place in the state of nature, and in this sense he assumes what has yet to be shown.[13] Although most individualists have allowed that moral values are important in shaping some of the needs and wants of individuals, they have tended to accept Hobbes's view that coercion is the significant co-ordinating mechanism in social life. They have, consequently, taken the really important motor mechanisms at work in society to be those which have arisen out of the perennial struggle for guns and butter.

Marxism and Individualism

Marx's approach to sociology, as I have noted, is not reductionist, in the sense that it does not seek to deduce sociological explanations from psychological laws. For him the issues relating to psychologism did not seem to be very significant — indeed, no other major writer has displayed such a lack of curiosity about the psychological dimensions of social life. Marx's relationship with individualism is complicated further by the fact that he was a stern critic of a position in social theory which has been characterized as abstract individualism. Crudely stated, the position is distinguished by the attempt to understand the institutions of social life as being primarily responsive to the needs, interests and purposes of individuals (conceived in the abstract). Marx believes, in contrast, that what we are is for the most part dependent on the kind of society we find ourselves in, and it is this that consequently determines at least some of our needs. What people require of government and of others varies, therefore, according to the period of history and the kind of society in which they are living.[14] It is in this sense that Marx is Hegelian in his approach.

The fact that Marx criticizes a crude form of individualism and that he was indifferent to the psychological dimension with regard to his own work should not be taken as grounds for thinking that he was hostile to all the core ideas of those who attempted a reduction of sociology to psychology. Indeed, far from dismissing the method of reduction, Marx complains that individualist writers are not rigorous enough in applying the technique. Thus, he criticizes those writers of the seventeenth and eighteenth centuries who attempted to conceive of political obligation as arising out of a contract between individuals whom they envisaged as having definite opinions about what it would be rational for them to agree to. Such an approach, Marx points out, is inevitably vitiated by the fact that the allegedly abstract individuals negotiating the postulated contract turn out, on examination, to display values which reflect the social presuppositions of the philosophers; this is because they always have the needs and interests characteristic of a particular historical period. As Macpherson has shown, a common presupposition of the early Contract theorists seems to have been a view of persons as essentially proprietors, and the question they were asking in effect was: what set of political institutions would be most satisfactory to a community of more or less independent property owners?[15] It is this notion that ideally society should be constituted to cater for the interests of property that really offends Marx (and, of course, Macpherson). He argues that just as bourgeois economists seem to assume the universal nature of the market without comprehending the connection between commodity production and the specific property relations of the capitalist period, so the philosophers of the Enlightenment assumed, as if it were a fundamental and natural fact, that there could be no more rational basis for establishing the state than the protection of property rights.[16]

Marx's polemic, then, is directed at specific assumptions which liberals in his day made about property relations; it is not aimed at the materialist assumptions of individualist writers or at their rationalism. Thus, the idea of abstracting from the observations of social behaviour certain common traits (in the manner of, say, George Homans) or the notion of establishing a hierarchy of human needs (as is characteristic of writers such as Maslow, Fromm and Bay) are not ones that Marx would necessarily have objected to. Indeed, in *The Holy Family* and later in *The German Ideology* there are suggestions that Marx approved the development of a materialist psychology.[17] Furthermore, he makes clear that his own work is predicated on the idea that what we are as people is determined by our social circumstances, and he treats psychological factors as dependent variables. But if this is so, then it surely follows that Marx's own psychological views include some conception of a residual universality (of a nature which is common to all mankind). If he takes for granted that individuals will respond to similar circumstances in much the same way, then what makes for the differences between people must be not their variable nature but the circumstances in which they are situated. If characteristic ways of behaving are to be somehow related to the fact that agents are of a given character, then one cannot expect, as Marx clearly does, that where material circumstances change human dispositions to behave in particular ways will also change.

In fact, what is striking about Marx's work, setting him apart from those attracted to holistic approaches in social science, is his total lack of interest in the psychological dimensions of life; his focus is almost always on the mechanisms by means of which he supposes that individuals come to have their choices foreclosed, and in this regard he concentrates almost entirely on sociological factors, paying little attention to psychological constraints. Marx's theory of ideology and consciousness, for example, ignores those problems relating to the mechanisms by means of which values are said to become internalized; and his materialist account, especially of the relationship between consciousness and people's interests as members of a class, provides a sharp contrast to the neo-Freudian preoccupations of many modern writers who call themselves Marxists.[18]

I have emphasized that Marx is not a psychological reductionist in his approach to sociological analysis; nevertheless, if we look at what he actually says in the few places where he talks about his conception of human nature, we find that the assumption that there are general characteristics common to all mankind (which, of course, is different from the view that people are much the same the world over) is given very clear expression. Marx tells us, for example, that every person (simply because he or she is human) possesses certain potentialities or powers, and that we claim our humanity by fulfilling this potential.[19] Along with these powers go needs; these are what is required for the fulfilment of powers. Needs change with historical circumstance as humanity comes to realize its potentiality (illiterate people have no need for books, yet access to books is necessary if we are to develop in more advanced cultures), but they are common to all mankind, for we must all hope to satisfy our needs if we are to develop properly. It is because our human potentiality is common that our needs are universal. What is distinctive about Marx's approach is that he recognizes that what people actually want does not necessarily correspond with what they need (in the deeper sense in which he uses this concept), and that our capacities will only come to be developed in a human way where the expansion of humanity's productive power (to satisfy our material needs) is linked with the achievement of freedom. In this regard he suggests that the development of human potentiality is contingent on the abolition of capitalism as a system of production and its replacement by socialism. Thus, although industrial production under capitalism may have reached the point at which all human needs could potentially be satisfied, we are incapable of using this resource constructively. Marx suggests that this will continue to be the case as long as the market method of resource allocation dominates by structuring our relations to each other in such a way that we come to see our needs in alienated class terms. In such circumstances we will be unable (or at least very unlikely) to comprehend our truly human interests. It is because he believes that individualist writers misrepresented alien class needs, by suggesting that the characteristic wants of the bourgeois period are the universal needs of humanity, that his polemic against them is so bitter. Marx's objection is not that there are no human needs but that whatever these needs might be, they are decidedly not the interests of the property-owning class.

Marx's Response to Hegel

Marx's response to individualism was influenced by his reading of Hegel, who also criticized the philosophers of the Enlightenment for misrepresenting the true nature of bourgeois property relations (what Hegel calls 'civil society'). Hegel does not object to the fact that they take these rights to represent a universal human need, for he is prepared to go along with individualist writers on this point; he criticizes them because they fail to appreciate the complex relationship which ought necessarily to exist between the sphere of life where property is dominant and other spheres of life, such as that within the family and the realm of politics dominated by the state. Hegel tells us that the motives of citizens in the area of economic life are for the most part appropriately characterized by particularistic egoism; that particularistic altruism is appropriate in family relationships; and that political life requires universal altruism. Hegel points out, quite correctly, that if rational egoism is set up as some sort of human ideal, in the way that individualist writers sometimes seem to recommend, then because the restraining force of the state (mediated by an impartial bureaucracy) may come to be undermined, the complex pattern of interlocking relations which characterizes life in advanced civilizations could deteriorate into anarchism.[20]

Individualist writers did, of course, perceive the importance of social institutions other than those in the economic sphere, for they stressed the significance of the family and the state. What is often lacking in their approach, however, is a realistic grasp of the importance of values; consequently, their sociology tends to be rather crude, for they mostly assumed that all human actors were motivated by rational egoism. Hobbes, to take the most extreme of the abstract theorists, is a case in point, for although he acknowledges the fact that our capacity to develop as individuals depends on social institutions, what he worries about when reviewing his own society is the viability of market relations (that is, civil society). What Hobbes envisages is a world in which there is no state, and he comes quickly to the conclusion that there can be no moral life in such circumstances. He tells us that our capacity to enter into relationships with one another depends crucially on the civilizing role of the state as arbiter of disputes and enforcer of agreements. He reaches this conclusion because of assumptions which he makes about the greed, suspicion and envy of mankind.[21] It follows from this view of the human predicament that individuals, no matter how strongly motivated they might be, will be incapable of developing mutual trust and thus of emerging out of barbarism as long as they are without the mediation of a state capable of enforcing contracts.

In recognizing the civilizing role of the state, Hobbes is in agreement with Hegel; he explains the problems relating to the establishment of order rather differently, however, and his perspective provides a sharp contrast. Hobbes distinguishes between what he calls obligation *in fore interno* and obligation *in fore externo*; he writes:

> The Lawes of Nature oblige *in fore interno*; that is to say, they bind to a desire they should take place: but *in fore externo*, that is to the putting them in act, not alwayes. For he that should be modest, and perform all he promises, in such time and place where no man els should do so, should but make himselfe a prey to others, and procure his own certain ruin, contrary to the ground of all Lawes of Nature, which tend to Natures preservation.[22]

The central idea reflected here is that rational individuals would (and indeed should) be disposed to accept the constraints of contractual relations, and that they would do so even in the state of nature if it were not for the fact that they cannot afford to allow others to get into a position where they might be tempted to abuse trust. A rational acceptance of social rules as obligatory entails, Hobbes tells us, that there be some security. The reason for this is that in most contracts the person who performs his or her part of the duties first would have to submit his or her own claims to the discretion of the other party and, as Hobbes explains, this would not be prudent. It is for this reason that Hobbes urges the establishment of Leviathan; he argues that we need to be equally dependent on a sovereign before the basis for social trust can be established.

It is significant that Hobbes's notion of moral development is limited to a conception of keeping trust. In this regard his moral horizons do not seem to take sufficiently into account the full range of human emotions, and he says little also about the development of character or about virtues such as loyalty, humility, generosity and love. In so far as he does concern himself with the subjective side of life, this is because he sees that rational choices can be inhibited by emotions such as greed and envy.

Nevertheless, within the limitations of his conception of what is involved in moral behaviour, Hobbes's reasoning is sound: if individuals were in a state of nature in which their power to harm each other was approximately equal, and if they could set up a sovereign who would guarantee and impartially adjudicate contracts, then it would be rational (because prudent) to enter into a Social Contract to escape the hazards of anarchy. Hobbes's problem is that circumstances of the kind required by his theory cannot be said ever to have been definitive of the human predicament at any stage in history, nor is it likely that such circumstances will exist at any future time. Furthermore, it is not easy to see how individuals could contract from the state of nature into a society in which everyone's relationship with the sovereign is the same. One problem here is that the administration of coercion, needed to uphold the agreements made by individuals, would itself require the involvement of number of persons apart from the sovereign and, because of this, could involve inequality; those who have the sovereign's confidence would tend to have more influence.

More important, if certain individuals were especially trained to use coercion, they might often be placed in circumstances in which they would be tempted to abuse this skill; they might even be in a position to threaten the sovereign himself or to replace him with someone of their own choosing. Inequalities of a kind very dangerous to most individuals would, therefore, be likely to follow the establishment of civil society. Thus, unless Hobbes somehow provided his negotiators with a promise of institutional protections they would have little reason for entering into a social contract. But Hobbes gives no such guarantee, and his negotiators would, therefore, have no reason to trust the sovereign or those who act as agents for such an authority. As Hobbes himself has shown, those who had the advantage would know that the weak could not afford to return to the state of naked coercion in circumstances in which an unequal balance of power had already been established, and they would, therefore, be tempted to abuse their position. What is wrong with Hobbes's account, then (as Marx seems to have realized), is that his prognosis that equality in the state of nature would lead to a war of anarchy between 'everyman and everyman' may well present less of a threat to the negotiators than the prospect of the rule of terror which they would see as likely to follow the institutionalization of a coercive instrumentality.

A different objection to Hobbes's account of the social contract, stated by Hegel and endorsed by Marx, relates to what they take to be his oversimplified understanding of the civilizing role of institutions and his unacceptable conception of what it is to act morally. The case against Hobbes along these lines was first put by Rousseau, who argues negatively that Hobbes's argument rests on a *petitio principii*, which can more plausibly be reversed: where Hobbes had assumed the brutish dispositions of natural man and the civil character of social man,

Rousseau tells us that the contrary is the more likely; where Hobbes assumes that individuals enter civil society on a basis of equality (because they are all equally vulnerable to each other), Rousseau tells us that the state of civil society originated in inequalities which are inherent within the state of nature itself. Rousseau's account of the origins of civility is, moreover, a brilliant parody of the accepted wisdom of his day. He writes: 'The first man who, after fencing off a piece of land, took it upon himself to say, "This belongs to me", and found people simple enough to believe him, was the true founder of civil society.'[23] Rousseau's point is that once property is established individual owners have to combine together to protect it. This follows, we are told, because a natural inequality of talent leads to a massive struggle to accumulate even within the state of nature. Furthermore, once inequalities of fortune are established, those who have not been successful become envious and those who succeed succumb to the driving passion for glory which Hobbes found so disturbing. In such circumstances the position of the rich becomes precarious, for their very ability to accumulate places their lives and property at risk; hence, they must band together to impose a lawful order, transforming 'shrewd usurpation into settled right' and subjecting the 'whole of the human race thenceforth to labour, servitude and wretchedness'.[24]

What is striking about Rousseau's position, in contrast to that of Hobbes is the way in which he reverses the analysis: if one postulates equality in the state of nature, then, so Rousseau tells us, there would be no reason for envy, greed or the 'seeking after power' to emerge as prevalent human character traits (as Hobbes seems to have assumed would be the case). Thus Rousseau reasons, because Hobbes takes these characteristics as natural he has got his causal connections all the wrong way around – it is precisely because of civilization that these unfortunate traits have emerged.

Hegel appreciates Rousseau's reasoning – or at least the sensitivity which the latter displayed in outlining the processes by means of which institutional arrangements affect the development of our dispositions and capacities. What Hegel objects to in Rousseau's account, however, is his negative view of the socialization process. In particular, he argues that Rousseau is totally mistaken in thinking that primitive people had a nobility which the civilized lack. Rousseau does not think that individuals can develop very far beyond the merely animal outside community – there was no noble savage; however, he does claim that simple communities have a better chance of allowing the development of desirable virtues which, he argues, would be corrupted by life in more sophisticated societies.[25] Hegel questions this judgement. While he acknowledges the force of Rousseau's criticisms of Hobbes and agrees that the life of the simple savage in the state of nature would not necessarily be brutish or short, he argues that the latter, because he stresses that such an unstructured social environment would prove incapable of producing arts or letters, is surely more perceptive than the former. Although Rousseau is sensitive to the fact that our capacity to emerge as human persons depends crucially on the development of social ties, Hegel tells us that he does not fully appreciate the point, for he does not comprehend the functional role of institutions. He criticizes Rousseau, for example, because he does not see the positive role of the state, which must necessarily represent the collective interest of all. Hegel argues also that Rousseau has been too hasty in denouncing private property. He tells us that it is through their property rights that individual citizens are able to establish themselves as persons with a definite identity of their own, and that it is through the institution of property that our private interests come to be accommodated socially with those of others.[26]

Marx and Engels reject Rousseau's pessimism about modernizing imperatives and where they were leading, and they recognize that Hegel is fundamentally correct to insist that nothing can be gained for mankind through a nostalgic longing to return to some notional state of primitive communalism. They are, nevertheless, as is well known, much more sympathetic to Rousseau's radicalism than to Hegel's views about property's being a prerequisite for the development of our human capacities. Furthermore, they take over his romanticism, for they accept as a fundamental tenet the notion of the latent goodness of mankind, and they accept also his view that once the corrupting influence of the private ownership of social resources (with its consequent gross inequalities) is eliminated, truly human virtues will have a better chance to dominate the human character than the anti-social traits of envy, suspicion and pride.

Briefly stated then, what Hobbes fails to provide, according to Hegel and Marx, is an adequate sociological understanding of modernizing imperatives. They tell us that even Rousseau, in their judgement the most perceptive of the individualist writers, fails to comprehend the way in which our human potentiality emerges from an historical process; while they acknowledge that he appreciates the social dependence of individuals, they believe that his pessimism over the effects of civilization vitiated this insight. Hegel argues that history should be seen as a process in which humanity comes to realize its potentiality, and that the role of the philosopher is to interpret change positively. What is important, Hegel tells us, is that the motor forces at work in history transcend the particular motives and ambitions of individuals. Thus, successful leaders, often acting for selfish reasons, can nevertheless (and without being aware of it) serve the purposes of progress in an heroic way.

Marx rejects Hegel's optimistic teleological approach as metaphysical. It is wrong, he argues, to see the state (or the institution of bourgeios property upheld by the state) as functional to the goals of 'Reason' or 'Spirit' (conceived as something imposed by history, apart from the specific interests of particular classes).[27] He argues that the important lesson to be learned from an analysis of Rousseau's contribution (especially in the light of Hegel's response) is that it is necessary to reach an understanding of the ways in which institutional practices can help or hinder personal development. In his *Early Manuscripts*[28] he tries to show how Rousseau's insight into the alienating effects of the property claims made by private individuals can be combined with Hegel's sense of historical progress to provide a more adequate account of alienation.[29] What Marx emphasizes is that history has no meaning (in the sense that we cannot say that there are designs or purposes at work which are independent of human actors), but that the impact of institutional practices on individuals is something which can best be understood as resulting from the unintended consequences of those choices that the majority of individuals are likely to make in any given set of circumstances. In the light of this analysis, Marx suggests that what we need is an account which traces the way in which specific roles and relations come to be established, starting from the premise that the enterprise of producing history results from the impact of the choices of many individuals. Such an approach is important, he tells us, because it is these very relations of production which, in turn, inhibit human development by setting up particular interests that conflict with collective goals. Marx believes that if we are to understand the relationships involved here, we must devote part of our attention at least to the acting individuals in order to see what happens to them within the social enterprise of production. In this regard he concludes that the particular interests of individuals should not confront collectively imposed goals and interests as something alien. Unfortunately, in practice (especially under capitalist relations of production) the relations between individuals seeking to realize their particular human needs and the claims of society with which they are confronted are contradictory. This is partly because social interests represent the negation of the aspiration to develop human potentiality, and because the goals of individuals serve in turn to undermine the debilitating structures imposed by the collectivity. The reason for this, Marx tells us, is that market resource allocation requires that the power of labour be sold as a commodity. In such circumstances it becomes possible, even imperative, for those who own the means of production to extract a surplus by competing with other owners, and they must, therefore, extract the largest possible contribution from their employees. What outrages Marx about this situation is the dehumanization which, he argues, takes place when labour is treated as a commodity. He is, of course, concerned about the poverty which he believes results from unbridled competition between capilists and about the psychological harm caused by the brutalization of work under the capitalist mode of production. These are, however, consequences which Marx takes to be inevitable, given the nature of the system of production he describes in *Capital*. It is, therefore, in Marx's view, quite pointless to complain that the capitalist owners cheat the workers, for they do pay the market price of labour power (which, Marx suggests, reflects the cost of producing the labourer — that is, a wage sufficient to support a family); it is also unhelpful, Marx tells us, to appeal to the better sentiments of humanity in the hope of inspiring social change. Thus, he tells us, moral outrage, in itself and without supporting theories explaining the causes of social evils, is hardly worth expressing.[30]

Marx claims to have located the fundamental problem (the primary cause of the alienation of humanity) in the fact that social choices are made by private individuals whose strategies are dictated by the exigencies of market competition. In sharp contrast to Hegel, who saw modernity as progressively increasing our human capacities, Marx (like Rousseau) believes that this is not necessarily so. Indeed, he is able to show that, contrary to Hegel's optimistic prognosis, under capitalism the vast bulk of humanity is forced to abandon its human dignity by selling itself as a commodity. Furthermore, he argues that the state has always represented the interests of particular classes and should not be presented as the agency of a universal or collective interest. Marx explains that what is required, if we are to transcend the alienation which inhibits human development under capitalism, is that the tyranny of the market be replaced by a system in which social resources can be controlled collectively, and that the imperatives established through competition for profit be replaced by democratic controls which will enable mankind to work constructively towards the realization of truly human goals. He optimistically believes that these goals will be achieved after the capitalist mode of production is replaced by a system based on social ownership of the means of production.

Marx's Methodological Individualism

Marx writes, at times, in a very modern way. It is as if, in reaction to Hegel's holistic, teleological theory of social change, he had anticipated the kinds of complaint which some modern philosophers make against metaphysical historicism. He writes, for example:

> The premises from which we begin are not arbitrary ones, not dogmas, but real premises from which abstraction can only be made in the imagination. They are the real individuals, their activity and the material conditions under which they live, both those which they find already existing and those produced by their activity. These premises can thus be verified in a purely empirical way.[31]

It is on the basis of statements like this, and also because Marx makes no attempt to qualify his admiration for the methods used by the classical economists (who represent what we may regard as a paradigm of the individualist methodology at work), that we may safely conclude that he is an individualist. If, for example, we imagine him making a methodological statement (contributing to the debate between reductionists and holists about the correct approach in sociology), we can see, in the light of the passage quoted above, that he cannot, without contradicting himself, allow for any causal agency other than acting individuals. What Marx means by a materialist explanation is precisely an account in which the point of reference is acting individuals, their motives, interests, and needs, in given historical situations. Thus, we are to explain historical change by reference to the choices which individuals are likely to make; but we do not explain the choices which individuals are likely to make by referring to the imperatives of history (conceived as some abstract teleological force which dominates our lives).

If we are to identify Marx with a label that serves as a characterization of his philosophy of science, it would be most appropriate to call him an essentialist or, perhaps, a realist. I make this suggestion because his approach is to seek out the mechanisms which he believes are actually at work in social life using the technique of strategy analysis. Marx strives to account for what happens by examining the ways in which the phenomena he is investigating are produced. In this regard his orientation is similar to that of those philosophers of science who assess theories by the plausibility of the processes which they suggest as possible mechanisms accounting for phenomena. What is typical of the realist approach is a reliance, first, on inductive reasoning and, second, on the method of reduction as an appropriate technique for displaying mechanisms. To find out how something works, realists inform us, we first reduce a mechanism to its simplest elements and then speculate about how it is constructed. For the realist, then, an adequate explanation must rely on some hypothesis about the processes at work to produce a particular result.

The importance of understanding 'how' is well illustrated by the philosopher Rom Harré, who asks us to suppose that we are looking for an explanation of the fact that many blue-uniformed men pass by a window. He points out that it would not be possible, simply by observing the men go by, to reach any causal understanding of what is producing the phenomenon. In order to provide an adequate explanation, we would want to know, for example, whether there was an airforce base in the vicinity. If we were told there was such a base, we would understand why so many men had passed by and we would suppose, without further evidence, that if the base were closed the number of uniformed men in the vicinity would decline rapidly.[32]

Marx clearly believes that his most significant economic discovery (that under capitalism labour power is sold as a commodity but can produce more than its own natural market price) gave him a scientific understanding of the mechanism at work under systems of market resource allocation. He claims a better understanding than that of bourgeois economists precisely because he thinks that they have no comprehension of the underlying mechanisms by means of which capital is accumulated. Thus, in Marx's view, they are reduced to generalizing about uniformities without having any adequate understanding of what produces them. It is for this reason, he argues, that they claim there are laws of economics which would apply in all systems. Marx criticizes this approach as misconceived; what these economists fail to appreciate, according to him, is that after changes in historical circumstances have taken place, different mechanisms may be at work in social life. We would be best advised, he tells us, to approach economic analysis with a willingness to change our presumptions about how phenomena come to be produced, for it may be that historical changes result in the establishment of totally new structures. This is certainly what Marx predicts will happen if the capitalist mode of production is ever replaced by socialism. He tells us that in the new situation people will behave differently, because circumstances would allow for responses based on principles more worthy of humanity than the hard-bargaining, 'out-to-get-what-I-can' which characterizes the particularistic egoism of civil society under capitalism.

Marx's method is based on the construction of an abstract model in terms of which he makes deductions by way of a strategy analysis. In this respect at least, his approach is not fundamentally different from that of the writers he criticizes, and it can best be described as individualist. Where Marx has an advantage over most other individualist writers is in the fact that his materialism is based on a sensitive appreciation of the way in which particular interests can conflict with the collective good; and he is, consequently, prepared to dismiss as ideological those theories which accept the actual wants of individuals (as these are manifest in given historical periods) as evidence of real, 'objective' human interests. What Marx stresses (and the classical economists seem to overlook) is that if the processes that produce people's actual wants are eliminated, we must expect the people to behave differently; this is because their responses will reflect other interests.

2
Historical Materialism and Consciousness

This brings me to the problem of consciousness in Marx's work and its relationship to his individualism. A task which any sympathetic commentator must tackle is to see whether one can defend Marx's use of strategy analysis and his reliance on such notions as 'objective interests', whilst at the same time providing a reasonable account of the importance of ideological and subjective factors in social life. The problem here is that if one emphasizes Marx's individualism too strongly, his position can be reduced to an absurdly lopsided fundamentalism, which it is not possible to defend.[1] If, on the other hand, one emphasizes Marx's sensitivity to the importance of ideological and other subjective factors in social life, then historical materialism as a methodological orientation gives way to holistic functionalism and idealistic historicism (a position which, as I have shown, Marx severely criticizes). Is it possible to find an interpretation of Marx which does not have him embrace either of these unacceptable points of view?

Lukács's Contribution

Surprisingly, in searching for a balanced interpretation of Marx's materialism, I find that it is useful to follow the lead of the Hungarian Marxist Georg Lukács. If I am correct in my reading of his essay 'Class Consciousness', he makes an effort to preserve Marx's methodological commitment to strategy analysis;[2] this is, therefore, a useful text to turn to for my purposes, despite the fact that Lukács is correctly seen as someone who champions a holist approach in social theory. As I show, although Lukács has certainly had a major influence on those who have attempted to revise Marxism in a Hegelian and Idealist direction, he says things in 'Class Consciousness' about Marx's treatment of the problem of consciousness which indicate that the Marxist method is not incompatible with what I have described as strategy analysis. We should note, particularly, that Lukács is clear that it is not the psychological dispositions of individuals which are significant in shaping social life; it is, rather, the total social environment which is important. It is because Lukács attempts to account for 'consciousness' whilst avoiding the pitfalls of psychologism, and because he remains true to Marx's strategy analysis approach, that his essay is a suitable point of departure for my purposes.

The problem with which Lukács concerns himself in the essay is reformism. He is involved in a sustained polemic against socialists who pursue short term goals within the framework of capitalist society (specifically, wage claims through trade union bargaining) without seeing that the aim of their endeavour should be to overcome the system of the private appropriation of the means of production itself. This, as I have said, poses a serious challenge to Marxist sociologists who are forced by the evident behaviour of most workers (who mostly support the short term strategies adopted by reformist leaders) to acknowledge that they display little that can be interpreted as class-orientated strategies. The question, then, is whether, in the light of this evidence, it makes sense to continue to analyse social life in terms of a class-conflict model.

What Lukács shows, in responding to this challenge, is that many of the theoretical problems (which are alleged to make nonsense of Marx's materialist account) arise because critics persistently confuse 'the perception by subjects of what they take to be their interests' with 'the perception of the objective conditions necessary for realizing these interests'. He points out, in this regard, that when Marx uses the notion of 'objective interests' to ground his analysis of conflict and to expose the illusions of shortsighted bourgeois theory, he is not at all concerned with the motives of the proletariat. Thus, factors such as what the working classes are conscious of as being in their interests to pursue or what their attitudes are to those who control most social resources do not seem to be of great significance to Marx. Lukács puts this point well: 'The essence of scientific Marxism consists, then, in the realization that the real motor forces of history are independent of man's (psychological) consciousness of them.'[3] The point here is that it makes sense to identify 'interests' as part of a strategy analysis even where there is no direct evidence that people are actually aware of these interests. When a sociologist does this, he or she is usually referring to situations which are structured in such a way that some significant consequences of an agent's actions are clearly not intended. In claiming that a course of action is in a person's interests, even where that person is not aware of it, the sociologist may even be anticipating future strategies. Marx, for example, is concerned with the likely interaction between the choices adopted by agents in situations where there is a clear class structure, and just as the bourgeois economist legitimately anticipates future strategies when reviewing the relations between buyers and sellers in a market, he grounds his predictions on an analysis of structured choice. What Marx does is to turn utilitarian economic assumptions against bourgeois economics itself: where liberals argue that each person acting rationally in his or her own interest contributes to the common good, Marx shows that this is not so at all; he argues that each rational calculator in fact (quite unintentionally) contributes to the ever increasing tensions between labour and capital, and he shows how this conflict of interests will eventually destroy market society itself.[4]

Marx's analysis of capitalism is also directed at Hegel's complacency about the inevitability of social progress. He is concerned to show that, contrary to what Hegel had argued regarding the role of the state and the importance of property rights, the opposite is true — for, Marx, tells us, under the system of capitalism the majority are dehumanized by the processes set in motion. My point here is that Marx is able to refute Hegel conclusively only because he is equipped with a sociological method which allows him to make controversial claims about the interests of the collective (and about what he takes to represent truly human interests); it is only because Marx the historian is able to trace alienation as a function of bourgeois property relations that he can take the final measure of Hegel's teleological metaphysics.

Sociologists are often in a good position to assess the possible consequences of the strategies which a subject group is likely to adopt; they are, therefore, often justified in making controversial claims about the interests of particular parties, particularly perhaps when an unintended consequence of a structured situation is detected. This would be the case even when the persons involved were not subjectively orientated towards the promotion or the prevention of the predicted outcome.

Even if persons themselves become conscious that structures

produce consequences of an unintended kind, they may not necessarily be influenced to take a different course of action, because the rationality of a shift in strategy orientation may often depend on how agents are themselves affected. Their best strategy may remain the same even if the outcome they think most likely is not their favoured one. It is this kind of situation which Marx describes as embodying a contradiction.[5]

What we are faced with here is the Hobbesian dilemma: individuals have a collective interest in co-operating with each other but because they must calculate from their individual perspectives, they have no way of promoting collective interests without placing themselves at risk. The logical point involved here is illustrated very clearly by Parsons who, as we have seen, is critical of Hobbes's solution to the problem of order. Although he concedes that the individuals in the state of nature outlined in *Leviathan* would have a common interest in entering into civil society, Parsons argues that they would have far more trouble than Hobbes allows for in finding a strategy to realize this desired collective goal.[6] It is clearly in everyone's interest that the state of nature be replaced by civil society; as individuals, however, they may well reason that any attempt to co-operate with others to achieve this common goal will leave them vulnerable to possible abuse. This supposition, in the situation outlined by Hobbes, would have been reasonable and would, consequently, have influenced each of them to adopt strategies directed at achieving other goals which would have been seen as having more chance of being realized or as involving less risk to themselves.

Parsons takes the problem of devising a strategy for realizing a collective goal to be insurmountable, given the assumptions of individualist theory about human nature. He points out, in this regard, that Hobbes's negotiators have no way of eliminating the possibility that fraud or force will be resorted to by one or other of them; and (because no strategy can be thought up to avoid this problem) Parsons concludes that no adequate account of social order, which assumes rational egoism, can be given. It is mostly in the light of this consideration that he suggests we reject Hobbes's reductionist methodology.

Hegel's response to Hobbes is similar: he finds that the postulate of rational egoism allows for a most unsatisfactory account of the phenomenon of loyalty to others, and that no adequate explanation of how it comes about that citizens acquire a sense of duty, which they must necessarily display if political co-operation is to be successful, can be given if egoism is assumed. If citizens are required to perform their civil duties not merely because they are fearful but to conform with enthusiasm, and must even make personal sacrifices where these are called for, then it makes little sense to try to account for this by postulating an agreement between egoistically motivated, rational individuals. If, however, the phenomenon of social order cannot be accounted for as a rational response by individuals to circumstances that reflect the human predicament, Hegel reasons, the rationality of political association (for we mostly agree that it would be rational to choose to live in civil society rather than in the state of nature) has to be something imposed on individuals; what is rational must, then, ultimately reflect the interests of the collective and not those of the individual.[7]

Lukács responds differently to the Hobbesian dilemma: he does not feel that he has to abandon the view that strategy analysis is the most appropriate method for understanding social phenomena; instead, he points out that Marx himself anticipated the problems which bother Parsons and Hegel. Marx's perception of the difficulties is captured in the following quotation:

Just because individuals seek *only* their particular interest, which for them does not coincide with their communal interests (in fact the general is the illusory form of the communal life), the latter will be imposed on them as an interest 'alien' to them, and 'independent' of them, as in its turn a particular, peculiar 'general' interest; or they themselves must remain within this discord, as in democracy. On the other hand, too, the *practical* struggle of these particular interests, which constantly really run counter to the communal and illusory communal interests, makes *practical* intervention and control necessary through the illusory 'general' interest in the form of the State.[8]

In modern times we have Mancur Olson's clearer statement:

Unless the number of individuals in a group is quite small, or unless there is coercion or some other special device to make individuals act in their common interest, *rational, self-interested individuals will not act to achieve their common or group interests.*[9]

Olson's theorem in Marx's hands is used to restate, in a more sophisticated way, Hobbes's view of the state as essentially coercive. The illusory 'general good' is imposed as an 'interest' alien to individuals because it represents specific class interests. It follows that the real basis for social order is an understanding of the forces which give rise to the domination of a particular class capable of imposing its interests, and not by reference to the notion that we are integrated by our shared values within a culture.

Olson's theorem has another, equally important role in Marx's work, for it provides the most important basis on which his conception of the contradictions implicit within capitalism is grounded. It is worth noting, as a preliminary point in this regard, that the notion of contradiction takes its place within Marx's general theory of the dialectical progress of history and is surrounded by such puzzling ideas as the 'transformation of quantity into quality' and the much criticized 'negation of the negation'. In fact, Marx's conception of dialectical change simply reflects a view of history taken from the Greek philosopher Heraclitus, in which, as Engels puts it, everything is seen to be in flux, in which 'nothing remains what, where and how it was, but everything moves, changes, comes and passes out of existence'.[10] The objective of science, from the dialectical point of view, must therefore be to understand the processes which give rise to change. It is not surprising, then, that dialectical theorists express these 'laws of change' in ways which give modern philosophers, who are used to thinking of science as the quest for nomological laws, a great deal of trouble. If, however, we keep in mind that the process Marx focuses on when he exposes the 'laws of development' at work in the capitalist period is based on Olson's theorem, we can see that there is nothing very unusual about his method. This is because it simply develops the theoretical approach of the classical utilitarian writers in a much more thorough way.

The utilitarians perceived that the interests of the traditional aristocratic elite were in conflict with modernizing imperatives, and that this class resisted the emergence of capitalism. However, it was Ricardo, working closely with James Mill, who first comprehended that rent (the income of the landholders) could be seen as a surplus which had been taken without anything having been given in return.[11] He provides the following theorem to justify this claim:

As the demand for corn increases so the land cultivated gets poorer and this leads to an increase in the cost of production, measured as the labour hours needed for cultivation. It follows that those who have holdings in the more fertile areas have a competitive advantage because they produce more cheaply, and they can, consequently, sell at a price which does not reflect their labour costs.

We can deduce from this theorem that the established landlords benefit greatly when the demand for corn forces the less fertile land to be brought into production. It follows, also, that it would be greatly to their advantage if they could prevent technological improvements from being applied to increase agricultural production, for this would make it unnecessary to bring larger areas of less fertile land under cultivation. In the light of these two considerations, we can say that the strategy of each individual farmer, if he were to act rationally, would be to increase the yield of his own land (for this would increase his income); at the same time we can postulate that he would hope that the yields produced by rival farmers would not improve – that is, his interests as an individual here conflict with those of landholders as a class.[1,2]

Marx applies a similar analysis to the strategies of the capitalist entrepreneur, and in doing this he turns Ricardo's theorem on its head. The Marxist theorem can be formulated as follows:

By increasing his capital investment in machinery (the organic composition of capital) the entrepreneur can improve productivity, provided the cost in labour hours gets lower (we have to include here the cost of building the machines in the first place). It follows that those who hold the more productive plants have a competitive advantage.

We can deduce from this theorem that surplus value accrues in the hands of those who control capital, because they are able to utilize technology to ensure that their factories operate below the necessary labour time. They can, therefore, realize as a profit the difference between their production costs and those of the rest of society. (We should note here that the surplus does not flow to capitalists in proportion to their holdings, but according to the success they achieve in obtaining a competitive advantage over rival producers.) It follows that the level of profit will decline as more and more entrepreneurs, maximizing their advantage by moving their resources where they think they will get the highest return, invest their surplus in a given industry. This process of reinvestment will continue, Marx tells us, until the point is reached at which further improvements in a given area only produce a slight change in the cost of production. We have a contradiction here, in that the cumulative effect of each individual's rational attempt to maximize profits is a steady decline in the level of profit. A further contradiction follows because there is a conflict between the interests of the owners of capital and those of the labourers they employ – the former must constantly keep their labour costs down, whilst the latter struggle to get as high a return as is possible for their labour time. We can see here, also, that while every individual capitalist will choose to pay workers as little as possible and will use technology to improve productive capacity by reducing the labour time that is necessary to produce commodities, he will, nevertheless, have an interest in seeing that rival entrepreneurs pay high wages. This is because each producer must sell what he manufactures or his investment will be wasted, and he cannot do this if the working population has no purchasing power. Thus, every individual capitalist will choose to make his labourers redundant where this is expedient and will pay those he employs as little as possible. He will rejoice, however, when other capitalists are forced to maintain full employment or when they are required to pay higher wages. There is a further closely related consequence of the fact that investment in technology may result in a growing pool of unemployed citizens: capitalism's own imperative leads towards self-destruction, because it increases society's productive capacity whilst it undermines the ability of the population to consume.[13]

These contradictions (the perceived unintended consequences of a particular mode of production) are the mechanisms in terms of which Marx models the processes at work under capitalism and which he believes will ultimately lead to the transformation of the system into socialism.

We may wish to reject this model as unilluminating, or we may decide to adapt it so that it is more readily applicable to modern circumstances. In either case, it is important to understand that the explanatory force of Marx's conception of social change depends on his strategy analysis of these contradictions. We should note also that Marx conceives of the driving force of history as resulting from the actions of individuals, their choices and goals, and not as something metaphysical.

For Marx, then, history is not law-governed but dialectical (in the sense that people make history but not on their own terms, for they do not choose the problems which they are required to resolve in their lives), and he sees the sociologist's task as that of comprehending how one set of structured circumstances give way to another. To appreciate this movement, Marx tells us, we must resist the temptation to treat structures as an objectively given, unchanging reality, and we must retain the sense that they are constituted by relationships between persons, which are subject to change. Every historical structure, he tells us, represents more than what is merely given, for there is always a latent possibility for change inherent in the contradictions which careful analysis can illuminate. Through sociological analysis, then, we are able to see the structural strengths and weaknesses of a given historical system, and we can comprehend the latent possibilities for change by identifying the real interest of individuals (as opposed to their actual wishes and wants, which merely reflect circumstances). Lukács puts the point in a complex way:

The relation with concrete totality and the dialectical determinants arising from it transcend pure description and yield the category of objective possibility. By relating consciousness to the whole of society it becomes possible to infer the thoughts and feelings which men would have in a particular situation if they were *able* to assess both it and the interests arising from it in their impact on immediate action and on the whole structure of society. That is to say, it would be possible to infer the thoughts and feelings appropriate to their objective situation.[14]

There are difficulties in reading this kind of statement in the light of Olson's theorem of collective action. I would, however, submit that there is enough evidence in his essay 'Class Consciousness' to make the fit — furthermore, it is the only way to make sense of what would otherwise emerge as a puzzling and possibly confused statement.

Regardless of whether I am right to interpret Lukács's views in the way that I have, we must note (if we are to understand Marx's attitude to consciousness) that the relationship between 'interests', 'the perception of interests' and 'the adoption of a strategy for the realization of interests' is a complex one. Something may be in my interests, yet it may not be a good strategy for me to take a risk to try and bring it about; I may have no rational reason, as a self-interested individual, for adopting such a course of action. It is often easy to miss the ambiguities involved, and where this is the case we may talk of vulgar individualism. A vulgar account of historical materialism would be one in which, after postulating class-structured social circumstances, the following deductions are made (quite falsely in terms of Olson's theorem): first, that contradictions within the system will generate a consciousness of its common interest on the part of the exploited group; second, that a radicalization of people's perceptions will enable them to change the system; third, conversely, that those who have a monopoly control over productive resources will perceive a common interest in maintaining the system of exploitation; fourth, that because of this consciousness they will be capable of mobilizing resistance to change.

Marx and Engels are sometimes guilty of suggesting a vulgar version of historical materialism, as they do in the *Communist Manifesto*. Lukács, as we have seen, rejects vulgar individualism. In terms of his observations, no individual would have an interest in supporting class-orientated actions merely for the sake of a collective class goal. We must therefore, he tells us, resist the temptation to explain such actions as resulting from any subjective conception of class interests.

A problem for Marxist theorists, as Lukács correctly sees, is that they must face up to the fact that reformist political and labour leaders often help achieve what working-class citizens actually take to be their goals (higher wages and better working conditions). The Marxist must, therefore, provide an analysis of class-orientated behaviour without making the fallacious assumption that it is somehow the result of a consciousness of class interests. He needs, then, to construct a model of the processes at work which avoids the pitfalls of reformism but which at the same time explains why such a strategy has been so attractive to those leaders who seek to better the circumstances of the working class.

In fact, this is easy to do, for a consciousness of society as divided along class lines is often surprisingly weak in those whose actual behaviour is most conducive to the attainment of class goals. For example, a judge sentencing a strike leader may have no notion of social class, and this very fact may contribute to the harshness of the sentence he or she delivers. Similarly, within the ranks of the workers the most radical behaviour threatening the system may often be that of people whose consciousness of class is low. An example here is black militants who see conflict in racial terms; also, the behaviour of the extreme Right may present an ironical case, for they sometimes make quite radical demands in the interests of the working classes. This way of considering class behaviour also illuminates the paradox that the bourgeoisie, while promoting its selfish individual interests, threatens its class interests in maintaining the system which allows for exploitation. Lukács puts the point thus:

> in the case of the other classes, a class consciousness is prevented from emerging by their position within the process of production and the interests this generates. In the case of the bourgeoisie, however, these factors combine to produce a class consciousness but one which is cursed by its very nature with the tragic fate of developing an insoluble contradiction at the very zenith of its powers. As a result of this contradiction it must annihilate itself.[15]

One form of Marxist analysis, then, consists in the demonstration that the support for, or failure to support, objective class interests is often an unintended consequence of actions directed at producing other goals. If we set out to examine contemporary social life using such a framework, we would want to show that behaviour makes some contribution to the maintenance of, or represents a threat to, the system of class relations. Our understanding of the functioning of social institutions would be reductionist, for we would be showing how the actions of individuals contribute to the maintenance of, or are disfunctional to, a given structure. The focus of this form of analysis would not be the subjective consciousness of class interests on the part of agents but the fact that most political behaviour actually serves the interests of class, and does so regardless of the motives of agents. Marx states the point:

> It is not a matter of what this or that proletarian, or even what the proletariat as a whole, at any particular moment, considers as its aim. The question is *what the proletariat is*, and what, consequent upon that being, it will historically be compelled to do. Its goal and its historical action is obviously and irrevocably prescribed for it by its own life situation as well as by the whole organization of bourgeois society today.[16]

Marx's judgement here has been questioned. It is suggested, as I mentioned earlier, that revolutionary changes have not occurred precisely because of what the proletariat considers to be its aims — it is said to suffer from the malady known as 'false consciousness'.[17] I have suggested, using Olson's theorem, that this kind of retreat from Marx's strategy theory is unnecessary, because the maintenance of a class system can be explained as the result of everyone calculating within a framework which no individual acting alone has any interest in challenging. This does not mean that it is not in the general interest of the working class to put an end to capitalist property power; it is just that the difficulties of organizing the class politically, so that it can act collectively, are not easy to overcome. One reason for this is simply that the spoils that are likely to result from revolutionary activity are so remote, and the chance of success such a long shot, that few are prepared to expend much energy, or take the necessary risks, to achieve revolutionary goals. Furthermore, those few activists who do take such risks are not likely to have much success unless the circumstances at the time of their initiative are propitious. This is because, as Marx himself makes clear, the attempted realization of a class goal can be successful only where the contradictions of the previous order begin to manifest themselves or, to borrow Olson's language, where structural developments reach the point at which they begin to provide a selective incentive for those whose interests run contrary to the prevailing system to act politically.

If we interpret Marx in the way suggested — that is, as an individualist aware of the fact that people are always situated within specific historical structures which determine the strategy options available to them — we can save him from some telling criticisms. In the sections which follow, I will review some of the more important areas of dispute. I look first at the debate about Marx's distinction between the 'economic base' and the 'superstructure' of society, and his conception of economic determinism; then at Karl Popper's review of what he calls historicism and his charges against Marx; finally at the conflict between Marxists and pluralists about the distribution and the nature of 'power' in liberal democracies.

The Base/Superstructure Distinction

Consider first the well-run Plamenatz objection to Marxism that historical materialism rests on a conceptual confusion of great importance. The problem arises, we are told, because of Marx's suggestion that the 'economic base of society' is the same thing as the 'property relations'. Plamenatz argues that 'property relations' must surely be constituted by norms of the legal order and must therefore be characterized as part of the superstructure, and that Marx's theory of historical change must be questioned because it requires us to explain changes in the superstructure in terms of changes in the base.[18]

Marx is certainly guilty of using terms in the way that Plamenatz suggests, and it follows, therefore, that if we read Marx's theory in a way which requires him to isolate economic factors (so that he can explain other phenomena of a political and legal nature in terms of them), then his materialsm can be shown to rest on a form of economic fundamentalism which is indefensible.[19] Even if we read 'economic change' as meaning 'technological innovations in the methods used in industry', it is difficult to see how this single factor could determine social change. Nor is it easy to defend the view that technological innovations, are fundamental in the sense that they can be singled out as not being determined by other social factors. It is not plausible, for example, to hold that technological development is independent of the level of scientific advancement and the political strength of those who may oppose scientific research, both of which might plausibly be regarded as falling squarely in the 'superstructural' sphere. Despite some passages which may be interpreted as supporting a theory of technological determinism, Marx never held the view that a particular mode of production (where what is referred to are the techniques used in manufacturing processes) would dominate social life to the exclusion of other factors. He would, for example, have regarded it as of central importance to distinguish capitalist relations of production from those he described as socialist; and he would, consequently, have wanted to distinguish between social systems even where they make a similar use of technological innovations in the manufacturing processes (as the Soviet Union and the United States often do). It was Marx's strongly held view that we should not blur significant differences between social systems by trying to isolate one causal factor at work. Thus, when he talks about a given economic system, he usually has in mind not only the level of technology used in production but what he calls the 'relations of production' embodied in the prevailing institutions (of which he regarded the property system as the most significant).

The claims of economic fundamentalism (the attempt to trace all social developments to transformations in the economic sphere only) are, in any case, so difficult to support in the light of historical evidence that it is implausible to attribute such a position to a writer of first rank. Are we to suppose that Marx, who was sensitive to the complex interrelationships which are involved in social life, would have been so dogmatically committed to the thesis of economic determinism that he would have wanted to explain all human history in terms of one factor only? Are we to suppose, for instance, that he would have explained the fact that some traditional institutions have disappeared in modern times (such as slavery), whereas others have persisted through many different stages of economic development (such as the English monarchy and the Catholic Church), without taking into account a wide range of considerations of a kind which cannot easily be regarded as purely economic? The evidence of his own historical work is surely enough to caution against taking such a view.[20]

It is interesting to observe that Plamenatz's charge is a species of the more recent complaint made against reductionism by Steven Lukes, and rests on a confusion between ontological individualism (the view that only persons and natural things exist in any meaningful sense — not banks, churches or armies) and methodological individualism (which is a doctrine about the special form which sociological explanations ought to take).[21] As long as critics believe in the myth that methodological individualists are committed to denying the importance of structure (what, after all, is a market?) they will continue to battle against an adversary of their own making. Strategy analysis, which is the most characteristic individualist approach, is based on the idea that we can identify socially important structures: those in which the actions of agents, who may be motivated by purely private concerns (the manifest function), produce quite unintended social results (the latent function). Sociologists who follow the reductionist methodological rule seek to show, usually by way of a reference to the typical behaviour of a number of agents, how we may come to understand the social implications of acts. In accomplishing this task they must necessarily refer to social facts which have an ontological status of their own. Social entities (such as markets) or structured relationships (such as those presupposed by commodity production) cannot be said to cause anything, however, for they have no purposes of their own — social consequences result, according to individualists, only because people choose to act in various ways. They hold, further, that if we are to understand the processes at work in social life, we must see how what one person chooses to do comes to affect the situations of others.[22]

Finally, it is worth noting that it is a presumption of Marx's treatment of norms and values, which gives his 'base'/'superstructure' terminology its point, that our commitment to values does not usually go very deep, and that we are likely to change our perspectives when we perceive that we have a definite interest at stake (as white South African sportsmen often do when they reach the level at which international competition is important to them). Thus, in Marx's theory, when the contradictions of a historical period reach the point where transformation is imminent, many of the values of the interlocking cultural system will also come to be undermined and questioned. Although Marx does not try to explain changes of this kind in a one-dimensional way, he is clear that what occurs here is not merely a matter of a change of consciousness. He writes, for example, in a scathing attack:

Since the Young Hegelians consider conceptions, thoughts, ideas, in fact all the products of consciousness, to which they attribute an independent existence, as the real chains of men (just as the Old Hegelians declared them the true bonds of human society) it is evident that the Young Hegelians have to fight only against these illusions of the consciousness. Since, according to their fantasy, the relationships of men, all their doings, their chains and their limitations are products of their consciousness, the Young Hegelians logically put to men the moral postulate of exchanging their present consciousness for human, critical or egoistic consciousness, and thus of removing their limitations....They forget, however... that they are in no way combating the real existing world when they are merely combating the phrases of this world.[23]

The point I stress here is that Marx is not overimpressed by the view that what is decisive in social life is shared values, for he is critical of the view that the true bond of human society is an integrated form of consciousness. He is, of course, prepared to recognize norms as constitutive parts of structures, but he wishes to explain the persistence of structures, or their tendency to change, by the interests which are served or which are in conflict with them. Those interests cannot, then, be the dependent variable (established through consciousness), for it is by reference to them that culture itself must ultimately be explained.

Marx and the Historicist Fallacy

Karl Popper's criticism of Marx's approach (which results from his influential philosophy of science) can also be challenged once we read 'historical materialism' as a form of strategy analysis. The case which Popper makes against Marx is part of his wider discussion of what he calls historicist social theory.[24] Briefly put, the historicist fallacy is alleged to occur when theorists mistakenly believe that because social life is the product of a historical process, there are no laws of society, and that each period of history is consequently characterized uniquely; that the challenge for social science must be to discover laws of historical development, as opposed to just plain, ordinary, social laws; that they are able to make predictions on the basis of any discovery of such laws of development and the presumed understanding of history which this provides. Popper calls the predictions of historicists prophecy, and he contrasts them sharply with scientific deductions from laws. In his view science is the endeavour to find laws which allow for specific as opposed to large-scale, long-term prognostications of the kind that he believes to be made typically by radicals in politics. In this regard he argues that scientists, as opposed to prophets, state their conjectures about the world in such a way that they are subject to possible refutation; and he argues that most historicist theorists are unscientific in their approach because their work is characterized by a tendency to avoid being specific. It is for this reason, he tells us, that their work is so difficult to prove wrong.

Marx, to Popper's great delight, is an exception amongst historicists, for he does make enough statements about the immediate future (such as his prediction of the increasing misery of the working class under capitalism) to have his conjectures thoroughly refuted by events.[25] The trouble is, however, that while Marx himself has a strong instinct for science, Popper tells us that his methodology is historicist and not scientific; furthermore, Marx's disciples have shown that they care little for empiricism and have held to the Marxist framework despite all the contrary evidence. Thus Popper suggests that if there is such a thing as scientific Marxism, it has been falsified by the evidence of history; and that what remains today is the very worst form of historicism, operating either as the ideology of totalitarian communism or as the basis for the visionary dreams of political extremists who, with no grasp of the complexities of social life, hope to transform their societies by revolutionary means into a Utopia.

In assessing Marx's methodology as science we must bear in mind that he is not a Popperian and had no special reason for assuming that his responsibilities as a scientist required him to articulate generalizations for possible refutation in the light of history. Although he is prepared to formulate a few 'laws' which he believes are applicable under the capitalist mode of production, Marx is sceptical of the attempt to formulate universal generalizations about social life. He sees his primary task as that of providing some understanding of the underlying processes at work in history, and in tackling this task he adopts what has come to be known as the resolutive-compositive method. His idea is to resolve social life into its most basic elements (acting individuals) and then speculate about how capitalist society could have evolved; it is in this way that he explains how capital came to be accumulated.[26] Like the English utilitarians, Marx begins his analysis by postulating a simple model of exchange relationships between individuals producing for themselves as independent units; and he uses it to show that the natural harmony of interests, which it was plausible to assume would have emerged naturally in these circumstances (because each producer is free to withdraw from an exchange if he or she sees no benefit in it), could have been undermined to produce capitalism. The answer he gives, as we have seen, is based on his account of what happens when labour power itself comes to be sold for its market price. It is through the construction of a model of this kind that Marx theorizes about social change. He does not turn to history in a crude, inductivist way, trying to perceive the laws of development at work, as Popper thinks some historicists do; rather, he operates with a model of what he takes to be the fundamental processes at work and tests its power to illuminate by looking at real history.

Popper is wrong, then, to suppose that Marxism must be dismissed as non-scientific. It is true that many Marxists are still influenced by Marx's conjectures, even though some of them appear to have been invalidated by subsequent events. It does not follow, however, that modern Marxists are necessarily irrational, for a perfectly adequate and scientific response is to see whether the claimed anomalies between Marx's predictions and the evidence of history can be accounted for in the light of his understanding of the processes at work. We need only reject his theory where we are satisfied that it no longer provides insight into what is happening, or where alternative accounts of the processes at work seem to be more plausible.[27]

The Pluralist Challenge

A common complaint made against modern Marxist writers is that they often confuse what they, as committed radicals, hope people will regard as being in their interests with what people actually believe to be in their interests. This confusion arises, it is alleged, because of the persistence with which Marxists have held on to a class model of society despite the evidence that very few people actually perceive their relationships with others as involving this kind of conflict. If people do not see their interests as being defined in class terms, then it would seem to follow that attempts to make sense of their behaviour using a strategy analysis which assumes these alleged conflicting interests must be unsatisfactory. To put this point another way: the difficulty for the Marxist is said to arise from the fact that the property-owning classes seem to have been able to maintain their hegemony not only by means of coercion but also through persuasion. What is remarkable about liberal democratic systems is the agreement, manifest in all sections of society, over the basic rights which entitle individuals to own and to control property. Even the leaders of labouring classes rarely challenge capitalism, for what they mostly demand are piecemeal reforms aimed at increasing the prosperity of the groups they represent.

Many radical writers have come to accept that there is a need to revise Marx's methodological approach to give cultural factors a more significant weighting. In understanding the distribution of power in society, so it is argued, one must turn from a crude counting of available resources (money, influence, organizational strength, and so on) towards an appreciation of the fact that power in class society rests ultimately on a successful appeal to legitimacy. In this regard it is suggested that no adequate understanding of power can ignore the processes by means of which legitimation is formed through engineered consensus. Moreover, with regard to liberal societies it is suggested that the very requirements of their institutional arrangements (the need for widespread political participation, the publicity and importance attached to surface conflicts, the parochialism and the real possibilities for improvement which these systems offer) generate a kind of repressive tolerance which serves to sustain the existing *status quo* and to prevent real threats to the system of class exploitation from finding political expression. The point, put simply, is that the political demands people make will always reflect the circumstances of their past history and their understanding of their present social environment and will, in this sense, be a cultural response. It is because they accept this view that many modern radicals have tended to pay more attention to psychological variables than did Marx and Engels; they hope to comprehend the impact of our consumer-orientated social life and the emerging culture of mass entertainment as contributing to class hegemony.

I have already provided reasons for regarding this kind of response as unnecessary. If we keep in mind Olson's theorem, we can, following Lukács, find an explanation for the muting of class conflict in liberal societies, and we can do this without abandoning the strategy-analysis approach so central to classical Marxism for some form of holistic sociology. We should not expect rational agents to act in ways which support class interests for, as Olson has shown, it does not follow that if a group (or class) has some reason or incentive to organize, individual members of the group (or class) would also have an incentive to support such an organization. Furthermore, given that politicians are likely to respond in ways which reflect their perception of how to advance their own personal careers, we can see that they will tend to ignore the remote threat of potential interests and concern themselves instead with the real gains in financial backing and good will which are more easy to obtain from those interest groups which are organized. We can see, then, why politicians usually favour particular groups and specific interests where they are in conflict with collective goals. They generally stand to lose votes where feelings are intense, (if they take a stand against vested interests, for example), but if they ignore collective interests, the impact on individuals is usually so slight that the political effects are likely to be insignificant. In any case, politicians know that a vote is a blunt instrument with which to punish leaders for ignoring an interest unless the need is felt so intensely that it overrides other considerations.

Those who think that the strategy analysis suggested here is not adequate to save Marxism may respond as pluralist behaviouralists do by arguing, first, that labour is organized in liberal societies and has a very significant political influence through the trade unions and the parties controlled by them; and, second, that the test of whether an interest is at stake politically must be behavioural — that is, when citizens or groups do not campaign, organize, write letters to Members of Parliament and so on no interest is threatened.[28] On these assumptions it follows that if the labour movement does not use its influence to promote the alleged class interests suggested by Marxist theory, then this should be taken as evidence that no such interests exist in reality.

Pluralist writers have tended to support these views by suggesting a conception of political power as influence. The advantages of this approach are clearly manifest in the response made by Robert Dahl to the claim that American society is dominated by a 'power elite'.[29] Dahl quite rightly insists that such a claim would not be satisfactorily supported if the only evidence provided were an accurate description of social connections between those members of society who are described as being in a position to influence others. What is required to establish the claim that society is dominated by a ruling elite, he tells us, is research into actual decision-making in key political areas. The thorough sociologist interested in researching into this problem must select for study a number of key (as opposed to routine) political decisions; identify the people who play an active part in decision-making; obtain an account of their actual behaviour while the policy issue was being reviewed and resolved; and determine and analyse specific outcomes of the conflict.[30]

Dahl's recommendations have undoubtedly brought a new rigour to debate, and I would suggest that as long as we are concerned to determine who has influence in political life, we must recognize the good sense reflected in his way of handling the problem. For many, however, and particularly for radicals who are concerned with 'power' in a much wider sense, the central issues cannot be resolved merely by focusing on political influence. The problem which Dahl seems to overlook is that radicals offer a different interpretation of the evidence relating to those who have influence, and their theoretical approach, in so far as it is a Marxist one, calls on a concept of interest which cannot easily be operationalized in the way that behaviouralists require. What Marxists show (and here again I follow Lukács) is that a good explanation of why a class may often fail to promote its interests politically, or even to be aware that it has an interest in a particular policy area, is that individuals may judge that their chances of influencing the course of events in a favoured direction are not good. The point here is that interests only become manifest as behaviour when people are motivated to make an effort to realize them and this means that sociologists, concerned solely with behavioural evidence, may fail to see how liberal processes of consultation and contest effectively favour some causes rather than. Even the policy a group chooses to promote — for instance, the welfare-orientated reformist programmes characteristic of parties reflecting labour interests — may not be the policy of first choice (which might be to work towards a socialist society), for political leaders, if they are to achieve anything at all, must necessarily formulate their aims in the light of some assessment of their capacity to influence. Thus, it may be that an active trade union is very successful in promoting policies such as higher wages and favoured industrial relations legislation which are in no way in the long-term interests of members (because they contribute to processes leading to inflation, which will erode the gains) but are the best expedients in the circumstances (because the union has no power to change the structure in which it is forced to operate). It might be said, superficially, that such a group is powerful by comparison with others who are less successful in promoting their policy objectives; such a judgement can be misleading, however, because the capacity of the group successfully to promote alternative policies, seen to be more beneficial in the long term, may be slight.

The Marxist criticism of the pluralist approach to the analysis of political power should be distinguished from that of Peter Bachrach and Morton Baratz in their interesting 'Two Faces of Power'.[31] What they argue is that it is necessary, when discussing political power, to look at how certain kinds of policy issues are prevented from becoming political. As they point out:

Power is also exercised when A devotes his energy to creating or reinforcing social and political values and institutional practices that limit the scope of the political process to public consideration of only those issues which are comparatively innocuous to A.[32]

What Bachrach and Baratz require is a redefinition of 'key political issue'. For Dahl and other pluralists, issues of significance are to be identified by observing actual conflicts as these become manifest in political life. But this focus may beg the question at issue, for if there were a power elite (or a ruling class) no significant conflict of interest — that is, no conflict which threatened the hegemony of the elite (or class) — would be allowed to emerge in the system. Bachrach and Baratz suggest that those who exercise hegemony often have a capacity to suppress issues which are seen to be threatening, and it is for this reason that an analysis which merely focuses on those conflicts that successfully emerge as political may be misleading. As an alternative approach, they suggest that researchers try to identify issues by looking for conflicts which could potentially

> involve a genuine challenge to the resources of power and authority of those who currently dominate the processes by which policy outputs of the system are determined.

Bachrach and Baratz believe, moreover, that this kind of conflict can be identified, objectively, by looking at actual behaviour. They seem to think that sensitive observers should still adopt a conception of power as influence, provided they are careful to choose for case study the politically important issues (defined, in their sense, as involving a threat to the hegemony of the ruling group) and provided that they do not restrict their focus to those cases in which there is a serious confrontation between groups with resources and influence, as Dahl recommends. Their idea is to trace the way in which conflicts are prevented from emerging as issues.

Bachrach and Baratz do have a valid criticism, and their position represents an improvement on that of Dahl; this is primarily because they are more sensitive than the latter to the difficulties which some groups experience in getting their concerns into the political arena. Furthermore, the instinct of these sociologists, reflected in their struggle to ground their research on behavioural evidence, is a sound one and should not be dismissed lightly. I would, however, suggest that Bachrach and Baratz are likely to have more difficulty than they seem to allow in locating fundamental conflicts of the kind they wish to examine. Certainly, it is true that one may find cases where two communities struggle for political power (the documentation they provide of the struggles in Baltimore between aspirant black leaders and the ruling white elite is a case in point); it is, however, not at all clear that this kind of struggle, although it may be fundamental in the sense that the hegemony of a ruling elite is threatened, can also be used to justify any claims about class conflict (or about the political importance of objective class interests). I would, therefore, suggest that we need a third sense for 'key political issue', which is defined theoretically in the way I have recommended, using Lukács's exploration of Marx's conception of 'objective interests'.

The problem we face here is one of interpretation, for what is in dispute is the question of what is to count as a 'key political issue'. I am suggesting that it is often important to make an assessment of interests before evaluating the significance of political influence; and

I claim that large sections of our communities are not aware of their interests, and that this is so precisely because they are politically impotent (women are such a group, and Marx argues that workers are similarly situated). Once we are prepared to make a judgement about interests which is not bound by an assessment of a group's political capacity to influence, even where such a judgement is not influenced by Marx's analysis but merely reflects intuitive common sense, it will be quickly apparent that the power of special groups sustained by competitive processes is the most serious danger facing liberal society today. Countries like the United States and Japan are, in fact, rapidly destroying themselves — their national health and environmental resources — because of the unbridled and totally unprincipled behaviour of the major producer groups. These interests, representing the most powerful industrial and professional organizations (and here I would include many of the trade unions), place their private interests before any conception of the public good. There is, moreover, no evidence that liberal political processes offer any adequate defence against this. Given the underlying logic of the situation, this is not surprising; nor is it puzzling that the objective interests of the working classes have failed to provide an adequate selective incentive to motivate individuals in a world still dominated by capital.

3
Marx's Ethical Individualism and his Conception of Democracy

In this chapter I wish to explore the ethical assumptions which inform Marx's political judgements and his theory of democracy.

A difficulty in appreciating Marx's views in the area of political philosophy is that he abandoned any systematic speculations about normative issues at an early stage in his intellectual development because he thought the task of explaining social phenomena far more significant.[1] Thus, he concentrated on providing a materialist account of capitalist social relations, explaining, for example, the nature of profit so as to show how capital comes to be accumulated, and he showed a definite hostility towards those whose approach was purely normative. He writes:

> Does it require deep intuition to comprehend that man's ideas, views and conceptions, in one word, man's consciousness, changes with every change in the conditions of his material existence, in his social relations and in his social life?
> When people speak of ideas that revolutionize society, they do but express the fact that within the old society, the elements of a new one have been created and that the dissolution of the old ideas keeps even pace with the dissolution of the old conditions of existence.[2]

There are many statements of this kind in which Marx makes the point that moralizing merely indulges the illusion that social life can be transformed if people would only act morally or rationally – that is, if there is a change of consciousness.

Some writers have taken Marx's remarks in this connection as suggesting that we should never abstract political theorizing from an understanding of the dynamics of social relations and, more controversially, that political philosophy needs to be replaced by a sociology of knowledge. They have consequently concluded that Marx would recommend that we seek out the social (ideological) role played by ideas, so that they can be seen as contributing to the hegemony of one class over another. Marx, then, is seen as encouraging socialist intellectuals to identify the ideas which function to sustain class hegemony in particular historical periods.

There is, as I have noted, some evidence that Marx held the uncontroversial view that political theory should never be isolated completely from economic analysis, and we find him claiming also that certain ideas could only have been articulated at given stages in history.[3] Further, it is significant to note that Marx had a very poor opinion of those leading intellectuals who failed to appreciate the forces at work under capitalism.[4] To this extent at least, Marx certainly points the way towards the development of a sociology of knowledge. Nevertheless, both of these claims fall far short of the judgement that liberal philosophy (as distinct from liberal economic assumptions) is systematically misleading. Marx regarded political theorizing as largely irrelevant to the forces at work in social life, and he did not suppose that ideas played any significant role in seducing the proletariat into apathy. The most he says is that the liberal state poses as an illusory agent of the general good, but according to his account it achieves this more by the tasks it performs on behalf of society as a whole (such as coping with natural disasters) than by putting forth misleading philosophical conceptions.

In so far as Marx assesses the role of philosophical ideas as political weapons, he certainly does not think that liberal ideals contribute to the hegemony of the bourgeoisie. Notions such as the importance of human autonomy, political liberty and rights, along with ideals such as the achievement of equality, did, of course, come most prominently into circulation as a consequence of the struggle of the bourgeoisie against feudalism, but Marx believed that these same ideas could be turned against the exploiters. The new ruling class was, in fact, caught in a trap of its own making, for in order to preserve the interests of capital accumulation, it necessarily frustrated the realization of true human autonomy, true political liberty and equality. Nor does Marx reprimand liberal philosophers – or even Young Hegelians such as Feuerbach or Bauer – for failing to articulate the true nature of these ideals; rather, he is concerned that they do not see how difficult it is for these goals to be realized under capitalist relations of production. Marx's judgement seems to have been that the normative task of articulating political ideals had actually been accomplished by Rousseau, Kant and the Young Hegelians, and that the real task in his day was to transform social life. This would be the historical role undertaken by the proletariat. He does not suppose that the emerging class would require new ideals; he assumed that it would provide the revolutionary force necessary to destroy capitalism — this is how the ideals of the bourgeoisie would come to be realized.

We can conclude that there is some licence in Marx for taking liberal theory seriously, and certainly it is worth exploring the degree to which his own conception of democracy was inspired by individualist ways of thinking. This will be the task of the chapter. I begin first by looking at the core ideas of what I call ethical individualism and show how Marx's romantic conception of the human potential is related to this tradition; I then look at his critique of liberalism and at his own conception of democracy; finally, I consider some serious problems with Marx's approach and review an alternative put forward by C. B. Macpherson.

Ethical Individualism

The way in which I use the label ethical individualist embraces a number of closely related ideals and a principle which I regard as lying at the core of a humanist approach to politics and ethics.[5] First, individualists place a value on the achievement of personal autonomy — on the development, that is, of a capacity to be self-directing and not simply a pawn of other people's manipulations, or subject entirely to the forces of nature and society. We can express this by saying that individualists comprehend the dignity of persons as somehow requiring that they be left free to realize aims which they have decided upon for themselves. Second, individualists refuse to accept that the purposes and values of actual individuals be subordinated to the claims of the collectivity; thus, the only reason which individualists accept as a sufficient justification for foreclosing on the choices of others is to ensure that everyone enjoys the maximum liberty compatible with a like liberty for all. It follows that although particular individualist writers will have their own distinctive conception of the good, they do not regard it as legitimate for this to be promoted at the cost of violating the autonomy of others.

Some liberal individualists assume that the ownership of property and the right to dispose of it as one chooses is somehow to be included in any adequate conception of human autonomy. They claim that without the right to privately owned property there can be no adequate fulfilment of our human capacity to be autonomous. Extreme liberals (those I call possessive individualists) consequently argue that the principle of freedom embodied in my second postulate should be read as including a prohibition against governments' interfering with the way in which individuals dispose of their own property. Other liberals (mostly those influenced by utilitarian ways of thinking) are content to suggest that the area of social life left to the private choices of individuals be maximized as far as this is compatible with general welfare;[6] of course, in terms of liberal economic assumptions, the most advantageous policies are usually those which do not destroy the incentive to accumulate private wealth but, even so, utilitarian individualists are sometimes prepared to allow that governments may foreclose on property rights.

Marxists reject both liberal positions because, in their view, any right privately to dispose of property necessarily undermines human autonomy. This is so, they argue, because in the circumstances of free competition to control productive resources the majority of those who have no property must abandon their capacity to develop any autonomy of their own in selling their labour power as a commodity.

Despite differences in the way the core commitments of individualism are interpreted as a result of these incompatible assessments of the impact of private property rights, and excluding Maoists and perhaps also some Leninists, there is, nevertheless, an emerging consensus amongst theorists that liberal humanist values must lie at the heart of any adequate justificatory theory of political life.[7] It makes a lot of sense, then, to seek out possible ways in which different approaches can be reconciled, and we may also conclude that we are likely to make progress in democratic theorizing by asking ourselves what Marxists have to learn from liberals and vice versa.

Before proceeding further, it is necessary for me to distinguish two very different approaches within the individualist tradition. I shall call the first 'want-regarding' individualism, and here I have in mind English utilitarian thought going back from J. S. Mill through Hume to Hobbes. The other is the tradition, heavily influenced by German thought, which embraces Marx, Hegel and Rousseau, but which, through the work of T. H. Green and writers such as A. D. Lindsay, has also had an important influence on Anglo-American ways of thinking about political institutions. I use the label 'ideal-regarding' to describe this humanist tradition.

In characterizing these positions I make use of a distinction, to which Brian Barry has drawn our attention, between what he calls ideal-regarding approaches and want-regarding approaches.[8] The difference between these is brought into focus by Barry when he asks us to consider the kinds of reasons which could be provided for taxing the consumption of beer in order to subsidize the activity of going to the theatre. Those who oppose any taxation of beer presumably hope to give people what they actually do desire, whereas those who wish to subsidize the theatre and to penalize the drinking of beer believe that some ways of spending one's leisure are better than others and hope to promote an appreciation of culture amongst the masses. To take another example, if we look at the institutions which prevail in the area of sexual relations, it will be found today, in the more affluent Western countries at least, that there is a commitment to leaving matters to the determinations established through personal choice. But why is there support for this form of allocation? Why is it that so many of us think that it is a good idea to leave sexual relationships to free competition? Some defend this commitment with want-regarding arguments: the suggestion is that people should be left to do what they want because only in this way will overall happiness be maximized; others employ ideal-regarding arguments, suggesting that the highest expression of true love must involve free choice, and that to establish sexual relations on any other basis would violate our dignity as people.

Both ideal-regarding and want-regarding arguments have had an influence within the liberal individualist tradition, but it is, surprisingly, the latter form of argument (derived from Hobbes and systematized by Bentham) which has been the most popular approach. Liberal individualists have, for the most part, endeavoured to defend a commitment to recognizing personal choice (giving individuals what they actually want) on utilitarian grounds. Even the concern of liberals to interpret social life as some sort of contract between rational self-interested individuals has often been premised on the assumption that the utility of institutions can be demonstrated in this way.

Want-regarding individualists, especially those who are also 'possessive individualists',[9] tend to subsume dignity under the ideal of autonomy and to conceive of the latter in terms of liberty. I mean by this that in their conception we can best realize our humanity by protecting as large an area as is possible within which the individual is not directly coerced by others. Want-regarding individualists focus, then, on how we can eliminate the domination of one person by another so that each person's choices are afforded an equal weighting, and they do not trouble themselves greatly to consider how humanity taken as a whole can develop a capacity to exert some influence in shaping the human destiny. The assumption is often made, of course, that where coercion is limited to the role of preventing one person from interfering with another's right to choose, our overall capacity to control our own lives will be maximized; also that this freedom will lead to greater want satisfaction than would be the case where interfering governments acted paternalistically.

Want-regarding individualism is, therefore, vulnerable to empirical refutation, for if the consequences of free choice in unbridled market competition do not result in an increase in overall happiness (as Marx argues), then it is difficult to see how a commitment to freedom (I include here the freedom to own and control property) can be defended using want satisfaction as the only standard.

A purely want-regarding approach is also difficult to defend philosophically. As Barry has shown,[10] the problem is that if one begins with want-regarding premises only, one cannot reach conclusions which discriminate between wants. Thus, if A's desire is that B (a member of a different racial group) should be required to use separate public toilets, and if this concern is an obsession, so that the want is stronger than any objection B may have to the discrimination, as consistent want-regarding theorists we would surely have to support the satisfaction of A's prejudice. A difficulty for utilitarian theorists is, then, that they cannot easily discriminate between wants in order to claim that some are better or more desirable than others. But individualists need to discriminate between wants, for most would hold, as J. S. Mill does, that C's desire to prevent D from practising his or her religion should not count as an acceptable reason for interfering with D's choices — that is, that the claim to freedom of each person should be compatible with everyone else's enjoyment of equal liberty.

Most of the classical utilitarian writers do not seem to have been aware of this problem.[11] Bentham thought it sufficient to require that each person's choices be counted equally, but he does not seem to have seen that, even allowing for this, he would still have to tolerate prejudice. John Stuart Mill was less happy about defending liberty in a purely want-regarding way, although even he seems to have supposed that individualist values could be defended on utilitarian grounds.

Many liberals have, however, been persuaded to abandon utilitarianism and have defended personal choice by making the ideal-regarding claim that our dignity as persons somehow requires that we act autonomously (so even if people make silly choices, leading to a decrease in their overall happiness, they should be required to stick by them). It is not merely that these writers became aware of the logical difficulties implicit in a purely want-regarding approach; more important, there was significant dissatisfaction with the moral dimensions of utilitarianism and with the passive, self-indulgent, materialist conception of human nature which seemed to be assumed by the approach. Frustrations of this kind can be found in the younger Mill's own work, for he was very much preoccupied with finding ways in which individuals could develop their capacities, and he argued in this context that progress meant not that people consumed more and more material goods but that they learned to refine their sensibilities and to discriminate higher from lower pleasures.[1,2]

What emerged in the late nineteenth century was an apologetic which shifted the emphasis away from the benefits of consumerism towards an appreciation of liberty as a value in itself. Bourgeois society was applauded because it allowed people to develop their capacity to be autonomous (of course, they could choose to spend their time under the influence of liquor or succumb to the squalor of poverty). What was thought to be important, however, was that people should be taught to handle freedom, for it was assumed that progress could not be made by looking backwards to a time when individuality was not deemed to be of value; furthermore, the new liberals argued that how we develop depends crucially on whether we are treated as responsible agents capable of making choices for ourselves or regarded as complex machines whose behaviour is manipulated by the rewards and punishments imposed by those in authority.

I describe ideal-regarding liberals as humanists, for they can be differentiated from those who remain content with a want-satisfaction approach by the fact that they embrace a conception of the essential nature of people. In this they are influenced by Kant, who has provided an account of our humanity in terms of an alleged potentiality that persons enjoy for acting in the light of reason rather than simply responding to stimuli. Thus, as against Hume and Hobbes, who accept that reason can only be the slave of passion, Kant distinguishes what he calls the categorical imperative. According to him, we not only need to reason in the light of some understanding of wants (if you want ...then you ought to do...) but we are also capable of perceiving rationally that we have a duty to act in ways which may seem to conflict with our inclinations. For Kant, the truly autonomous person is not swayed by passion but chooses to act one way or another only after making the rational judgement that it is the right thing to do. It is, then, he argues, only by developing our capacity to reason and not simply by passively satisfying our wants that we will come to realize our truly human nature. What is thought to be important, then, is that people be taught to handle freedom responsibly, and this requires that they be forced to develop their capacity to reason.

Humanist individualism was also influenced by both Hegel and Rousseau who, as we have seen in Chapter 2, stress how our development as persons — even the shape of our dispositions — is intimately connected with the kind of society in which we are nurtured. It is accepted that there can be no development of our individuality outside community with others, and that even our capacity to reason is to a large extent the product of social interaction.

In the light of these assumptions, it is not surprising that humanists should wish to assess institutions by the opportunities which they afford to individuals. At its best, according to humanists, communal life should not impose on individuals in a way which destroys their personal autonomy but ought to provide rights which, as Green puts it, are a 'power of acting for his own ends — for what he conceives to be his good — secured to an individual by the community on the supposition that its exercise contributes to the good of the community.'[13] A central issue with regard to the conception reflected in this quotation (which I have taken from T. H. Green's *Lectures on the Principles of Political Obligation*) relates, of course, to his qualification 'for the good of the community'. What Green seems to have in mind here is that if an individual is to claim something as a right, then he or she ought to recognize that a similar right should also be enjoyed by other members of the community. What is good for the development of any single person's individuality must necessarily also be good for others, and they have an equal claim, therefore, to have their potentiality protected. Green could not, then, have approved those situations (as in ancient Rome and Athens or in modern South Africa) in which the emancipation of some is accomplished at the cost of enslaving others.

A central concern for the humanist individualist is to decide just where one person's claim to an entitlement involves the violation of the claims of others to equal dignity and respect, so that their development as persons is jeopardized unfairly. This is the problem which I will explore more fully in Part II. At this stage I wish, first, to note that

Marx should be regarded as a humanist individualist and, second, to show that his dispute with writers like Green (and Hegel) relates to their economic and sociological assumptions and not to their humanism.

There can be little dispute over whether Marx is an individualist, for he places great value on the achievement of autonomy. It is true that he emphasizes how bound up each of us is within our community, so that we may never satisfy our potentiality merely by retreating into a private sphere in the way that J. S. Mill at times seems to suggest. Marx clearly shares the Kantian conception of human essence as a potentiality to achieve autonomy, and his critique of liberalism arises out of his claim that the prevailing conditions in liberal society actually serve to frustrate our efforts to be self-directing. It should be noted also that his radical assumptions about property in no way entail (as it is sometimes alleged) that the purposes and values of actual individuals be subordinated to the claims of the collectivity. Indeed, a careful reading indicates that Marx's own understanding of class conflict entails a strong condemnation of any situation in which some are subordinated to the claims and purposes of others. Marx's individualism goes further than that of most liberals in this regard, for he is concerned also with the way in which the economic system itself comes to dominate, emerging as a seemingly autonomous power that sets goals for humans which they themselves do not choose and which are alien to their development. We can say, then, that Marx is a humanist and also an individualist (in the sense in which I have elected to use this label).

Marx's commitment to the central values of individualism is informed, as I have said, by very different assumptions from those of liberal theories, and certain features of his orientation need to be noted. I shall discuss briefly his romanticism and his rejection of 'possessive individualism'.

It is significant that Marx is much more influenced by Rousseau and by German romanticism than are most liberals. This accounts, in part at least, for why he seems to be more clear-sighted about the negative impact of the Industrial Revolution. Marx's romanticism is also responsible for his greater optimism, for he genuinely believes that it is possible for a society to exist where there is total harmony between the interests of individuals and the good of the collectivity. Marx supposes, in this regard, that in a future communist society individuals will express their individuality only in socially constructive ways — that in developing themselves they will at the same time, and necessarily, contribute to the good of the whole community.

As is to be expected, this romantic aspect of Marx's individualism has often been unfavourably compared with the more pessimistic 'realism' of most liberal writers who assume that it will always be necessary for the state to impose some sort of harmony upon the anarchistic inclinations of individuals. While I accept that there is some force to this criticism, its importance (as I show more fully in the next chapter) has been greatly exaggerated. In any case, as will become clear when we review Marx's notion of democracy, it would be wrong to conclude from the fact that Marx believes in a future society in which there is a natural harmony of interests that he necessarily has an unrealistic conception of the need for democratic control; the state, for Marx, disappears only where control lies firmly in the hands of the people.

The most important distinguishing feature of Marx's humanism is his complete rejection of 'possessive individualism'. He argues that the development of individuality cannot be dependent on our personal possession and control of property because this is incompatible with any harmonious development of communal life, and that human autonomy in the social world can only be achieved where communal choices are made collectively. Thus, in so far as we are dependent on community, our individual development is vitiated by the antagonism generated where there are private holdings in property; further, our autonomy (both individual and collective) is lost when the market substitutes its own imperatives for human choices.

It is interesting to observe that T. H. Green, in stating his view that a right to hold and to dispose of privately owned property should be upheld by the state, actually takes the trouble to address himself to what he takes to be the main objections of his socialist critics. He claims, first, that our development as persons requires that society should secure for us the power to acquire and keep the means of realizing a will (that is, a right to property); he then observes that if such a right is to be meaningful, we must be capable of making good or bad use of the opportunity afforded. Thus, Green concludes, if individuals are to be treated as persons responsible for their own well-being, inequality will necessarily result. As he puts it:

If we leave a man free to realize the conception of a possible well-being, it is impossible to limit the effect upon him of his desire to provide for his future well-being, as including that of the persons in whom he is interested, or the success with which at the prompting of that desire he turns resources of nature to account. Considered as representing the conquest of nature by the efforts of free and variously gifted individuals, property must be unequal; and no less must it be so if considered as a means by which individuals fulfil social functions.[14]

Green goes on to suggest that the increase of private wealth in this way does not diminish the opportunities or resources available to others. This is because the opportunities for ownership available to others are not jeopardized and because accumulation results from increasing the total wealth available and not from taking away what others own. He concludes that there is no reason why individuals should not be entitled to enjoy the fruit of their endeavours, nor any justification for preventing them from passing it on to their children.

These arguments, which are typical of liberal theorizing about property rights,[15] do not meet the full thrust of Marx's critique. The issue is not merely that the inequalities generated by market exchanges cannot be justified in the way that Green supposes (see my discussion of Nozick's restatement of Green's arguments in Chapter 8), but also that capitalist relations involve an alienation of our capacity to subordinate nature to human purposes. The point to note is that Marx's critique of individualism emerges from within the assumptions of individualist humanism itself, and this point is generally missed by liberals who try to dispose of socialist ideals by providing arguments to justify inequality when the real dispute is about the alienating effects of capitalism.

I turn now to consider two characteristic features of Marx's conception of democracy: first, his challenge to Hegel's idea (derived from Hobbes and reflected in most liberal political theories) that the state ought to (and necessarily does) stand autonomously apart from civil society, imposing some structure on the potential anarchy; second, Marx's rejection of any form of elitism and his conception of democracy as rule from below.

Marx's Critique of Hegel's Notion of the Autonomous Bourgeois State

In his *Critique of Hegel's Philosophy of Right* Marx correctly identifies the idea of an autonomous state imposing rationality upon the particularistic forces of civil society as a crucial weakness. As we have already noted, Hegel thought of civil society as the sphere of life in which the conflicts and disputes manifesting the particular interests of individuals and groups were paramount. These conflicts were, nevertheless, held in check to some degree and, through arbitration and collective decision-making, synthesized by the activities of the state. In Hegel's conception the general good of all was somehow mediated by the main political institutions of the modern German state. Thus, the hereditary sovereign, although essentially feudal, nevertheless represented the collectivity precisely because he or she did not have to rely on any groups representing specific interests to gain power; the bureaucrats, because they had tenure of position and secure salaries, were also able to stand for the general interest against forces asserting the claims of particular interests; finally the Assembly of Estates provided the instrumentality by means of which the conflicting interests of civil society eventually came to be harmonized.[16]

Marx rejects this view of the state as an agency of the collectivity. In the first place, he is not prepared to accept that the state is as autonomous as Hegel seemed to assume, for in his view the instrumentality more often than not serves the interests of the dominant forces of civil society. He also points out that the state is a complex set of institutions which are manned by actual people, who are themselves involved in particular social relationships. Thus, Marx suggests, to the extent that the state is autonomous of civil society the instrumentality serves the interests of the bureaucratic officials whose personal ambitions and material well-being prosper with the growth of state power. For these reasons, then, Marx is highly critical of Hegel's political judgement.[17]

Marx allows that the role of the state in the bourgeois period was distinctive, in that forces at work in civil society asserted themselves against the shackles of feudal politics in a way which created an illusion of independence, because political liberty and equality were established as basic rights. But he points out that the so-called free state which was established in France as a result of the Revolution and in America where the feudal order had no deep roots in no way embodied the universal interests of all. Indeed, Marx argues that the contrary is the case: for if abstract idealism manifests itself in a purely political form, it allows the emancipation of the forces of egoism and crass materialism. As Marx puts the point:

But the perfection of the idealism of the state was at the same time the perfection of the materialism of civil society. The shaking-off of the political yoke was at the same time the shaking-off of the bonds which had held in check the egoistic spirit of civil society. Political emancipation was at the same time the emancipation of civil society from politics, from even the appearance of a universal content.[18]

It is for this reason, then, that Marx found the anti-feudal programme of Young Hegelian writers so inadequate — in his judgement there could be no purely political emancipation.

If one regards the state as somehow embodying the collective goals of community, and if, moreover, one regards it as being essential that these be imposed upon the particularistic egoism which informs individual behaviour in civil society, the question of which social forces are allowed to have political influence becomes a matter of vital importance. Ideally speaking, the essence of the state as the embodiment of pure reason would be best preserved where there is total autonomy from the influences of civil society, so that the state co-ordinates and controls impartially and is not itself determined. This was Hegel's reason for supporting hereditary monarchy and for thinking that bureaucrats needed to be protected from the corrupting forces of civil society. The Young Hegelians were, of course, unhappy about Hegel's undemocratic political commitments, and particularly with his sympathy for constitutional monarchy, but they were, nevertheless, sufficiently influenced by him to have their own reservations about placing unbridled power in the hands of the people. Clearly, if one starts out with the assumption that the state ought to be the embodiment of universal values, one's democratic commitment with regard to such issues as the extension of the franchise to women, to poorly educated workers and peasants and perhaps even to Jews will be influenced by whether one thinks these groups will use citizenship rights responsibly. It is because he posed the problem of Jewish emancipation in this distinctively Hegelian way that Bruno Bauer (whose opinions Marx challenged in a series of articles in the *Rheinische Zeitung* during 1843)[19] argued against the extension to Jews of the responsibilities and privileges of citizenship.

I shall briefly discuss Marx's dispute with Bauer because his opposition to the latter's attitude reflects an approach to political issues which remained characteristic throughout his career. The arguments on both sides of the dispute also clearly illustrate the Hegelian view of the political sphere on the one hand and Marx's reasons for rejecting it on the other.

Bauer seems to have believed that if the political sphere could come to embody secular standards based on impartiality and a respect for competence, it would impose these rational standards upon society. From his perspective, the extension of political rights to Jews seemed to be almost contradictory: for, as he puts it, as long as a person remains Jewish:

The restricted nature that makes him a Jew will inevitably gain the ascendancy over the human nature which should join him as a man to other men; the effect will be to separate him from non-Jews. He declares through this separation that the particular nature which makes him a Jew is his true and highest nature in the face of which human nature is forced to yield.[20]

Bauer's view rests on the assumption that there is a contradiction between religious prejudice and political emancipation; thus, for him progress depends on freeing the state from the shackles of religion. Bauer's point, put simply, is that if people are religious, there will be conflicts between those of different faiths. It follows from this that if there is to be emancipation, then religious sentiments should not be encouraged. It was on this basis that he argues that Jewish emancipation would be a step backwards (or, to put the point the Hegelian way, that a state which presupposes religion could not be a true or actual state). What Bauer suggests is that instead of asking for recognition of themselves as Jewish, so that they have privileges similar to those of Christians, Jews should renounce religion itself and work for the emancipation of Germany; that is, they should join in the struggle for a purely secular society instead of worrying about their circumstances as Jews.

Marx suggests that the lesson to be learned from a consideration of the religious issue is not (as Bauer thought) that political emancipation is impossible without the abandonment of religion, but that political emancipation taken in itself, because it is fully compatible with the practice of religion in the private sphere of civil society, is not the final form of human emancipation. Real, practical emancipation means freedom from the circumstances which produce a religious response. In its wider application, Marx's point is that the Hegelian way of posing the political problem sanctions the illusion that the political sphere, considered in abstraction from civil society and represented by the state, can come to embody general interests. But, Marx argues, the reality is the very antithesis of this, for the consummation of abstract idealism, as this manifests itself in political forms, allows for the emancipation of the very worst forces of egoism and crass materialism in civil society. Liberty in such circumstances does not mean liberation from religion, but rather religious liberty — just as it does not mean liberty from property, but rather the liberty to own property (including the labour power of others).

Marx's criticism of what he took to be the essential weakness of liberal ways of theorizing about politics — that they regarded the state as imposing upon civil society, whereas in fact it is subordinate to the forces of the latter — although articulated when he was only twenty-four, informed his political judgement throughout his long career. Thus, for example, in his commentary on the *Gotha Programme* (drawn up by leaders of the German Socialist Party, who endeavoured to set out in point form some basic commitments over which they could all agree)

Marx criticizes the fact that political freedom is listed as a primary objective.[21] What these socialists are asking for, Marx scornfully observes, is nothing more than what has already been achieved in Switzerland and the United States. In his view, the authors of the *Gotha Programme*, because they think of the state as autonomous, fail to comprehend that the final conclusion to the class struggle cannot be produced under the 'free state' form characteristic of the bourgeois period — they fail to see that the 'free' state of the bourgeois period serves the interests of capital. Marx suggests, in contrast, that what the workers will have to aim for is the subordination of the state to the people, and that for this purpose they should establish a revolutionary dictatorship of the proletariat to transform capitalist social relations.

Marx's notion of dictatorship in this context is not altogether clear. As we shall see, however, in reviewing his notion of democracy as control from below, it is highly unlikely that he had in mind any model of elitist leadership commanding the state instrumentalities so as to transform civil society. Such a conception would have been Hegelian. What Marx was proposing was the subordination of the state to revolutionary forces in civil society — the state was to reflect the interests of the emerging proletariat and would, to this end, have to be controlled by workers.

Marx, the Extreme Democrat

I turn now to explore this idea that Marx is an extreme democrat.[22]

We can begin by noting that Marx's understanding of the subordination of the state to civil society (outlined in the previous section) was complicated in his more mature period, for he came to accept a class view of political conflicts. Thus, although (as we have seen) Marx first viewed the state as an instrument of factions within both bureaucracies and civil society, he later put forward the view that the state served (*in the last instance*)[23] to maintain the hegemony of one class over another. Politics was in this sense determined by economics and reflected class divisions. (This view is most clearly stated in the *Communist Manifesto*.)

The sense in which Marx views the state as serving the interests of the capitalists can best be interpreted as relating to certain functional tasks necessary to sustain and to facilitate the accumulation of capital. The bourgeois state, in his conception, is the vehicle in terms of which the class of accumulators can co-ordinate itself, superimposing collective choices on the resistance of the wider society. Some form of collective action is necessary to repress threats from subordinate groups or classes, to assure the provision of services in the interests of the whole class which are not easy for individuals to supply for themselves (such as energy supplies and roads); to provide for defence against foreign invasions; to maintain the rule of law and to arbitrate where there are disputes between rivals.[24]

Marx's judgement here about the role of the state is qualified, as Hal Draper has shown in his recent work,[25] by the following observations. First, Marx does not mean that the state will never be opposed by factions of the capitalist class. Indeed, a characteristic feature of the role of the state in sustaining class hegemony is that it must impose certain objectives in the face of opposition from groups within the very class whose interests are being served. As we noted in the last chapter, not all capitalists will approve of burdens imposed upon them in the name of the public good, and even where they do, it will be in their interests to ensure that they contribute as few of their own resources as possible; they endeavour, in short, to make someone else pay. It follows from this that Marx does not assert that there will not be conflicts of interest within the ruling class, or that these will not produce political struggles. Finally, Marx allows that in some circumstances, particularly where the struggles between factions within the bourgeois class become so marked that no particular group emerges with sufficient support to govern effectively on behalf of that class, the state instrumentality may fall into the hands of some other class, or even a dictator. What Marx shows in his discussion of Louis Bonaparte[26] (and as has been conclusively demonstrated by the case of South Africa, which remains capitalist even though the state instrumentality is in the hands of the urban proletariat) is that, regardless of who has political control of the state, prosperity under capitalism will be facilitated until such time as revolutionary forces emerge in civil society. Apart from anomalous periods in which the state may fall into the hands of an adventurer, such as Louis Napoleon became in his later years (or, as Hitler clearly was), the state will serve the interests of the bourgeoisie.

Marx's conception of the state as an instrument of class rule was integrated into his theorizing about democracy. He argued, for example, that communism (by bringing an end to class conflict) would eliminate the need for an instrument of coercion. In these circumstances governments would come to reflect democratic forces and would no longer serve to sustain exploitation.[27]

There are a number of aspects of Marx's view of the replacement of state control by democracy which require commentary in the light of past misunderstandings. I shall deal with his claim that the state will 'wither away' (the phrase is Engels's), his conception of the 'dictatorship' of the proletariat and his attitude to civil liberties and the issue of reformism.

MARX AND THE 'WITHERING AWAY' OF THE STATE

Marx views the state, as we have seen, as an essential instrumentality of class domination. It is through the state that the ruling class organizes itself to defend its interests against revolutionary pressures from below. Also, only the state instrumentality can provide the adjustments necessary to ensure that exploitation can proceed with maximum efficiency, and it is the state which supplies the means whereby conflicts within the ruling class itself are prevented from escalating to the point where they threaten the capacity of the class to rule. In Marx's view, these tasks arising out of the struggle between classes will become unnecessary once society is transformed so that there is no longer any exploitation of one group by another. Engels summarizes Marx's idea here by saying that in a future socialist society the state will 'wither away' and the administration of persons will be replaced by the administration of things.[28]

These views have given rise to a volume of criticism, for they would appear to display a naive Utopianism. Are we to suppose that future societies (presumably characterized by even greater use of complex technology and embracing millions of citizens) will be able to dispense with bureaucratic rule? Are these societies to have no inspectors to secure standards protecting health, safety and the environment? Will there be no parliaments and courts for the resolution and adjudication of disputes? Will there be no need for police to coerce those who may act in ways which are disorderly or criminal? Will we not need democratic rights to be embodied in constitutional documents and protected by processes of judicial review? If we take the 'withering away' conjecture as an answer to these questions, then it would seem as if Marx is defending a judgement which goes against all that history has taught us about the problems of administration and human nature. Most important, Marx seems to overlook the fact that the cost of securing equality in social life, at least in those countries in which there is an advanced division of labour, is an expanding bureaucracy and inefficiency.[29]

Even if we have reservations about this judgement (for it is debatable whether, in the long term, free enterprise systems will show that they are inherently more efficient than those which are subject to centralized planning of resource allocation), it is beyond contention that people will be governed in future societies and that the most pressing problem will be to find ways in which citizens can hold elected representatives and bureaucratic agencies in check. The question we need to ask, then, is whether Marx is committed to the view that future communities will be able to do away with government and administration.

Hal Draper, using particularly Engels's work on anthropology, and especially his discussion of the origins of the state as a guide, has suggested that Marx always had in mind that certain functional tasks in any society would have to be accomplished, that the state, besides ensuring the continued domination of one class over another, also had to perform certain general functions.[30] Thus, in any society, whether communist, primitive or class dominated, there will have to be some potentiality for reaching communal decisions to mobilize and deal with contingencies (for example, floods and wars) and to commit social resources in one direction rather than another; there will also be a need for adjudication where there are disputes between individuals or between them and the state, and some coercion will be needed to ensure that order prevails. In the bourgeois period, according to Marx and Engels, these tasks are undertaken by the state in ways which reveal a definite class bias; even so, it is often the case that what is accomplished by government agencies is in the general interest (in dealing with health hazards, for instance, and in helping people after natural disasters). In a future socialist society, in contrast, there will be no serious discrimination against any segment of society in the way that priorities are chosen; also, it will be possible for the community as a whole to be involved in administrative tasks. This will arise because where there is full reciprocity in social life the community will be able to rely more and more on public opinion as a means of social control, for there will be no groups or factions who collectively feel resentment about being treated unfairly. Furthermore, the community will easily reach agreement about what is to be done for, again, no particular group will regard its interests as being seriously threatened by any decisions which are made in the area of resource allocation (this is because the gains and burdens will be shared fairly). And since there will be no deep conflicts between rival communities, the means of coercion can be left in the hands of the people without fear of civil war or revolution.

A sympathetic reading of Marx suggests, then, that his notion of the 'withering away' of the state refers only to the fact that its central role in sustaining the conditions necessary for the exploitation of the labour power of one class by another will eventually disappear. Once this has occurred, the community as a whole will be able to co-operate in accomplishing the other functions which are necessary in all societies. What is distinctive and controversial about Marx's view is that he thinks that the community will be able to do this without establishing specialized agencies potentially hostile to the majority.

'THE DICTATORSHIP OF THE PROLETARIAT'

The above interpretation of Marx's view of the 'withering away' of the state is supported, in part at least, by his notion of the 'dictatorship of the proletariat'.[31] Clearly the initial stage after a revolutionary change will be one in which the state will have to be used for class purposes, for there will be a need to coerce those who resist revolutionary change. Thus, it is not surprising that Marx should suggest that a dictatorship by the working people over the reactionary forces which survive from the bourgeois period would be necessary in the initial period of social transformation. What Marx proposes is the subordination of the state agencies to the revolutionary forces of civil society, so that the emerging interests of the proletariat are protected. Thus, although he uses 'dictatorship' to describe this period, Marx in no way suggests that the state should be under the command of a special party or elite; rather, he seems to suppose that the capacity to use coercion would be subject to democratic control.

If we think of a totalitarian government as one under which the state becomes autonomous, isolated from forces in civil society, destroying all resistance and imposing itself in every social sphere by way of an all-pervasive control, then no thinker could be more against totalitarianism than Marx.[32] The transition he has in mind is one in which democratically accountable authorities use the coercive instrumentality of the state to ensure that it remains fully responsive to democratic forces in civil society. Thus, after the initial period there will be no further need to maintain any substantial army or police force, for the role of sustaining order will become a matter for the community to undertake collectively. There is an element of Utopianism here, to be sure, but those who see the shadow of a totalitarian dictatorship are reviewing Marx's remarks in the light of the Stalinist experience.

MARX'S ATTITUDE TO CIVIL LIBERTIES AND THE ISSUE OF REFORMISM

Marx's view of the state as necessarily having roots in civil society (so that it could only be an instrument of the collective good after civil society itself had been transformed by democratic forces) led also to his dismissive contempt for the strategy suggestion that socialists first control Parliament and then use the instrumentality to transform civil society by introducing independent productive co-operatives.[33] In terms of Marx's analysis of the relationship between the state and civil society, no such transformation of the latter would be possible by purely political means. This is because an agency such as Parliament is necessarily the servant of the prevailing and dominant forces in civil society. Thus, unless the proletariat confronts the bourgeoisie as a revolutionary force, the imperatives of the economic relations in society will continue to assert themselves whoever is elected to Parliament. Marx's point is that workers' representatives would be incapable of carrying through a programme of change successfully without the mobilized force of the people behind them. The reason for this is that any move seriously to frustrate the accumulation of capital would lead to a severe breakdown of economic life; consequently, a united bourgeoisie would struggle, by fair means or foul, to bring about a change of government so that what they regarded as responsible economic management could resume. For Marx, potentiality for social change must necessarily arise first in the form of antagonistic groups within the sphere of civil society; these will then have to organize themselves so that they can eventually act collectively as a class. It is only after the organization of the working masses is accomplished that there will be any chance of forcing changes upon the bourgeoisie.

If Marx is sceptical about reformism as a strategy (because the focus is not placed on the necessity of organizing the working people for class confrontation) he nevertheless regards the framework of liberal freedoms and the right of democratic representation as assisting the revolutionary struggle against the bourgeoisie. This judgement is again informed by his conception of democratic forces emerging within civil society, for he argues that political rights enable the proletariat to express its frustration with capitalism and to organize itself as a class.

The struggle to overthrow the system of class exploitation requires, then, that workers organize to confront capital (in the form of the employer) at their place of work, and that they organize themselves as a class for political struggle. In both of these endeavours the liberties enjoyed in bourgeois society actually serve to threaten the hegemony of the bourgeoisie itself; this is because they enable the proletariat to organize by affording it legal protection.[34] Marx tells us that it is precisely because the bourgeois state is troubled by the existence of effective democratic rights that it will, whilst paying lip-service to the ideals of freedom as an abstract commitment, endeavour always to ensure that they are not realized in practice.[35] Thus, although the legitimacy of the bourgeois state is based on abstract legal principles — said to ensure control by the people and allegedly embodied in constitutional provisions which, in form at least, appear to be democratic — in practice, partly because the formal political liberties of bourgeois constitutionalism go hand in hand with social inequality and partly because of the practice of bourgeois politicians who happily violate rights wherever this seems expedient, every liberty (apart from the right to own and dispose of property) will be severely restricted by bourgeois governments whenever this is expedient. For Marx, then, the struggle to organize workers must embrace a determination to protect rights and to expose the manipulations and hypocrisy of the bourgeoisie.

Problems and Perspectives Relating to Marx's Democratic Assumptions

It is necessary, finally, to review some substantial criticisms of the assumptions which lie at the heart of Marx's way of theorizing about democracy. As we have seen, he conceives of the historical task of communism as bringing about a reconciliation between the personal and the collective perspectives; he does not want to destroy individuality by subordinating it to the public, nor does he wish to destroy the state so as to free the personal, as some anarchists recommend. Marx's goal is to show how the dichotomy between the two is the result of structural features characteristic of capitalism, and that where these are transformed (that is, where communism is triumphant) political problems (as these are conceived of by liberals: the protection of a sphere of privacy against the state, the control of the elites who necessarily govern, the establishment of welfare distributions in the name of justice) will disappear also. A communist society, Marx would have us believe, will not be threatened by the state, for the means of coercion will lie with the people; nor will forces in communist society appropriate wealth in a way which requires coercion to redistribute resources in the name of justice. What we would have under communism, then, is a society in which the claims which individuals make upon each other are accepted as constructive and complementary rather than as threatening to personal well-being and development. In Marx's view, as we have seen, we develop our capacities and talents in community with others, for it is through non-coercive co-operation that we develop as people. Communist society, in Marx's conception, facilitates this process by eliminating the alienating effect of the particularistic egoism characteristic of those societies in which one person's development seems to be possible only at the expense of others. But how plausible are these assumptions?

Most of those who have thought about the Utopian aspects of Marx's theorizing have not been persuaded by his romanticism. The problem is that the supposition that there could be a society of the kind Marx has in mind when he talks about communism is implausible. This is because it is hard to accept that the only significant conflicts between persons are those which arise out of class antagonisms, and this is especially so if we envisage that there will be insufficient resources for everyone to be able to do as they choose all of the time; yet if we do not suppose that there will be some shortages of valued resources, we expose ourselves to the critics who charge radicals with insufficient realism. Kolakowski puts the point thus:

> At the present time it is obvious to all except a handful of New Left adolescents that socialism cannot literally 'satisfy all needs' but can only aim at a just distribution of insufficient resources — which leaves us with the problem of defining 'just' and of deciding by what social mechanism the aim is to be effected in each particular case.[36]

Kolakowski suggests that the idea that conflict will disappear when class antagonisms are eliminated presupposes an unprecedented moral revolution; further, that if we are to accept Marx's account of communist society, we need to suppose that full participatory democracy is both feasible and desirable in modern society, and that bureaucratic instrumentalities will not impose themselves in undemocratic ways.

These criticisms must be well taken even by those who are sympathetic to Marx's endeavours. Clearly, if there is to be a Utopian society, people will have to have ways of ensuring the accountabilty of those who govern. Nor can we rely, as Marx seems to, on the supposition that the people will be able to govern without a framework of 'law', for even if we hypothesize that everyone is motivated by the very best intentions, they will, nevertheless, have to have some notion of what it is right for them to do. Also, we must surely suppose that mistakes will be made, and those whose lives are adversely effected by these judgements must surely be entitled and encouraged to bring forward their complaints. It follows, then, that Utopian communities will need laws enabling citizens to gain access to information and ensuring that they have a right to express their viewpoint; citizens will also need to be secure in the belief that elections to office will be held periodically and that the procedures at these times will be fair.

Nevertheless, as I show more fully in the next chapter, it does not follow from the fact that one is sceptical about Marx's account of Utopia that one must necessarily regard his judgements about capitalism as in themselves unrealistic. Also, most contemporary radicals will readily concede that Marx's conception of democracy (although clearly along the right lines) is not adequately worked out in detail, and they may feel free to accommodate liberal constitutional principles (perhaps along the lines I suggest in Part II). Indeed, if we look carefully at both sides of the debate and are prepared to allow Marxists the right to supplement Marx's description to provide greater realism, we find that the only assumption which is required to sustain his case (that socialism is a better type of society) is that the incentives which arise from the right to own and control wealth are not essential for economic efficiency. Yet the assumption that the desire to accumulate private wealth is the only motivation compatible with the complexities of a modern industrial society is itself highly questionable. Marx can, then be defended against those who dismiss his critique of capitalism as purely Utopian.

Unfortunately, it is not merely Marx's conception of Utopia which no longer seems credible; much more worrying is his account of the revolutionary transformation from capitalism to socialism. As we have seen, Marx argues that the process of social change will require the destruction of the bourgeois state and its replacement by the dictatorship of the proletariat. Of course, as I have made clear, Marx was firmly committed to arming the people, and he was totally opposed to any form of elite leadership. But, even so, are we to suppose that it is possible for a revolution of this kind to occur spontaneously, without strong leadership of a dictatorial kind? Even if this is so, will there not be a serious political danger that some elite group monopolizing violence will triumphantly assume control over the dictatorship?

In responding to these issues a few radicals have simply accepted the need for some form of political leadership. What is needed, it is thought, is an organized party of disciplined revolutionaries who will be prepared to initiate changes on behalf of the working people. Thus, they argue, a full revolution will involve a first stage in which leaders succeed in co-ordinating resistance to the bourgeois state with the purpose of coming to power themselves; a second stage, once they are in power, which involves the consolidation of their control by the elite so that they can use the state instrumentality for revolutionary purposes; and a final stage in which social relations are transformed through use of the state, now under the command of the revolutionary elite who act on behalf of the proletariat. This model of revolution reasserts the Hegelian view that political instrumentalities must impose rationality upon civil society; the revolutionary task is to make social relations more rational by establishing socialism. The revolutionaries cannot wait upon a time when the people themselves will demand socialism, for this will not occur spontaneously. It follows, then, that it is only after the revolutionaries have made their contribution and have successfully established socialism as a viable set of social relations that it will be expedient to allow democratic institutions to re-emerge and political freedoms to be enjoyed.

An elitist approach to revolutionary change may be applicable in the circumstances of the poorer Third World countries. With regard to the more advanced capitalist systems, however, revolutionary elitism must be rejected as dangerous and undemocratic (and certainly in conflict with Marx's own commitment to the democratic control of the revolution by the people). The problems arise primarily because of the scale of the changes which it would presumably be necessary to undertake. For example, what are we to suppose that the idea of revolutionaries taking over the state instrumentality means in practice? Are all the present incumbents of the vast bureaucratic agencies (most of whom are conservative and have absorbed bourgeois ways of addressing problems) to be told that their services are no longer required? If so, what is to become of them? If not, who is to be weeded out and by what criteria is the selection to be made? What of the police and the military? Can these agencies really be changed at the command of a small, cohesive ruling elite which has recently gained power, or are they likely to remain (as in Chile) ready to turn against the revolution at the first serious attempt that is made to transform society? It is not merely the agencies of the state which are likely to be resistant to changes imposed by a revolutionary elite for experience shows that people are reluctant to give up their private holdings in property, however small these might be. What level of ownership, then, is to count as being incompatible with socialist objectives, and how are confiscations to be made effective in the face of the resistance of large sections (if not the majority) of the population? The elitist model of revolutionary change requires us to suppose either that society will be receptive to radical changes without the use of a great deal of coercion and disruption, or that coercion will prove productive. But neither supposition is at all plausible: the first conflicts with the view that most people will only support socialism after capitalist relations have been destroyed, and the second requires us to suppose that coercion as an instrument for changing social life is likely to prove productive. But those who are faced by bayonets are not likely to make loyal socialist subjects, nor will citizens who have witnessed the destruction of family members and friends be easily persuaded of the merits of the new order. Furthermore, those who use coercion are inevitably corrupted by their involvement; certainly, in their constant vigilance against enemies they will be likely to keep the activities of the state secret, and there is no doubt also that in order to make the transformation process palatable, they will use the media to mislead the people.

Even if we leave these problems aside (supposing that a revolutionary socialist elite will have the genius to find solutions once they come to power), we may also question whether a revolutionary vanguard party would actually be able to seize power in a modern state. It is possible, of course, for a group to seize power through a conspiracy within the military, but I assume that this is an option which is practical only for movements representing the extreme right-wing of the political spectrum. With regard to left-wing conspiracies, however, most observers concede that in the present state of political consensus (even where social conflicts are quite sharp, as in Britain today) it is most unlikely that a revolutionary group could come into power after co-ordinating a general confrontation between the major classes — that is, after successfully challenging the bourgeois state. The possibility that this kind of revolution will ever succeed is, indeed, so remote as to make the conspiracies of vanguard revolutionaries politically irrelevant; unless the masses are involved there will be no serious threat to the *status quo*.

What, then, is to be done? Are we to succumb to bourgeois pessimism and give up hope of achieving socialist objectives? One optimistic answer has been provided by C. B. Macpherson, who has found it necessary to revise his own Marxist perspective to take into account features of the late capitalist period not anticipated by Marx himself. The central focus of Macpherson's approach is the changed role of the state, for he is not prepared to go along with Marx's judgement that the political realm must necessarily serve the dominant forces within civil society. In this regard Macpherson points out that it is no longer plausible to separate the political realm from the economic in

Marx's rigid manner, for late capitalism exhibits a much more politicized economic life than was the case in earlier stages of development. What Macpherson suggests is that the more significant involvement of the state in economic life has been a response to crises of the kind which Marx predicted, but that the latter failed to comprehend the role which the state would play in stabilizing the capitalist system.

Consider first the involvement of the state in the economic sphere. Macpherson lists the following roles which seem either to be new or to have expanded so much in scale as to make it reasonable today to talk of a political economy: the provision of welfare benefits; the undertaking of large-scale infrastructural supports; the management of the economy so as to prevent unpredictable market fluctuations or to allay the damaging side-effects of unbridled appropriation.

With regard to the provision of welfare, it is clear that the state today controls huge sums for investment in services such as health care and education; the state has also come to cushion the effects of capitalism by taking over the provision of insurance where this seems necessary and sometimes by providing pensions and housing for the poor. These involvements should be considered alongside the state's undertaking of large-scale infrastructural supports (for example, the provision of resources such as urban transport systems and energy supplies), as well as the role of the state as a funder of research on a truly massive scale. As Macpherson notes, the state does not merely control vast amounts of capital: it also regulates the market in various ways to prevent fluctuations and to moderate the damaging impact which enterprises often have on the environment or on the health of consumers. The most important control which the state can manipulate here is the flow of money, but it also operates through boards to administer schemes aimed at stabilizing markets which would otherwise fluctuate unpredictably or in ways which could threaten the stability of the system of capital accumulation by private investment.

All these tasks which the state undertakes (and I have not mentioned the role of the state as co-ordinator of the defence budget) are necessary to anticipate or to cope with crises. Furthermore, the effectiveness of the state depends ultimately on the viability of the prevailing system of capital accumulation. The state, then, despite the size of its involvement in economic life, still plays a distinctively class role. Indeed, by undertaking the management of welfare and by supplying infrastructural supports, the state benefits the capitalist forces in society by setting them free from the burden of providing these services, and perhaps (although this is debatable) it also increases the efficiency with which these supports can be provided.

Macpherson argues, nevertheless, that what is interesting in the new situation of late capitalism is that it is now becoming increasingly difficult for the capitalist class to act collectively using the state, for there are often too many conflicts over how to proceed; also the state now has a capacity to act with more independence from, and sometimes even against, the interests of the ruling class itself. Indeed, he notes an irony, for the initiatives of contemporary bourgeois states, even though they are generally directed at facilitating the process of accumulation, have often been imposed, in the face of the opposition of various powerful factions within the bourgeoisie, by politicians responding to democratic forces. We are back, then, with a conception of the state as imposing a degree of rationality on a reluctant class, but in this case the driving force which ensures that political leaders commit the state instrumentality in an endeavour to stabilize and cushion the effects of the unbridled market is the majority of citizens exercising their rights. Up to a point, as we have noted, this responsiveness, imposed by those who must necessarily bear the harsher effects of a system whose imperatives are inherently irrational, has the effect of preventing the collapse of the system itself, and it is ultimately self-defeating.

Following Habermas,[37] Macpherson concludes from an analysis of this predicament that there is a persistent legitimation problem in modern capitalist systems. Thus, when the state gives in to the forces of capital by tolerating their activities even where the effects are disastrous for some groups (such as those who find themselves poisoned, unemployed or poor), it has to account for itself democratically, and this is often difficult to do persuasively, despite all the available resources of deception. On the other hand, Macpherson believes that the legitimation problem is complex, for in some cases political leaders are able to dominate the forces of capital because of the leverage resulting from the state's role in those areas of the economy in which it has become an essential subsidizer or in which its role as regulator is crucial. Also, the state is able to deal with competing groups independently, forcing each in turn to accept compromises which it would not otherwise have tolerated. Sometimes, then, the forces of capital will be unhappy with the performance of modern governments.

If this analysis is correct, a reformist strategy of piecemeal adjustment towards socialism makes sense. What is hopeful is the fact that capitalist relations are being increasingly exposed as irrational, and it is not inconceivable that in the foreseeable future large numbers of people will simply withdraw their support from politicians who constantly give in to the forces of capital. Macpherson notes in this regard that there are sections of the community (for example, the personnel of the public sector, recipients of welfare benefits and the well organized sections of labour in declining industries) which have a real interest in insisting on large-scale state intervention in the economy, so they may defend this even where their actions jeopardize the effective functioning of the capitalist system. Macpherson is also encouraged because, as he notes, more and more people are seeing unrestrained expansion as having a negative impact on the quality of life; also, people are beginning to organize themselves to oppose capitalism at the community level and are demanding greater democratic participation at their places of work. Macpherson suggests that these developments are an indication that people are beginning to question the capacity of the market to provide a rational commitment of resources. Significant numbers of citizens are finding themselves engaged in conflict with the anti-democratic forces of capital.

The critical question today is, then, whether in any society it will be possible, as a result of growing disenchantment with the performance of capitalism, to co-ordinate a socialist front party — which in the circumstances will also be a party supporting the maintenance of democratic rights (including the protections afforded to trade unions) — so that the reactionary forces representing those who would rather abandon liberal democracy than free enterprise can be adequately confronted. We can say, also, in the light of Macpherson's analysis (which I believe to be sound), that the debate between those who support 'reformism' and those who advocate 'revolutionary struggle' which so preoccupied Lenin and Marx is now a dispute of purely symbolic importance between socialists.

4
Marxism and Utopia: Macpherson's Contribution

In recent years radical political theory has embraced a self-conscious moralizing Utopianism which needs to be distinguished sharply from Marxism properly understood. Radical moralists have been concerned primarily with the negative way in which liberal theory has come to think about politics. They have shown little patience with theories which set horizons pragmatically, and many have rejected the typically liberal view that the central problem of politics is 'the antique and yet ever recurring problem of how citizens can keep their rulers from becoming tyrants'.[1] This goal, say the new Utopians, is much too restrictive; they point out that the classical democratic theorists had no such limited vision, and that their concerns went far beyond such a narrowly defined commitment to speak of democracy as a theory of society and not merely as a mechanism for controlling rulers. The classical writers, we are told, were generally concerned with the quality of life encouraged by social institutions and with ideals such as liberty, fraternity and dignity. Modern liberal writers, on the other hand, are criticized (often quite unfairly) for jettisoning this idealism and for accommodating their horizons to the facts of the contemporary 'real world'.[2]

It is suggested that we need to re-articulate our ideals (liberty, good government, moral autonomy and so on), and then try to inspire change in the direction of these desirable goals.

Given their penchant for arguments of the kind outlined, it is not surprising that radical theorists have acquired a reputation for being excessively moralistic. They are also often criticized on the grounds that the mere citation of ideals does not provide any adequate philosophical argument for the moral positions adopted. In this regard it is unfortunate that so many radicals react so fiercely against individualism; this is because they fail to appreciate the significance of adopting a method in ethical discussion which does not take moral values or an idealized conception of human nature as given.

I shall argue in this chapter that some contemporary radical theorists are guilty of moralizing with no firm philosophical argument or sociological evidence to offer in support of their viewpoint; and that, properly understood, Marxist theory should not be regarded as a polemic of a moralizing kind. In developing these points I take C. B. Macpherson's work as an example of what I call a Marxist position and contrast it with the perspectives of liberal writers on the one hand and those whom I label Utopian moralists on the other.

The Poverty of Radical Idealism

The concern of most radical political theory has been to provide an alternative to individualist approaches. Radical moralists complain that the abstract approach, used by utilitarian liberals and by individualists, has built into it untenable assumptions about the human predicament, and especially about the human character. They argue further that we need to resist the temptation to think in the negative way characteristic of so much liberal thought. If, for example, we do not find many citizens involved in active political participation, then, it is argued, we (as democrats) should be concerned to find ways to improve this state of affairs. This, the radicals concede, may well require that we establish social programmes for socializing people to become participants in the democratic process (for legitimation of this form of elitism they often cite J. S. Mill as an authority). The aim of the radical democrat is to galvanize the masses so that our institutions actually elicit democratic citizenship and promote character development.

There is no doubt that some commitment to the ideal of participation can be found in the work of most great democratic theorists. Furthermore, critics justifiably accuse modern utilitarian theorists (and here I think of those pluralists such as Dahl and Joseph Schumpeter who approach democratic theory with what is essentially an economic analytical framework) of shifting emphasis from the concern of classical writers with democratic ideals towards what they take to be a more realistic commitment. By defining democracy in a way that is compatible with a good deal of citizen apathy, many modern liberals have abandoned as an impractical goal the ideal of widespread participation in political life. Furthermore, their preoccupation with the need for expertise and their stress on the importance of competent leadership fly in the face of such traditional slogans as 'rule by the people, for the people'. The utilitarian approach, which provides the model of representative government accepted by most liberal writers today, has as its central concern the goal of ensuring that governments are responsive to those whom they govern. Where modern liberals have considered the question of whether citizens should develop their human potentiality through political activity, the answer has tended to be negative. Participation in political life is seen as a burden which most ordinary persons can well do without. It is suggested, in this regard, that where political issues are not overwhelming and hostility between sections of society is muted, citizens will get on with pursuits which they regarded as more urgent; it is suggested, further, that in these circumstances the resolution of policy problems will be left to professional representatives in consultation with bureaucrats, and that this state of affairs is desirable.

In assessing the idealism of the radical critics of contemporary liberal democratic theory we are faced with two difficulties: first, there is confusion over the place that a commitment to liberal values and political processes is to have in their conception of a future democracy; second, it is not clear precisely what sort of personality or character training the radical writers have in mind as suitable to promote democratic dispositions. One suspects that these critics do not share the conception of democracy suggested by liberals; presumably, they would also reject the liberal ideal of the democratic character. But none of these moralists has described a viable alternative set of institutional arrangements which could be said to have more to offer than the political processes recommended by liberal writers. It is difficult, then, to know what conception of the democratic character the radical moralists are working with. If the new critics are merely suggesting that we somehow train citizens to participate more fully and responsibly within the institutions of liberal society, then it would seem that they are hardly in conflict with the prevailing wisdom on these matters. Liberal theorists have, in any case, shown some sensitivity to the elitist elements in their theory, and many would support reforms aimed at encouraging more widespread political participation.[3]

Despite the rhetoric, then, there may be very little conflict between the moral critics of the pluralist conception of democratic systems and some of the more sensitive liberal theorists. That this is so, however, is obscured by the fact that the idealists sometimes write as though they believed that greater participation in political processes on the part of the working masses will make a significant difference, not merely psychologically, but to the balance of power between competing groups in modern liberal societies. This is an important claim, which deserves careful consideration.

I should point out as a preliminary observation in this context that left-wing writers of a moralistic persuasion cannot be allowed to have things both ways: if liberal societies are characterized by class conflict, it follows that democratic participation cannot be accepted as a panacea (unless one supposes that the working class will be disposed toward radical rather than reformist strategies); if, on the other hand, the class nature of liberal society is not regarded as a fundamental problem standing in the way of the realization of democratic ideals, then these radicals are moving away from Marxist perspectives.

I suggest that the moralist critics misrepresent the political realities. Even allowing for the kinds of reforms which they suggest, such as the introduction of widespread industrial democracy and participation in other sub-political institutions like universities and corporations, real autonomy over the aspects of life which matter is not possible. This follows from the class nature of liberal society. My argument here depends on establishing some sense of 'what really matters' in social life. One crude way to establish criteria for what is significant is by reference to the major conflict area of resource allocation. All societies face the political task of making decisions about what to produce, how much to produce, for whom to produce and how to produce, and it is these decisions which can most plausibly be identified as of vital political significance. Ideally, democrats are in favour of some form of direct vote on each allocation as it may arise, but almost everyone who has thought about the complex issues involved here allows that such a solution is not practicable. The question is, then: how would widespread political participation in sub-political institutions be likely to effect the allocation of a society's crucial resources?

It is important to note that where capitalist relations of production are unfettered by government intervention in economic life decisions about the allocation of resources are left to the mechanism of market competition. Investors are given the right to allocate social resources (which they hold as private capital) to projects which they think viable; they are also given the right to withdraw resources already allocated. In modern systems, however, because it is apparent that the exercise of these rights by private individuals often places workers in extremely precarious and dependent positions, governments interfere very considerably in the area of resource allocation and set limits on what private investors may be permitted to do with the social resources they hold; they also invest public funds, thereby taking responsibility for some resource commitments. Governments generally achieve political goals in liberal systems by acquiring significant sums of capital through taxation and by using political authority to bridle the market system (by controlling the activities of monopolies, by protecting consumers by policing standards, by issuing licences as a form of control, by borrowing from abroad, by regulating the rate of interest or by offering subsidies to some producers). Whenever governments act in these ways priorities have to be established, and there is usually an extended process of consultation and negotiation to determine which members of society are to benefit and which are to pay. It is this process of consultation that constitutes the essence of political life in liberal systems today.

It is not clear why more participation in intermediate institutions should be thought to affect the outcome of the struggle to determine allocations in liberal systems. Participation within trade unions, corporations, agricultural co-operatives, Churches and other organizations, however desirable this might be for other reasons, cannot be justified on the grounds that it will alter the balance of power between these often conflicting groups. More participation may liven up the routine of much contemporary life (or make it more tedious), but it will not necessarily change the basis of power in capitalist societies; nor will such participation produce a 'general will' focused on collective goals such as environment protection, public transport, consumer protection or the elimination of high rates of inflation. Moreover, the central problem (that participation in decision-making relating to resource allocation by all concerned citizens is not a practicable goal) would remain with us even if reforms directed at providing for more participation at the sub-political level had been implemented. Furthermore, the liberal response to this problem (that we ensure responsive government by forcing political elites to compete for public approval) is not even under challenge and remains the most sensible proposal, given the circumstances outlined above. We must, then, declare the new moralists to be Utopian, in the sense that they offer no solutions to the democratic problem of how the crucial social decisions about resource allocation should be made.

Does this mean that we must fall back on a conception of the democratic commitment in which institutional processes (free elections, parliamentary government), the rights of expression and the rule of law are regarded purely as defence mechanisms protecting us from possible abuse on the part of those elites which must necessarily exercise power? This is certainly the conclusion which many contemporary political scientists seem to have reached after reviewing idealistic arguments for participatory democracy. Such a pessimistic conclusion is not inevitable, however, for we are surely entitled to retain the idealism of those who aspire to promote a world in which our human capacity for autonomy is maximized. It is certainly true that if we could offer citizens a more effective voice in debates over those aspects of their lives which I have listed as being of first importance (those involving resource allocations), then capitalism as a system would undoubtedly be abandoned because citizens would perceive the contradictions between market forces and the claims of justice. To this degree, then, participatory theorists of democracy are right — effective democratic rights would ensure social changes making for vast improvements. The problem is, of course, that as long as liberal social systems are characterized by market resource allocation so that critical policy choices are simply not made politically, and as long as they are typified by systematic exploitation and inequality, no substantial progress towards meaningful participatory democracy, beyond what has already been achieved, is possible.

This is certainly the judgement articulated and defended by Macpherson, who is strongly critical of what he regards as the Utopian tendency of many democratic theorists. Macpherson takes J. S. Mill as an example of this kind of idealist, and criticizes him for failing to see that his goal of a fully effective participatory system is incompatible with capitalist relations of production. Macpherson is, however, equally severe with those whom he accuses of abandoning democratic ideals, for he finds the complacent attitude of those who rest content with a purely negative conception of democratic institutions (as mere protective mechanisms against possible tyranny) entirely unacceptable. In this regard Macpherson warns us against allowing our ideals to be shaped by unduly pessimistic assumptions about future possibilities. He concedes that modern societies will not be efficiently governed through popular initiatives, but he argues that provided our present circumstances are changed sufficiently so that most citizens have different expectations about what it is possible to achieve through political activity (and if, also, there is a more equitable distribution of resources), most of the ideals of Utopian democratic theory will come to look more realistic. The central difficulty, he suggests, 'is not how participatory democracy would operate but how we could move towards it'; he is, however, clear that moralistic demands for more participation will be in vain unless they are linked with some conception of how capitalism as a system of resource allocation is to be replaced by socialism.[4]

Idealism and Utopia

The kind of moralistic radical polemic that we have been discussing is very typical of the exciting campus rhetoric of the 1960s, which culminated in the political outbreaks of 1968. The intellectual inspiration for much of the activism of these years came from theorists loosely identified as the New Left. These writers wanted to link the contributions of Marx with those of Freud, using their own reading of Marx's discussion of alienation as an excuse for adding a psychological dimension to Marxist sociology.[5] It was argued that a theory of culture was needed which could support the vague ideology found in Marx's work. It was in this way that the New Left hoped to avoid what they regarded as the crude materialism of writers like Engels who, they claimed, had read Marx in a way which placed too little emphasis on the psychological dimension of alienation.

So successful was this attempt to utilize Freudian perspectives within a very broadly interpreted Marxism, focused almost entirely on the early *Economic and Philosophical Manuscripts of 1844* which Marx and Engels had regarded as being an immature work, that it is only in recent years that the Freudian revisionism is beginning to be questioned.[6] We are left with the impression that some radicals actually invite the label Utopian — or at least that they do not regard the scepticism with which liberals have greeted their Utopian speculations embarrassing. No successful attempt has been made to save radical theory from the charge of unbridled Utopianism, and it is not often realized that Marx himself criticized very severely political rhetoric of a moralistic kind.[7] Like that of other great Utopian theorists, such as Plato and Rousseau, Marx's orientation to political philosophy is basically sociological; he saw himself as a scientist eager to learn about the processes at work in social life, not as a dreamer or speculator about the nature of the good life. The central question which interested all three of the Utopian writers mentioned above concerns the problem of moral corruption: why is it that people seem incapable of relating to others in a moral way? It is because Plato, Rousseau and Marx pose this question in a way which allows for a sociological analysis of the problems that their contributions should be sharply distinguished from those of Utopians whose primary concern is to recommend ideals and values, to consider what society looks like ideally when people do act in a moral way. The Utopian moralists are mostly concerned to criticize the *status quo* and to recommend their conception of the good society. For them social relations as we find them are intolerable, and they set out to provide standards against which we may measure our moral achievements and towards which we ought to strive. In this regard their work is premised on the assumption that people, provided they can be brought to comprehend the evil of their ways, will struggle to improve their behaviour, and that Utopia will be established provided we all resolve to act morally. Sociologically orientated Utopian writers have no such confidence in humanity's goodwill, and they consequently hold all forms of moralizing in the greatest contempt. For them, it is more important to understand the causes of evil than to preach against it.

In modern times the sociological orientation and the moralistic tradition in Utopian theory have, however, become hopelessly confused. One reason for this is that a good deal of the inspiration for the revival of Utopian moralizing is, understandably enough, traceable to both Rousseau and Marx. Rousseau's plea for social simplicity, though ultimately conservative and contrary to the imperatives of his time, is still able to move the modern reader — much more than his own contemporaries, who regarded this aspect of his theorizing as very much the work of an eccentric. In our day we are increasingly aware that the quality of our lives may indeed have suffered as a result of industrialization. It is not only the pollution and destruction of the physical environment which worry most of us but the dreadful burden which industrial work, with its dreary monotony and long hours, places on the human psyche. Rousseau, then, may well have been right: we should never have committed ourselves to such an enterprise.

But while much of the criticism of industrial life comes from Rousseau, his perspectives are ultimately pessimistic, for it is not possible to return to a pre-industrial era. We have to turn to Marx for any viable hope of a better future. It may not be possible to turn back but we may push forward towards a time when technology no longer enslaves but liberates. The *Communist Manifesto*, written jointly by Marx and Engels, is surely the most optimistic tract in the whole history of political thought; Marx and Engels describe how, at the high point of technological development, we come to the end of class struggle itself and participate freely in the fruits and joys of communal life. The language is such that we can almost feel the driving imperatives of history taking humanity forwards.

Most modern Utopians follow Marx in thinking that technological innovations will simplify social relations; they argue, nevertheless, that human ingenuity is not put to constructive use, and that there has been too much production for its own sake, regardless of the costs as measured in terms of the quality of our lives. Furthermore, they complain that not enough attention is paid to the nature of work by those who set social priorities, and they suggest that technological innovations can free producers from the burden of having to adapt to machines (it is hoped that automation may eliminate the need for assembly-line production based on human labour power). What will be achieved in the future, it is thought, is a simplification of work roles, leading to greater social mobility and the possibility of job rotation. This kind of simplification, it is argued, will also permit more democratic controls to emerge. It is suggested that more participation in public life is both necessary and possible, and that democratization will benefit from the fact that developments in electronics are serving to facilitate communications. We need, it is urged, more community use of social resources like schools, theatres and parks; and we also need more leisure time and better facilities for helping people to use it wisely. These kinds of suggestion are clearly influenced by Marx's conception of the human potential; but while they are in the spirit of Marx's enterprise, it is clear that much Utopian speculation is shakily founded on his analysis of the causes of our present miseries. For one thing, almost all modern Utopian writers reject any attempt to construct social theories on pessimistic individualist assumptions about how people actually behave; and they also reject attempts to theorize which take egoism as a given feature of human motivation, along with an idealized conception of rationality, as is the case in strategy analysis. The Utopian radicals hope that their moral appeals will persuade a significant portion of humanity to forego the search for ways to serve their own self-interests in order to promote collective goals. They argue also that it is precisely the so-called realistic assumption that aggression and selfishness are endemic which lies at the heart of many mistaken liberal ideas about the nature of political reality. Indeed, a common criticism of bourgeois theory among modern radicals seems to be that it has lost sight of humanity's potential — of the fact that we do seem to be capable of forming ennobling relationships based on trust and of fulfilling tasks of creative responsibility. We find in the work of writers like Fromm and Marcuse the idea that what is wrong with our present circumstances is our narrow, one-dimensional conception of our own humanity, and that all we need for effective social reform is a change of consciousness; it is as though they actually believe that revolutions can come from a heavy barrage of Utopian propaganda.

It is interesting to observe that although Rousseau, Plato and Marx share the view that moral development is an innate potentiality shared by all humanity (and that in some circumstances this disposition will determine behaviour), they are at one with Hobbes in their analysis of the human character as we find it, for each of them makes a cautious estimate about how much good will we can expect from individual actors. As Marx puts it: 'The bourgeoisie...has left remaining no other nexus between man and man than naked self interest, than callous "cash payment".'[8] Rousseau opens the *Social Contract* by asking whether legitimate government is possible, taking men *as they are*, and his answer reveals that he would endorse the much criticized 'real world' assumptions of contemporary liberal democratic theorists. Before we can hope for the emergence of moral attitudes and of a social life based on right and not might, Rousseau tells us, there must be a basic equalization of power; he argues that where people are forced to co-operate from a position of equal bargaining strength they will ultimately develop the capacity for moral dealings − they will see that they need to respect principles of justice in relating to one another.[9] In this sense the equality of power, which includes an equal need to co-operate, forces individuals to be free − it prevents inscrupulous individuals from using a power advantage to set up a fraudulent basis for legitimacy. About the chances of a people ever establishing a society on such a basis Rousseau is pessimistic; like Plato, whose *Republic* served as something of an inspiration, Rousseau never really believes that his ideal can be brought into effect.[10] The model is suggested as an heuristic tool; its purpose is to show what moral relations could be like and, in this regard, it is moralistic. For all three of these Utopians their ideal is constructed from an extrapolation of their theories of social corruption. In answering their question relating to the limited nature of social life these theorists at the same time construct models which provide them with a programme for reform. It is because they can expose those factors in the social situation which inhibit moral development that, *ipso facto*, they produce the remedy − simply a situation without the offending features. For Plato this involves setting up a society in which reason rules the passions and appetites; for Rousseau the solution lies in establishing true equality; Marx sees the problem as requiring the elimination of class conflict. All of them justify their Utopian models with social theories which take human nature as they find it and not as they would like it to be. In this they deserve to be sharply distinguished from the moralistically inclined Utopians.

Marxist Utopian Theory

Having distinguished a sociologically orientated Utopianism from moralizing approaches, we may now consider the relationship between a Marxist version of such an approach and liberal individualism. I shall do this by reviewing the work of C. B. Macpherson.

Macpherson has made a significant contribution to radical democratic theory and, it is not surprising, therefore, that his work is often dismissed as of no consequence on the grounds of his alleged Utopian and supposedly unrealistic assumptions. Certainly, a great deal of optimism and a moralistic fervour is manifest in Macpherson's work, and a superficial reading may easily leave the impression that he is somewhat too abstract in his approach. Even his general claim that the basic criterion of democracy is the effective and equal right of individuals 'to live as they may wish' tells us nothing about how any actual society in which this criterion has been realized would look. As one critic complains, Macpherson fails to compare political regimes in terms of functional fidelity with any of the concepts of democracy which are identified in his work; and the same critic goes on to suggest that Macpherson 'provides an object lesson in how not to do comparative analysis'.[11] Clearly, many readers respond in this way when reading Macpherson; his speculative reflections and what often appears to be a simple-minded optimism leave him vulnerable to the charge of moralizing. It is interesting to note, however, that in his recent *The Life and Times of Liberal Democracy* Macpherson makes an effort to model the view of democratic processes reflected in rival conceptions of the democratic commitment, and he tries, with some success, to spell out his own framework for Utopia. But this work has only recently been available, and his critics are right to claim that his previous contributions contained no adequate discussion of the procedures for social decision-making which he proposed for his ideal democratic society. Like most Utopian writers, he has a penchant for vaguely stating ideals and aspirations without providing any adequate illustrations in the form of made-up examples or by citing practice. Furthermore, until the appearance of his latest publication his conception of democracy as a kind of society rather than as a network of institutional practices suffered from the fact that he had presented it in an excessively abstract way. Certainly, this has been the verdict of most liberal critics.

I agree that there is some substance to these charges against Macpherson's style of theorizing (although, as I have said, most of the unsympathetic commentary will need substantial revision in the light of *The Life and Times of Liberal Democracy*.) Nevertheless, I wish to suggest that such an appraisal can be misleading. We must not suppose that Macpherson is unaware of the difficulties upon which his critics have focused; nor must we suppose that we can dismiss his Utopian theory merely by making the obvious point that it is not grounded empirically in the same way as conventional approaches. Part of the purpose of a writer like Macpherson, as I endeavour to show, is to challenge the assumptions upon which so much unreflective social theory is grounded. It is for this reason that the objection that Macpherson's work is Utopian may often be beside the point. What concerns him is the way in which we think, and he wishes to recommend a conceptual framework in terms of which we can best comprehend the democratic commitment. For this reason it is unfair to treat his work as though he were doing badly something which he has no intention of accomplishing.

Macpherson's contribution may serve to illustrate some of the differences between Marxist and liberal approaches to democratic theory. What is significant to note is how difficult it is for a Marxist to avoid exposing him- or herself to the charge of Utopianism. The problem is that liberal theory has for some time — indeed, since its inception with Hobbes — based itself on what might be aptly described as a 'reality requirement'. Marxists, in contrast, have been at pains to point out the ideological purposes served by descriptions of behaviour as this is manifest under capitalist relations of production and by the aim of squaring aspirations in democratic theory with what seems possible in the light of the findings of such a sociology. Macpherson, in particular, has made an effort to expose and to challenge fundamental premises, which he claims liberal writers mistakenly accept as part of the human predicament. Indeed, it is precisely because he has taken liberal theory seriously enough to devote a great deal of his time to the reading and exposition of the classical liberal writings that his criticisms are so illuminating, even to those who disagree with his point of view.

Liberal theory has, as I have said, premised itself on what we might call a 'reality requirement'. What I mean by this is that the liberal way of conceiving of the democratic commitment asks us to make a responsible attempt to come to terms with what are taken to be the realities of the modern predicament.[12] Responsible approaches are to be distinguished from those (such as that which Macpherson is alleged to provide) which associate the democratic commitment with the goal of realizing some ultimate ideal such as justice for all or the full development of our human capacities. These approaches are irresponsible, liberals tell us, because they assume that we can have everything that we desire, and that no hard choices establishing trade-offs between competing values will have to be made. But, we are told by liberal writers like Dahl, Berelson and Schumpeter, the reality is such that unless these choices are made our speculations are Utopian, for we must not retreat from serious dilemmas into generalized abstractions about what it would be good to promote which cannot be given specific content in the real world. Thus, for example, we may all agree that it would be desirable to establish a society in which all citizens were able to develop their full potential, but it is unlikely that we will reach agreement when we each try to spell out how we conceive of such a society, and this is especially so if we assume that human nature will change dramatically.

Contemporary liberal writers have been particularly troubled by 'reality requirements', for they have been confronted by the findings of sociology relating to the problems imposed by the imperatives of rapid modernization. They are also aware of the complex interrelationships characteristic of contemporary industrialized societies. Unlike their precursors, such as Pareto and Mosca who came to accept the pessimistic conclusion that democracy is impossible to attain in modern conditions, contemporary liberals urge that we abandon the classical conception of democracy and accept a less ambitious aspiration as satisfying democratic ideals. What they suggest, in effect, is that we regard those institutional arrangements which require leaders to compete periodically for the people's vote as adequate fulfilment of the democratic ideal of self-government.

The realism of liberal writers is often laced with a certain optimism, for they sometimes argue that once a compromise with idealism is made to allow for the circumstances of modern life, and provided we have the resolve to find practical solutions to our problems, some progress can be made towards reaching agreement about the democratic commitment. Liberals suggest that provided we are not taken in by a rhetoric which promises without proscribing, we will come to see the arrangements set out in those institutional systems which are based on the principle of political equality as the best possible in a less than perfect world.

Of course, I exaggerate and oversimplify the subtle arguments of writers as different as Robert Dahl and Sir Isaiah Berlin, to name two of the most prominent liberals I have in mind. Nevertheless, it is true to say that each of these writers hopes in his own way to force agreement on his audience by requiring that we clarify the choices we must all make in coming to terms with the real world. Dahl, following the economist Joseph Schumpeter, is concerned about factors such as the importance of expertise, the scarcity of time and the significance of size where we are dealing with urban configurations as limiting the range of alternative institutions which could be recommended as functional. Berlin is concerned to distinguish 'freedom' as an ideal from 'autonomy', and he suggests that although we might hope to realize the former by establishing typically liberal institutional protections, we cannot recommend the latter as a practical ideal. In his celebrated lecture 'Two Concepts of Liberty' he argues that a failure to keep this distinction and his strictures in mind can lead to the acceptance of the notion that coercive interference with the choices of some by others is justified.[13] Each of these writers, in very different ways, forces us to confront a 'reality requirement'. Any attempt to avoid the choices which, through analysis, they impose on the conscientious reader is considered Utopian — and is, as such, irrelevant to the theoretical task of deciding what institutional arrangements should be accepted by persons of reason and good will.

Although there are sophisticated and subtle differences between them, there is a hard core of agreement between liberals. I refer to the careful distinction which they make between social and political spheres of life. Realistic political argument, it is contended, must address itself to two separate and quite distinct problems: the question of how we can establish political institutions which enable all citizens to have an equal chance to voice their preferences and have them counted (this is the democratic problem); and the question of how we can achieve social justice and general affluence so that everyone can enjoy the good life (this can be the goal even of a fascist). The virtue which distinguishes leaders who are democratic from those who are not, according to liberals, is not their attitude towards the goal of establishing social justice; rather, it is their attitude to liberty (conceived as political equality amongst citizens). Liberals are adamant that it is a conceptual confusion of great significance to confuse the demand for democracy with a demand for social equality or with any ambition to realize some ultimate ideal such as the maximization of human capacities, no matter how these are conceived. They believe, also, that once we are clear about the distinction between these very different problems, we will come to value liberal democratic institutions for what they are — the most equitable arrangements for allowing everyone as much chance as is possible to influence public decision-making.

What is significant, from our point of view, is that Macpherson is not prepared to accept the liberal way of approaching issues in democratic theory. In particular, he argues strongly against the suggestion that we can regard questions relating to the ideal of social justice as easily distinguishable from those which relate to democratic ideals. Macpherson makes clear that if he were to accept the ground rules for political debate as these are laid down by liberal writers, then he would have to accept their pessimism also; this is something he is not prepared to do. It is for this reason that so many of the criticisms of and objections to his contribution are beside the point: one cannot dismiss a theorist of Macpherson's stature simply because he does not approach problems in the conventional manner. If one were to challenge Macpherson in any significant way, then one would have to confront his reasons for rejecting the liberal approach to policy issues. The point is that Macpherson explicitly rejects what he regards as the narrow vision of liberal political theory, and he sees the pessimism of so much bourgeois theory as reflecting a model of social life which has quite unacceptable assumptions built into it.

In Macpherson's view, liberal arguments are essentially circular because they assume that people are so perverse in their attitudes to one another that no Utopian vision has any chance of being realized. The crucial charge with which he confronts liberals is that despite all the permutations of the apologetic and all the sophistication of modern writers, at the base of their approach is the deeply pessimistic view that modern industrial societies must invitably embody inequalities of wealth and status if they are to function at all adequately. Liberals who accept this conclusion do so, Macpherson tells us, because they assume that work is a cost (an expenditure of energy) which has to be extracted by means of coercion or by way of an incentive. If society tries to hold a carrot in front of the donkey (the producers) to get it to do the work necessary for the system to function efficiently, then those who contribute more, because they work harder or have more talent, will achieve higher status. On the other hand, if society were organized to drive social production by means of the stick, a vision of totalitarian control begins to look menacing; individuals in such a world would be forced to work for others who had the coercive power to extract the effort from them. Liberals, understandably enough, reject coercion as a solution to the problem they set themselves — the question of how society is to establish a work discipline. It is for this reason, also, that they have come to condone what in the light of their premises must be the alternative: a system of incentives and consequent inequalities. The problem of how society is to control elites which exercises the minds of many modern liberal writers also follows from this way of visualizing the human predicament — because once there are inequalities of status and power, those who have these advantages may threaten to establish forms of tyranny. Liberal institutions are required, it is suggested, precisely because they offer an adequate defence against tyranny. If elites are required to compete for the right to govern, citizens have some assurance that a cohesive and threatening power group will not emerge. This assurance is further strengthened if competitive political processes are adequately supported by a free-enterprise economic system which ensures that some substantial resources remain in the hands of individuals who are not part of the governing elite. Responsive and responsible government can be sustained, it is suggested, as long as liberty and private property are protected.

In contrast to liberals, Macpherson rejects this kind of pessimism, and his conception is such that the problem of extracting labour in the form of a commitment to work is not seen as overwhelming. He insists that the incentive model of motivation favoured by liberal writers is an unreasonable basis on which to build a democratic theory, because there is no reason why all our expenditures of energy need to be regarded as a cost. Macpherson's own contribution, his effort to retrieve democratic theory, is based on an assessment of the human condition which is decidedly more optimistic. It is not necessary to bribe or to coerce people to work, he tells us, for activity is not something which always has to be extracted. In his conception, human beings are naturally industrious and it is only in circumstances in which there is no freedom that the problems which bother liberal writers become important considerations — we have to be bribed or coerced to work for others but no incentive is needed to get people to work for their own well-being. The problem for the democrat, as Macpherson sees it, is to make sure that producers are free from exploitation. Once this is achieved, the alienation of market systems and the fearful and sullen responses of those working in systems based on coercion will be replaced by an enthusiasm generated by self-determination. Macpherson believes that extraction is assumed by liberals to be a necessary part of the human situation because their pessimism is a legacy of the 'possessive individualism' which modern writers have inherited from the seventeenth century.[14]

It is not often appreciated that Macpherson criticizes liberal writers for making claims about human nature which are not supported by the evidence of history. For example, he accuses Hobbes and Locke of assuming bourgeois characteristics to be typical within their state of nature. In making this point, Macpherson suggests that they have not been able to free themselves from their own cultural horizons and presuppositions. If liberal writers assume that incentives are necessary in economic life, then they show that they are not prepared to move to the level of abstraction necessary to avoid their own prejudice. It is, therefore, open to Macpherson to complain that their own expectations about how individuals behave are still influencing their deliberations. This is a point which Macpherson has taken from Marx, who writes of Bentham:

he that would judge all human acts, movements, relations, etc., according to the principle of utility, would first have to deal with human nature in general, and then with human nature as historically modified in each epoch. Bentham does not trouble himself with this. With the dryest naïveté he assumes that the modern petty bourgeois, especially the English bourgeois is the normal man. Whatever is useful to this peculiar kind of normal man, and to his world, is useful in and for itself.[15]

Modern liberal writers have made some effort to meet this objection. It is worth noting, however, that it is only with the publication of Rawls's *A Theory of Justice* that we find a fully worked out liberal theory which gets clear of all assumptions about human nature. And, as we shall see, when strategy analysis is used at the level of abstraction that Rawls requires, what emerges is a position in political philosophy which is very different from the 'possessive individualism' criticized by Macpherson.

There are a large number of problems which spring to mind when one confronts a Utopian perspective which has the degree of abstraction characteristic of Macpherson's approach. It is only fair when dealing with Macpherson's work, however, that we recognize that he speaks from within the Marxist framework and that his own assumptions are not purely idiosyncratic. We need to do him the courtesy which he so willingly extends to others and to situate his core assumptions in the context of the theory within which he is working. It is all too easy to set up a Utopian writer for parody and ridicule, but we should remember that what may appear to be simplistic and naive is often in reality carefully thought out. Marxist writers, in contrast to moralistic Utopians, should not be accused of merely parading values and ideals with no theory to back their inspiration. Marx himself, as we have noted, is highly critical of what he calls Utopian theory, and his own perspectives are inspired throughout by a carefully constructed model of how modern societies actually work. It is, then, in the light of his sociological analysis that his optimistic prognostications and his belief in our potential for moral development should be viewed. The same consideration should be applied when reviewing Macpherson's development of the Utopian aspects of Marxist theory.

Like Marx, Macpherson's vision is built around a conception of people as having a potential for being fully responsible for their actions and in control of their own destinies. Marxist objections to liberal society reflect the concern that because citizens have been forced to sell their labour power as a commodity, and because social priorities are determined in large measure by the market, they have had to forfeit something essential to their humanity. The force of Marx's polemic is not derived from any claims he may make relating to the unjust way in which resources are distributed by the market; nor does he object to capitalism because market allocations often result in great poverty. What Marx and the modern Macpherson find intolerable is that people as we find them in liberal societies have no control of their own destinies and are, therefore, the object of forces which prevent the free development of their capacities. What we find in their condemnation of capitalism is a protest against a dehumanized life in which people are the slaves of a system of social coercion which alienates them by not allowing them to take responsibility for their own destinies. For Marxists the bourgeois citizen is a pawn; at the heart of their ethic is a concern for freedom which they conceive as self-determination. Marxists suppose that it is possible for social intercourse to be mutually advantageous, and their ideal requires that individuals realize their potentialities co-operatively so that no-one is forced to confront the demands of others as something alien, negating his or her self-fulfilment.[16] It is noticeable how closely Macpherson's democratic ideal reflects these core assumptions of the Marxist ethic. He writes:

What is essential in modern democratic theory? As soon as democracy is seen as a type of society, not merely a mechanism of choosing and authorizing governments, the egalitarian principle inherent in democracy requires not only 'one man, one vote' but also 'one man, one equally effective right to live as fully humanly as he may wish'. Democracy *is* now seen...as a kind of society − a whole complex of relations between individuals − rather than simply a system of government.[17]

It is significant that despite the requirement that 'man be governed by his own nature and its requirements, and by that alone', nothing is said either by Marx or by Macpherson about the nature of the truly human character. (Marx does, it is true, make some romantic statements, but he never says enough to convey anything more than an overwhelming optimism about the innate goodness of humanity.) It is significant also that both Marx and Macpherson refuse to specify the nature of what they take to be the good life — it is up to the individuals of any future society to choose how best to fulfil their nature. This agnostic position about the good life (which is somewhat similar to Rawls's 'thin theory of the good' in *A Theory of Justice*) follows from the Marxist premise that human interests and needs evolve historically. Marxist theorists can be specific about the mechanisms at work in society which prevent individuals from developing themselves (just as Rawls thinks he can be specific about the 'primary goods'), but it would be presumptuous of them to lay down guidelines about what constitutes the good life because what people ought to choose must depend on their future interests and capacities. For example, it would not be possible to say that women ought to value their present status as wives and mothers as a fulfilment of their 'feminine nature', for it may turn out in the social systems of the future that different forms of family relations will evolve which will make it unnecessary for anyone to choose to sacrifice their own personal development in the way that contemporary mothers often seem to do. Marx and Engels are prepared to say, with regard to their attitude to family life, that love relationships which are not freely chosen are less than ideal (they are committed to the individualist ethic to this extent at least); they are also prepared to argue that relationships will not be ideal as long as there are status differences between men and women. Engels is clear, however, when he speculates about the future of marriage, that it would not be appropriate to say how the institution ought to evolve in terms of some conception of the good. Thus, he tells us that although he personally associates love with sexual exclusivity and monogamous cohabitation, it may be that people in a future society in which envy and notions of ownership have less prominence within the culture may find that life-long and exclusive commitments are inhibiting, and they may choose different patterns of relating to one another without necessarily hurting the people they love.[18] The point is that in pondering this kind of variable a Marxist simply has to be agnostic about the future.

A problem with this way of thinking, as already mentioned, is that the aspirations lack specificity. It would, however, be quite misleading to accuse Marx of wishful thinking, as few theorists have been more concerned than he to support their speculations empirically. Marx attempted to provide a materialist explanation of the reasons why we have been unable to realize our potentiality as moral beings. The crucial insight upon which he builds his model is that moral relations between people will never be possible as long as the social world is such that some are able to ensure that the labour of others is under their control — or, as Macpherson puts it, as long as the relations of production are 'invasive'. Individuals are alienated because until there is equal access to productive resources, those who can sustain their monopoly will also be able to extract a payment from the individuals who must necessarily get their co-operation before they can work. Under capitalism this is done purely as a market transaction because labour power must necessarily be sold as a commodity at a price which reflects the costs of producing the labourer rather than at a price which reflects what the labourer is capable of producing. It follows from this diagnosis of the ills that a cure is at hand: a world without 'invasive' relationships. The Utopian aspirations follow as a deduction from the critique, for if the crucial problem for mankind is freeing itself from servitude, then it follows that there must be some conception of liberty — that is, a Utopia. The point is that if a Marxist writer extrapolates certain idealizations for the future, these carry with them at least some plausibility, contingent on the strength that their model has exhibited as a tool for analysing the real world. Even if we do not believe that the Utopia which Marx promises will ever come into being, we must concede that his mode of proceeding is not merely speculative. For those who accept his analysis of the ills of capitalism, his prognostications for the future follow logically as a deduction from his explanatory model.

Once the human predicament is perceived in terms which reflect the reality of power relations, the thrust of one's theorizing must be negative. In so far as theorists are able to move in a positive direction, it is because they are able to wish away impediments to the development of our moral potentiality. This is why Macpherson's efforts to construct his theory around the analysis of the three basic impediments (lack of means of life, lack of access to the means of labour and the need for protection against invasions by others) goes some way towards setting democratic theory on the right track. This way of proceeding may not allow for very great precision, but what we have to understand is that Utopian theory, which is not merely moralizing, is always the corollary of a critique; unless one is prepared to endorse the entailments, one cannot produce an adequate model to explain the contradictions which beset reformers in their efforts to achieve social harmony.

The trouble with this way of thinking is that it reverses the pattern of entailment which more conventional approaches assume should apply. Liberals, for example, reject the abstractions of Utopian theory as unrealistic and then believe that they are being worldly-wise when they accept anomalies (often quite clearly perceived) in the real world. It is surely better, however, to follow the Marxists and to try to be clear-headed about the world we know, even if this does mean that we are at times a little dewy-eyed about what life might be like in different circumstances. Suppose even that the pessimists are right and that Utopia is merely a logical possibility which has no chance of being realized in the real world, we should still be prepared to face the fact that our present systems fall short of the ideal. It is no use pretending that the relations between people can be moral when they patently cannot be, short of Utopia. What we have to realize is that a theorist like Macpherson is critical of present realities only because he is at the same time overwhelmingly optimistic about future possibilities. It is surely better to err in this direction than to embrace the alternative, which is to be so totally pessimistic about the possibility of there being a better world that one ends up complacent (even apologetic) about the iniquities we find about us.

5
Problems with Marxism as an Ethical Theory

In this chapter I deal with some further points of disagreement between liberal writers and Marxists, and particularly with the debate between Macpherson and Sir Isaiah Berlin over the concept of freedom.

Criticisms of the Marxist Approach to Ethics

If we look at the objections which have been directed at Marxist approaches to ethical issues, we find a number of points which are constantly reiterated.[1] First, it is suggested that Marxist writers have made little substantial contribution, for they have usually dismissed political and ethical philosophy as peculiarly bourgeois indulgences. Second, it is suggested that Marxist writers tend to make claims about the relationship between political ideas and particular periods in history without adequately demonstrating these alleged links with reference to the work of specific philosophers. Third, it is argued that in so far as they do concern themselves with the philosophical literature, Marxist writers have shown little appreciation of moral reasoning, and that they are particularly cavalier about the important logical distinctions which have been made by liberal writers of first rank. Fourth, it is noted that Marxist thinkers display little embarrassment about asserting their own values as absolute standards, whilst they regard the values of other thinkers as relative (reflecting historical circumstance and particular interests).

In so far as a Marxist ethical position is discernible, it is often regarded as derivative (mainly from Kant). Furthermore, Marx's contribution is seen as negligible, for his humanism is simply asserted and he fails to make important qualifications or to note distinctions where these are thought to be relevant. As Eugene Kamenka puts it, after describing Marx's debt to Kant:

one must remember that it [the Kantian strain in Marx] is a simplified, Prometheanized Kant — a Kant without the conflict between duty and inclination, without frank elevation of the noumenal will over man's empirical nature, and without Kant's recognition of the independent requirements of logic or 'reason'.[2]

It is also asserted that Marxism is characterized by sloppy conceptualization. Criticism, in this regard, is directed at such notions as 'human needs' and 'objective interests' (as opposed to the needs which people actually manifest in given historical circumstances, or the goals which they consider to be important). With regard to political and ethical philosophy, the claim that Marxist writers are casual about their use of concepts has focused mostly on their ideal of freedom. Sir Isaiah Berlin, for example, has argued that anyone committed to realizing the Kantian ideal of people as beings fully responsible and in control of their own destiny, as Marxists clearly are, has entered a maze of conceptual entanglement.[3]

In this chapter I will not respond to all of these criticisms, for many must be well taken. Marx and Engels do not make a substantial contribution to political and ethical philosophy precisely because they think such speculations pointless. The pressing problem for them is not that of promoting a change in our consciousness of what is morally right or wrong; rather, they want to show how society can be transformed to make the Kantian ideal of autonomy a more realistic aspiration.[4] It is not surprising, then, that neither they nor their followers (apart from Macpherson) bother very much with the logical distinctions in terms of which we can delineate the various positions adopted by liberal political philosophers.

Marx and Engels differ from liberals in that they perceive that what shapes the human predicament ultimately is not a failure of will (as, for example, Kant seems to suppose) but the class structure characteristic of particular periods of history. It is precisely because they see the problem of alienation as a social one and not as a psychological one that their scepticism represents an advance and not a regression to a less sophisticated position. Thus, Kamenka is misleading when he suggests that Kant's approach is greatly superior to that of Marxists.

Where Kant supposes that we have a divided nature, in which 'reason' competes against the forces of our natural inclinations, Marx analyses the conflict sociologically. He traces the causes of our failure to relate morally not to the sensuous nature of humanity (as though this were something ordained by God to test our commitment to duty, our willingness to act autonomously) but to social circumstances which often produce a tension between universal and particular interests. Marx's insight here rests on a logical point which is completely missed by Kant (and by Kamenka): it is the case that the rational choices of individuals reflect particular rather than universal perspectives. This is because humanity will be alienated as long as the universal interests of the collective society are not congruent with the particular interests of individuals. Pure reason, then, is impotent.

It is for this reason, also, that Marx and Engels are correct to criticize those who seek personal solutions to ethical problems; as long as our needs as individuals reflect our class situation we will not make much headway in changing the world purely through moral exhortation. Clearly, given this distinctively sociological approach, it follows that people cannot be expected to make truly human choices unless they are free (and the way in which Marx uses the notion of freedom leaves us in no doubt that what he means by the concept is the elimination of particularist class perspectives). Thus, the need for workers to sell their labour power as a commodity, and so give up their autonomy, cannot be wished away by moral persuasion. Even those who treat others as commodities, replacing human workers with machines where expedient, are trapped by circumstance and would lose their power were they to assert a human universal perspective rather than submit to the imperatives of the market. Conversely, given the relationship which Marxist writers postulate between 'interests' and people's beliefs and values, it follows that where there are no sinister interests the choices made by individuals will come to reflect human values. There is nothing paradoxical about Marx's and Engels's apparent rejection of all absolute moral values and their simultaneous prediction of the rise of a truly human morality: Utopia will follow the elimination of class conflict.

Marx's ethical perspectives, then, are coherent. Furthermore, those elements of his position which appear to be simplistic or contradictory when viewed out of context are easily explained when we take into account the role which notions such as 'objective interests' and 'truly human needs' play within his theory. But to say that Marx's position is coherent is not to pronounce it adequate, or to claim that he has said the last word on the subject. Political radicals need to be involved in moral argument at a much deeper level, and they need to come to terms with the substantial contributions which liberal philosophers have made. There is a need, particularly, for a properly worked out democratic theory which can serve to provide both a basis for criticism of liberal systems and the foundation upon which socialist institutions may be planned. Socialists can no longer afford to hope that all will be well after revolutionary changes have smashed capitalism (as Marx and Engels seem to have done), and they therefore need to articulate some conception of political rights. What is needed is a theory which can provide the inspiration for a conception of socialist legality. Marx, unfortunately, has not provided much of a lead in the area of jurisprudence, and the result has been that radicals have tended to embrace a political rhetoric which, because it proceeds on the basis of well intentioned moralizing, often degenerates into naive Utopianism. Few Marxist intellectuals have attempted actually to grapple with the arguments of liberal writers; nor have they provided us with an alternative approach which is acceptable.

Macpherson stands out as one of the few radicals who have taken the trouble to respond to liberal political theory. Consequently, his work provides a useful point of departure for my purposes, and I have devoted some space to the discussion of his contribution. It is also useful, especially if we are looking for an adequate political philosophy which reflects the fundamental values of those who are on the political Left, that we look at the contribution of the liberal philosopher John Rawls. As I try to show in Part II, Rawls develops his position by way of a strategy analysis model (going back to Rousseau and Kant for inspiration) which is in many respects similar to Marx's model of class conflict. He tells us, for example, that in speculating about a hypothetical situation in which we suppose that people are negotiating the terms of their future social relations, we must keep in mind that rational individuals would be likely to take advantage of any superiority they may have over others; conversely, when people must negotiate from a position of weakness they would be prepared to accept terms which would not have been agreeable had they been bargaining from a position of equal strength. The difficulty is that power enables those who control it to force others to agree to terms which they would otherwise reject as unjust. Thus, even if we are to suppose that some form of Social Contract had taken place, the mere fact that citizens had made an agreement would not be morally significant unless it could also be shown that each individual had freely entered into it (I use the concept free here in a sense which is closer to Marx's use than to that of traditional liberalism). The central idea on which Rawls bases his theory of justice is Rousseau's notion that the constraints of equal power could have the paradoxical effect of forcing people to be free. The claim, put simply, is that if others can marshal resources which are approximately equal to our own, then we will have to negotiate and bargain in our dealings with them rather than dictate our terms. Rousseau and Rawls use this insight as the key to a rational defence of democratic principles: adequate political justification involves taking other people's perspectives into account by recognizing well grounded claims to reciprocity.

Marx's position is much closer to that of Rousseau and Rawls than is often realized. Where he differs fundamentally from them is in his view that abstract theorizing is not very useful; for him the theoretical challenge is to develop an adequate understanding of the social system so that we can come to change it; he wants to establish circumstances in social life which will ensure that the dignity of all individuals is respected. Rawls, by contrast, prefers to develop a theory of justice in the abstract. He asks us to suppose circumstances in which individuals are constrained by the fact that they must bargain with others from a position of approximate equality, and to work out by means of strategy analysis the kinds of agreement they would reach. It is in this way, he believes, that we can develop a satisfactory theory of the democratic commitment.

Rawls's approach does not pre-empt more traditional Marxist responses and has a good deal to recommend it. In any event, most of us are not overoptimistic about the possibility of a socialist revolution in advanced capitalist societies. Even if we do suppose that some sort of revolutionary change may come about, so that property interests were destroyed, there would still be a need for some fully worked out conception of the democratic commitment which could help us to determine the rights of citizenship. Experience has shown, moreover, that the need for democratic controls may be even more necessary to prevent terror politics after the destruction of capitalism than during the period in which individual, particular interests are dominant. This is because intermediate groups under capitalism, as owners of resources, stand autonomously between the state and the citizen, and they are, therefore, in a position to bridle the coercive instrumentality by insisting on the rule of law.[5] But, without the protection of intermediate groups who have an entrenched autonomy through their control of social resources, there is every temptation for a ruling elite to emerge which uses coercion as the basis for claiming authority.[6] Such a development must be anticipated by socialists. What is needed, therefore, is an adequate conception of law which can be fully integrated within a socialist theory of the democratic commitment. We would, of course, expect that under socialism the need for state coercion would be very much less than under other systems which are not just (as Rawls also argues).[7] But this would be the case only when the institutional system actually protected the dignity of citizens. For this to occur, I shall argue, the allocation of values will have to be made in a way which does not violate what Rawls has exposed as the basic conception of justice.

The Marxist Concept of Freedom

In earlier sections I have shown why Macpherson argues that the liberal way of viewing political life is thoroughly ideological, and I have reviewed his claim that we need to retrieve democratic theory from the effect of the theoretical presuppositions of liberals. I have also defended the Marxist use of such concepts as 'truly human needs' and 'objective interests' (as opposed to people's actual interests and actual needs). I turn now to consider the conflict between liberals and Marxists over their different conceptions of freedom. Marx, as we have seen, uses 'free' to refer to a state of affairs in which individuals are able to realize their capacity to relate to others as fully autonomous and equal people. It is alleged, however, that this use of the concept involves a serious conceptual confusion. The problem is said to arise out of the refusal by Marxists to distinguish the sphere of politics from other areas of life in the precise way that liberals recommend. In response, Marxist writers have declared liberal theory to be misleading. If we are to do justice to the arguments advanced by both sides in this polemical dispute, we need to look more closely at the concept of freedom which, I shall show, is used ambiguously by both liberal and Marxist writers.

Macpherson's main interest is those concepts which are associated with 'ability claims' of the form 'X has the capacity/capability/ability to do A', 'X has the power to do A' and 'X has the freedom to do A'. He tells us that democratic theory should be concerned with the maximization of human 'powers', which he explicates as the 'ability to exercise human capacities'; and he contrasts this view with the liberal concern with a narrow conception of power as the ability to influence policy-making. What Macpherson objects to most strongly in the approach of many liberal writers is their predilection for elevating freedom (conceived narrowly as the absence of constraints imposed by others) to a place of priority within the framework of ideals to which we ought to be committed. By stating the democratic commitment in what is virtually a tautological way (quoted above, p. 102), Macpherson insists that the conceptual debate be focused on 'capacity' and 'power' rather than on 'freedom' and 'autonomy'. In this regard he launches a counterattack against his liberal critics by distinguishing two concepts of 'power', one of which, he argues is seriously misleading.

In assessing Macpherson's charges against liberal theory, we should note first that 'freedom' and 'power' are both members of a family cluster of closely related terms; both are used to distinguish various ways in which the 'ability claim' 'X can do A' can be said to have point.[8] When we attribute to someone the ability to do something, we may have in mind skill (some special talent: Jimmy Carter's athletic ability is above the average for men of his age); opportunity (the availability of certain necessary resources: they have built a track along which he can run in the morning); or freedom (the fact that the agent is not prevented: there is no Cabinet Meeting before breakfast, so Jimmy can run).

It would seem to be appropriate sometimes to say 'X can do A' meaning that an agent has the power to perform A if he or she so chooses. However, the link between 'power' and the ability attributes (capacity/capability/ability) is more complicated than that between them and the three interpretations of 'ability' listed above. The problem is that 'ability' is either a manifestation of 'power' or a precondition for the exercise of 'power', and it is not surprising, therefore, that the precise boundaries between the concepts is difficult to specify. I would suggest that 'ability claims' are more passive than are attributions of 'power' with regard to the three listed enabling conditions for acting in a particular way. We say 'X has the capacity to do A', provided he or she has acquired the necessary skills, has the opportunity and is free. When we attribute the 'power' to perform an action, however, this implies something more than that the necessary conditions for the performance are satisfied; we usually mean that the subject can ensure that these conditions will be met. For instance, if a person with power is not free, then he or she has the capacity to become free (Carter can cancel the Cabinet Meeting to ensure that he is free to run in the morning); if the powerful lack opportunity, then they have the ability to acquire what is necessary (Carter is able to order that a track be built in the White House garden). 'Power' is, then, limited by a person's capacity to establish the conditions necessary for doing what he or she wishes; and the powerful are able to achieve their objectives more readily than is usual, for they have a wide-ranging ability to alter the circumstances of their life as it suits them. Macpherson is right, therefore, to define a person's power as his or her ability 'to exercise human capacities', and he is right also to distinguish between 'power' and the enabling conditions (skill, opportunity, freedom) which make the performance of an act possible.

Turning from a consideration of 'power' to the more controversial 'freedom', we have already noted that the concept, in its most common usage, relates to one of the necessary conditions for the exercise of the capacity to act in various ways. If X is not free to do A, then this must be because the agent, although he or she has the necessary talent and opportunity, nevertheless cannot perform the act in question. It is important to note that freedom is but one of a range of factors which determine our capacity to do things, and we may be frustrated in our endeavours for other reasons: even though X is free to do A, our subject may lack the talent or there may be no opportunity to accomplish the task. Thus, a citizen of the Soviet Union may be talented enough to read certain controversial American publications in English, and the material may well be in a library to which he or she has access (that is, we can say that the prerequisites for the performance of the act in question, opportunity and ability, are satisfied). However, our citizen would not be 'free' to read the publication if some political authority had ordered that it should not be made available. It is also easy to imagine a situation in which permission is granted by an authority and the controversial literature is available in the library but our citizen cannot benefit from these opportunities because he or she cannot read English, or the case of a citizen who has the necessary authority and can read English but experiences grave difficulties in getting the material required from the library.

Liberal writers have, for the most part, recognized the importance of all three different types of condition which have to be met if we are to exercise our capacities, and they have stressed the distinction between liberty and the worth of liberty. Nevertheless, they have tended to hold to the view that freedom, conceived narrowly, as I have said, as the absence of constraints imposed by others, is politically by far the most important of the conditions. In this regard they have argued that restrictions of liberty should be treated more seriously than those which result from lack of opportunity or from poorly developed skills. Macpherson, in contrast, has tended to regard all three impediments as equally serious, and he has concentrated on maximizing capacities (taken generally to include skill, opportunity and freedom). He has also been critical of those liberals who have been excessively preoccupied with the establishment and maintenance of liberty.

One advantage which emerges if we follow Macpherson's suggestion here is that once we see 'freedom' (narrowly conceived) as merely one of a number of equally important conditions which are necessary if we are to exercise our capacities, we can blur the boundaries between constraints more easily. The important question, in Macpherson's view, is whether a constraint (be it the need for permission, lack of opportunity or the required development of a special skill) arises directly or indirectly out of the actions of others. Moreover, he is prepared to extend the concept beyond the very narrow focus of liberal writers (on freedom from proscribed constraints) and to claim that the value of liberty arises as an issue if what inhibits our capacity to act as we choose can be traced to the direct intervention of others or to their failure to act. For example, a government may deliberately prevent the exercise of a capacity by withholding opportunity (discouraging the publication of books in the vernacular) or by subverting educational advancement (discouraging the teaching of English in schools), without specifically proscribing the activity. Thus, they achieve indirectly — often with greater efficiency — what a straightforward banning of literature backed by coercive sanctions might have accomplished. Macpherson sees such a situation as raising the issue of freedom for, in his view, the important question is whether or not someone is responsible. He is prepared to argue that a restriction of freedom occurs whenever we are faced with frustrating circumstances which are the consequences of other people's decisions.

There is substantial agreement between Macpherson and most liberal writers on this point. Indeed, one reason why lack of freedom has always seemed to be much more objectionable than other inhibiting factors is that it is in many ways (indeed, essentially) the result of the power exercised over us by others. We do not normally mind if people alter the circumstances of their lives to develop their capacities, provided this is not accomplished at our expense. The most obvious way in which people have been able to extend their capacities has, however, been through the subjugation of others to their own will. It has never been easy to alter the availability of resources or to extend skills. Thus, in most cases in which people have succeeded in extending their personal powers this has involved controlling the lives of others whose co-operation with, or non-resistance to, their purposes has been significant. It is this insight which lies at the heart of the liberal concern with liberty. As Sir Isaiah Berlin puts it:

> I am normally said to be free to the degree to which no human being interferes with my activity. Political liberty in this sense is simply the area within which a man can do what he wants. If I am prevented by other persons from doing what I want, I am to that degree unfree; and if the area within which I can do what I want is contracted by other men beyond a certain minimum, I can be described as being coerced, or, it may be, enslaved.[9]

Macpherson's position must be distinguished from that of most liberal writers, however, because he finds it necessary to extend 'freedom' to cover all impediments subject to the discretion of others and is not concerned exclusively with liberty. He uses the terminology 'invasive relationship' to describe the kind of situation in which some people are able to extend their capacities by foreclosing on the freedom of others, and he also talks in a technical way about the 'net transfer of powers' from some to others.[10] Transfers occur, in Macpherson's account, wherever there is unequal access to material resources which are necessary for the exercise of our capacities to be productive through labour. This is because where some own the means of production (the natural resources and machinery necessary for labour to be productive), or can control it through coercion, they can extract part of the labour power of others by demanding a transfer in return for some limited right of access. In such situations individuals have to pay by giving up some of their power in order to work at all.

This brings me to the central point of difference between Macpherson and most liberal writers: for reasons which I have never found convincing, liberal theorists are reluctant to count property claims ('trespassers will be prosecuted') as constituting a violation of the freedom of others. This is the case despite the obvious fact that one person's fence demarcating his or her property manifestly bars others from entry. Berlin, for example, is reluctant to regard Macpherson's worries about the invasive possibilities involved here as raising an issue of freedom. The situation is one which, Berlin tells us, should more properly be considered as raising the question of the availability of resources. The justification which Berlin offers for treating some impediments as a 'lack of freedom' while others, though acknowledged to be important, are deemed not to involve the issue of freedom, is that to count as an interference with freedom constraints must involve the deliberate actions of others. He seems to believe (and his position here is shared by most liberal writers) that it makes a significant difference whether the constraints imposed on others are purposive and intentional or incidental (resulting from actions directed towards some other end). Berlin wants to treat property claims as similar to the types of constraint which are beyond human control (such as lack of natural ability) or which do not involve political anxiety (for nobody thinks that liberty is in jeopardy simply because we cannot jump up to the moon or live for a thousand years). He assumes that (under capitalist relations of production) the impediments imposed by inequalities of wealth are generally an indirect consequence of people exercising their freedoms. As Berlin sees the issues, one person's good fortune in acquiring wealth is not directed, whatever the unintended consequences, at preventing others from becoming equally prosperous; and he regards the freedom to contract and the freedom to acquire property (privately owned) as a necessary prerequisite enabling people to make the most of themselves. For these reasons Berlin argues that it is misleading, when we complain about inequalities of wealth, to suggest that we are demanding freedom. The situation is more properly described, in his view, as one in which we are demanding a restriction of freedom (the freedom to contract) in the name of some conception of social equality or perhaps justice.[11]

Macpherson responds to Berlin's position with characteristic vigour:

It is not a matter only of whether I can *get* what I want but also of whether I can *do* what I want. And...differences in access are at least as important in determining what I can do as what I can get. On these grounds we may conclude that the unequal access to the means of life and labour inherent in capitalism is, regardless of what particular social and political theory is invoked, an impediment to the freedom of those with little or no access. It diminishes their negative liberty, since the dependence on others for a living which deficiency of access creates diminishes the area in which they cannot be pushed around.[12]

A further complexity which makes the concept of freedom somewhat elusive, and which contributes to the bad reputation radicals have acquired for using political concepts loosely, needs to be noted. The problem I have in mind arises out of the fact that those with power may often use their discretion (for their power enables them to interfere at will) in a manner which is conducive to the extension of our capacity to do various things. We can say 'X is free to do A' even when the exercise of that capacity is subject to the discretion of some other person (Carter's staff may run because he has allowed them time off and access to the track). It is significant that it would not be appropriate to attribute 'power' in this kind of case, and we do not say 'X is powerful enough to do A' when he or she must ask permission before acting. What is implied by the attribution of 'power' is an ability to ensure co-operation (Carter's staff do not have any capacity to ensure that he will give them time off). The claim 'X is free to do A', in contrast to the claim 'X has the power to do A', merely indicates that the necessary condition, that of not being hindered, is met (Carter has not prevented his staff from doing what they want to); it does not suggest that X has the ability to alter the situation if the permission to do A were withdrawn.

It is for these reasons that Berlin writes, with regard to the negative conception of liberty which he defends:

The third characteristic of this notion of liberty is of greater importance. It is that liberty in this sense is not incompatible with some kinds of autocracy, or at any rate with the absence of self-government. Liberty in this sense is principally concerned with the area of control, not with its sources. Just as a democracy may, in fact, deprive the individual of a great many liberties which he might have in some other form of society, so it is perfectly conceivable that a liberal-minded despot would allow his subjects a large measure of personal freedom....The answer to the question 'Who governs me?' is logically distinct from the question 'How far does government interfere with me?' It is in this difference that the great contrast between the two concepts of negative and positive liberty, in the end, consists.[13]

We must resist the temptation to go all the way with Berlin on this point. While he is clearly right to claim that we do speak of 'freedom' even where this may be subject to the discretion of others, it must not be forgotten that the fact that we have to ask permission is in itself an imposition of considerable importance. Consider, for example, the difference between those countries in which the right to travel is something to which every citizen is entitled as of right and those in which passports are issued solely at the discretion of some political authority. There may well be a great deal of travelling on the part of the citizens of both countries, so that the degree of freedom, in Berlin's sense, must be judged to be the same. Most of us would not, however, accept this observation as grounds for complacency but would be greatly concerned *for freedom* if but one passport were refused by an official for what appeared to be an arbitrary reason. Our worry here relates to the fact that permission may be withdrawn at any time, and to be subject to this contingency is to be crucially dependent on another person's potential interference. Even if no one were refused a passport, the requirement that we have to ask permission is itself an imposition which ought to be objected to in the name of freedom.

One might see this kind of case, as Berlin does, as merely related to the distribution of power, but the connections with 'freedom' are so close, and the two concepts themselves so inextricably associated in our minds, that it is surely better to salvage from Berlin's conceptual analysis the intuitive links we all make when we talk about 'freedom' as an ideal. We surely do mean by a free society one in which permissions are not required, and we do associate freedom with the ability 'to live in accordance with one's own conscious purposes, to act and decide for oneself rather than to be acted upon and decided for by others'; this ideal, in turn, is associated in our minds with the democratic concept of liberty as 'a share in the controlling authority'.[14] These commitments follow from the forebodings which the thought that our lives may be subject to the discretion of others conjures up in our imaginations. Berlin is right to see that these fears are focused more squarely on 'power' than on 'freedom', and his conceptual distinction is a sound one; but it is these fears, nevertheless, which come to mind (and properly so) when we talk about the ideal of a free society. The reason for this is simply that the degree of freedom enjoyed by a community is in practice a function of the power relations which manifest themselves. If we are to preserve freedom, then we cannot afford to allow others to gain power over us.

Once we are prepared to think of 'freedom' in the broader, more positive way suggested by Macpherson, we can begin to see some traditional policy problems in a new light. I think here particularly of the widely held view that there are important, unresolvable conflicts between values — such as, for example, between liberty (to drive faster than 100 kph on a motorway) and safety, or between equality and efficiency in economic life, or between the claims of personal entitlement and social justice. In terms of Macpherson's account, we have a ready way of coming to some judgement about how competing claims of this kind ought to be balanced, for the apparent conflict between competing values does not take on the overwhelming significance which it does in liberal approaches.[15] The reason for this is that once we accept that what is basic in social life is a commitment to maximize people's ability to 'live as fully as they may wish', we can see that the three kinds of potential impediment listed above (skill, opportunity, liberty), which correspond in a loose way with Macpherson's suggested focus for democratic theory (the lack of the means of life, the lack of access to the means of labour and the need for protection from invasions by others), must be taken into account when discussing political issues. In this regard it is significant to note that it makes as little sense to say that we have a basic political right to liberty as it does to talk about there being a right to a skill (the ability to read) or to an opportunity (a place at Harvard University). None of these claims can be considered more basic than the others; social resources have to be distributed between people, and it follows, therefore, that their individual claims to equal concern and respect (their right to 'live as fully as they may wish') must take priority whenever choices between competing claims have to be made. Thus, if your claimed right to the liberty to perform a certain act (plant trees in your own garden) has a seriously damaging effect on the interests of others (the trees overshadow your neighbour's property), or if your use of an opportunity (a place at Harvard University) prevents others from enjoying the same advantage, then conflicting claims will have to be settled in a way which treats each person involved with equal concern and respect. We need a theory to help us resolve problems of conflict of this kind which reflects a concern to respect the right of each person fully to develop his or her capacities.

By exposing the presupposition of liberal theory and by carefully clarifying the fundamental issues, Macpherson has undoubtedly pointed us in the right direction. It is, however, John Rawls (as I show in Part II) who has shown us the way forward towards a more adequate theory of the democratic commitment.

PART II
RADICAL INDIVIDUALISM

Introduction

I want now to distinguish and defend a radical individualist approach to problems in jurisprudence and political philosophy by reviewing the work of John Rawls and Ronald Dworkin. These writers have recommended a conception of rights and of justice which should be especially welcome to those whose intuitive response to political issues inclines more towards that of Marx than towards the pessimism of liberal writers.

It is true that both Rawls and Dworkin are committed liberals, and that the former clearly thinks that a capitalist economic system (suitably corrected by welfare adjustments made by a sensitive government) could give rise to an allocation of resources and benefits which might plausibly be described as just. This is the aspect of Rawls's contribution which is correctly challenged by Macpherson. Thus, although he concedes that *A Theory of Justice* 'has the substantial merit of taking us beyond the warmed-up utilitarianism of much current liberal theory while avoiding the gross idealism that tempts or afflicts anti-utilitarians of the centre and right',[1] he argues that Rawls's enterprise is vitiated in a way similar to that of his nineteenth-century precursor, the liberal humanist T. H. Green. Both writers are concerned to move away from a utilitarian conception of the human character (as essentially a seeker after material pleasure), and they share a conception of democratic community in which individuals develop their capacities in harmony with others; neither perceives, however, that these ideas are incompatible with a system of production based on relations in which some are able to transfer (for their own benefit) some of the powers of others.

Macpherson argues that liberal humanists like Green and Rawls simply assume that social life will have to embody class inequalities, and that their central concern is to show how these can be justified as fair. But, Macpherson suggests, we do not have to assume class conflicts of the kind they take to be endemic to the human predicament, so we do not need the kind of theory Rawls and Green endeavour to provide.

I am prepared to go only part of the way with Macpherson. I cannot agree that the problem of justice is peculiar to societies in which there is class exploitation; rather, 'the circumstances of justice obtain whenever mutually disinterested persons put forward conflicting claims to the division of social advantages under conditions of moderate scarcity.'[2] This statement from Rawls is surely correct, and he is justified also in claiming that these conditions will be manifest in all modern societies in which there is a reasonably complex division of labour. Macpherson seems to suppose that a future socialist society will not be characterized by scarcity or conflict and that, therefore, a theory of justice of the kind that Rawls seeks to provide will not be a vital necessity. But, this is wishful thinking, for socialists will have more use for such a theory than would liberals, for they will need to allocate resources by making value judgements and will not be able to rely on an 'invisible hand mechanism'.[3]

Rather than dismissing Rawls's contribution out of hand, we should ask ourselves whether it is possible to distinguish his individualist humanist values (I describe these on pp. 00—00) from his capitalist market assumptions. Can what Rawls calls his general conception of justice:

All social primary goods — liberty and opportunity, income and wealth, and the basis of self-respect...distributed equally unless an unequal distribution of any or all of these goods is to the advantage of the least favored[4]

be regarded as independent of his political, social and economic assumptions? Dworkin certainly thinks that this is the case, for he tells us:

Rawls' most basic assumption is not that men have a right to certain basic liberties that Locke or Mill thought important, but that they have a right to equal respect and concern in the design of political institutions. This assumption may be contested in many ways. It will be denied by those who believe that some goal, like utility or the triumph of a class or the flowering of some conception of how men should live, is more fundamental than any individual right, including the right to equality. But it cannot be denied in the name of any more radical concept of equality, because none exists.[5]

Brian Barry reaches a similar conclusion in his summary judgement, for he tells us that the significance of *A Theory of Justice* is that it is a statement of liberalism which 'makes private property in the means of production, distribution and exchange a contingent matter', and it introduces a principle of distribution which could 'suitably interpreted and with certain factual assumptions, have egalitarian implications'.[6] Those who are persuaded more by Marx than by Mill in their assessment of liberal society may find, therefore, that they share a commitment to the idea that people have a right to be treated with equal concern and respect; they may also agree that this ideal should be reflected in the design of the basic institutions of social life.

Even Macpherson, as we have seen, shares this ideal. Indeed, we can reformulate Rawls's general conception of justice to read: 'All persons have an equal claim to the means of social life, to a share in the means of labour, and to have their dignity and privacy protected.' In his explication of what this democratic ideal entails, Macpherson emphasizes two requirements: participation in political life and equality. His notion of Utopia is a society which has a structure based on Lenin's idea of democratic centralism, in which authorities form a pyramid-like hierarchy, each level of which is elected from immediately below. Macpherson also insists that for these democratic structures to work meaningfully, it is essential that there be substantial social equality, and that widespread democratic participation at the base level be encouraged.[7]

What is interesting about Macpherson's model is that no mention is made of the importance of political rights. I do not wish to imply that he thinks that political rights are unimportant. Nevertheless, he is noticeably reluctant to give any support to the idea of entrenching a Bill of Rights and his model of participatory democracy (perhaps because it is so strongly influenced by Marx's idea of encouraging government from below) leaves little room for the possibility of judicial review. Macpherson seems to rely entirely on the spontaneity of democratic forces in a reconstituted society, on the assumption that provided we have rule by the people we will ensure justice. Yet I would argue that the most meaningful forms of political participation emerging in modern advanced systems today are those which arise out of the distinctively American conception that a democracy is a society in which citizens have rights which are protected. Citizens in that country are confident that their rights will often be upheld by a court, and they have sometimes successfully challenged and frustrated the ambitions of a government by forcing issues to adjudication. Even simple victories (for example, having the right to publish documents of national importance upheld; gaining acquittal after being arrested at a political demonstration; successfully suing a government agency for invading privacy without due cause, or for discriminating on political grounds in its employment policies) often represent a significant advance over the democratic practice of systems in which such successful challenges by citizens are not possible. Indeed, I would go so far as to claim that unless rights are taken seriously in this way no convincing claim can be made that a system is a democracy.

Of course, a society can succeed in taking rights seriously without establishing a system of judicial review or entrenching a Bill of Rights. Some commentators even think that a democratically elected Parliament is the best guardian of rights; and many, especially those writing in Australia and the United Kingdom, are persuaded that such a body is all that is required for an effective democracy. Macpherson and Marx may, therefore, be justified in their judgement that a fully socialist society would not need to institutionalize rights. We should note, however, that even if we are prepared to place our faith in democratic processes, we cannot avoid the philosophical problems relating to the nature of justice. This is because democratic citizens would have to make difficult choices between competing values, and to accomplish this adequately some properly worked out conception of justice would be required. The leading journalists and intellectuals in a democratic society would, therefore, have a responsibility to ensure that people understood the policy issues of the day and that the claims of competing parties in the name of justice were well stated. Democratic practice would also require that those in the lowest stations of life were capable of asserting themselves, and to do this they would have to be encouraged by more sophisticated and knowledgeable advocates. The basic institutional arrangements, including the conventions of the system, must be of a kind, then, which would ensure that rights would be taken seriously. We can say that a truly democratic system would be one in which people were confident enough, and had sufficient rights, to cause trouble if a matter of justice were in the balance.

I conclude that an adequate theory of democracy would provide some model of representative institutions of the kind that Macpherson offers in his *The Life and Times of Liberal Democracy*, but it would also require a conception of law which reflected a commitment to take democratic rights seriously. It is because I believe that radicals have, for the most part, neglected to concern themselves sufficiently with the development of such a theory that I have chosen to review the work of Rawls and Dworkin. All committed democrats share the view that persons be treated as equals and with dignity and respect; perhaps we may come to share the theory of rights which Rawls and Dworkin have derived from this commitment. I shall explore this possibility by delineating, first, the core commitments of the theoretical position I call radical individualism and then by applying the theory to a range of policy problems.

6
The Point of the Rights Thesis

It is important to distinguish radical individualism from the more traditional individualist approaches — utilitarianism and possessive individualism.

Possessive Individualism

Consider first possessive individualism. This characterization is taken from Macpherson, who uses the term to describe the core commitments of liberal political and social theory.[1] Macpherson has in mind the Lockean tradition within liberal thought, and he argues that contemporary writers have carried over into modern debate assumptions from the formative years of the seventeenth century. He is concerned especially with their attitude towards the institution of property and with the assumption made by many liberals that individuals owe nothing to society for the skills which they acquire when they are trained to accomplish sophisticated tasks. Macpherson argues that most modern liberals still cling to a conception of individual rights which takes freedom from coercion to be the fundamental political value, so that what is regarded as important is that individuals be free from any relations other than those they have entered into voluntarily. And he accuses them of conceiving of political society as a contrivance for the maintenance of orderly exchanges between people who are considered to be the owners of their own capacities and for the protection of the property which these individuals may acquire.

It is significant that what is characteristic of possessive individualism is that it is grounded in a special conception of natural rights that is regarded as fundamental. Furthermore, it follows from this conception that governments have no legitimate authority coercively to redistribute wealth in the name of some ideal of public policy (such as that of maximizing average utility), or even because of a humanitarian concern for the welfare of the poor. If individuals have rights, and if these rights establish entitlements, then attempts to redistribute property rightfully acquired may well constitute an abuse of the legitimate claims of those who succeed in life − it may involve exploiting the rich! If I choose to work hard and to cultivate my property while you lie idle enjoying leisure, and if, moreover, I take the trouble to store up my produce while you consume yours, then it would surely be an abuse to require that I share my accumulated assets with you. Robert Nozick, whose views I take to reflect a rigorous and consistent possessive individualism, goes so far as to argue that any attempt on the part of a government to act in the name of distributive principles of justice or on principles which reflect a commitment to some social purpose (such as the maximization of wealth, the establishment of equality of opportunity, the elimination of poverty) necessarily involves exploitation − for if the rich do not want to give up their assets for these purposes, they must be coerced.[2] Yet provided the property held by the rich is acquired legitimately in the first place (for the possessive individualist this means that they must have been acquired through processes which respect the choices and freedom of others), then presumably they have a right to them. Thus, any attempt coercively to appropriate a part of these privately owned resources for public purposes would violate the rights of the individual owners. This view is clearly based on the premise that our human dignity requires that we be free from all relations which we do not enter into voluntarily, and that we have a right to our privately owned assets.

Illustrating this view and his conception of basic rights, Nozick asks: why should we ever accept as just, distributional requirements which allow that some can benefit from the achievements and efforts of others? And he suggests that unless we can provide answers to this question we are obliged indirectly to acknowledge the claims of a conception of justice based on the principle of natural freedom. This he formulates as requiring 'from each as they choose, to each as they are chosen'. He argues that we are not entitled to expect that the efforts of some (their choice to work hard) be used in order to subsidize others and that, in so far as this is possible to determine, each person is entitled to a return from any form of co-operation with others which reflects the value of their contribution. For these reasons Nozick believes that any adequate account of justice must focus on the choices which are made by free individuals contracting with one another. In this way he builds a theory of justice on the back of a theory of entitlement, so that, as he puts it, we might say that the core principle of justice is:

From each according to what he chooses to do, to each according to what he makes for himself (perhaps with the contracted aid of others) and what others choose to do for him and choose to give him of what they've been given previously (under this maxim) and haven't yet expended or transferred.[3]

An important distinction, which is crucial to Nozick's conception of justice as a form of entitlement, is that between what he calls historical principles and what he calls end-state principles. As he puts it:

The entitlement theory of justice in distribution is *historical*; whether a distribution is just depends on how it came about. In contrast, *current time-slice principles* of justice hold that the justice of a distribution is determined by how things are distributed (who has what) as judged by some *structural* principle(s) of just distribution.[4]

It is Nozick's claim that any attempt to focus on end-states (it is desirable that 10 per cent of the candidates who sit the examination fail) must confuse and confound our thinking about justice (are the candidates entitled to pass?); for, he insists, what is crucial to our comprehension of the issues in this area is that we recognize 'that past circumstances or actions of people can create differential entitlements or differential deserts to things'.[5]

The central difficulty with the possessive individualist approach is that not many of us are prepared to ignore end-states in the way that Nozick recommends. Experience has shown that market relationships can give rise to unacceptable consequences. This is because people, who are required to be responsible for their own destinies, do sometimes make silly decisions, and the consequences of this in a world of free market competition may well determine life-long prospects; our humanitarian concern for others, then, cautions against any blanket acceptance of the principle of natural freedom. We may also suppose that our sense of what is fair will be violated by the way the process of free market competition allocates resources, for often success in exchange results from luck or from deception. No matter how talented, industrious or conscientious one may be, success in competition is often attributable to good fortune, and this cannot be guaranteed. For example, someone who accepts a reasonable risk in not taking out insurance cover may end up with a severe loss, though the decision to accept the risk was well thought out. Even if we do not accept that this might be so, the fact that the majority of those who make the same choice do not suffer any loss is surely unfair and totally arbitrary. Yet these kinds of anomalies occur again and again where resources are allocated purely through market competition. Another problem here is that those who start with few resources in a competitive situation are at a very great disadvantage and are unlikely to succeed. It follows that once inequalities are established and some individuals emerge with large private holdings, even if these are acquired in the first place through industry and fair exchange, their future dealings will not necessarily be fair, for they will be in a position to force competitors to accept unfavourable terms (which will, of course, be the best available, given the competition). Even if we disregard the issue of fairness, the mere fact that there are going to be winners and losers in every market system raises special moral problems. For example, most of us are concerned to protect those who are not capable of competing effectively. This may be because they suffer from a fatal weakness (a need for alcohol or the urge to gamble, perhaps, which undermines their capacity to make responsible choices), or it may be that they are so burdened by circumstance that their confidence is destroyed and others take advantage.

What is required to support the individualist ideal, despite these recognized problems, are assumptions about what might be likely to ameliorate the consequences of unbridled competition. Arguments by means of which the more tender-minded possessive individualists have comforted themselves have usually included the following claims: we can educate people to take responsible choices so that they act cautiously and can care for themselves; even if education is not a sufficient panacea, we can rely on the fact that people in general have a capacity to act in a caring and generous way towards those who are less fortunate, and we can, therefore, assume that those who suffer the harshest effects of competition will be cared for even without state intervention; although market relationships do produce some unfortunate results, any alternative system, and especially one which required a government to intervene in economic life, would be worse by far.

Utilitarian Individualism

The assumptions listed above have never seemed convincing to the majority of philosophers who have set out to defend liberal political perspectives, and they have consequently abandoned the possessive individualist approach. Thus, contrary to what Macpherson at times seems to imply, it would be true to say that the legitimizing political theory of liberalism has been hostile to the notion that there are natural rights, in the Lockean sense. Most of the leading writers have followed Bentham and have rigorously condemned the notion of natural rights as metaphysical. In place of the assumption of natural rights, they have been concerned to maximize the general good by promoting efficient policies, and they have, consequently, attempted to provide ways of measuring the impact of government initiatives.

One advantage the utilitarian approach enjoys over possessive individualism arises out of the more pragmatic attitude which theorists have been able to adopt to the individualist ideal of maximizing the area of life left to personal choice. Thus, although utilitarian individualists have generally defended the principle of natural freedom (which possessive individualists regard as a principle of justice), they have done so only because they were convinced by the argument that human happiness will be maximized by a policy which allows people to do what they choose. They certainly have not regarded the principle as a natural entitlement which can be claimed regardless of the social consequences which might be thought to follow. Thus, utilitarians have felt free to recommend paternalistic policies where this could be shown to be more beneficial, and they have often justified politically imposed restraints, provided their consequences could be shown to be better than those that would have followed from unfettered liberty. This kind of paternalism is thought to be particularly justifiable in areas of life in which there is heightened emotionalism or in which people are thought to be incompetent. So, for example, utilitarian arguments can be provided for prohibiting practices such as duelling, gambling, euthanasia and even abortion. In all these cases it might be felt that the judgement of individuals is clouded by their emotional responses in a way which makes their own choices an unreliable indicator of their real interests.[6] For similar reasons utilitarians have justified the imposition of a minimum age of consent to protect children from making mistakes which result from their immaturity, and the same reasoning applies to the certification of idiots so that they are not treated as fully competent individuals.

Even in the economic sphere of life the utilitarians have been able to build in a commitment to welfare. Paternalism here follows partly as a result of a deduction which can be made from the psychological assumption of marginalism: if a person has so much of one commodity that he cannot use it all, then in order to maximize pleasure what is left over should be given to those who do not have enough. Intensities also apply here, for the more one has of something, the less further supplies are likely to be appreciated. It follows that a principle which distributes in such a way that those with the most receive even more is not likely to maximize general happiness. William Godwin argued that the only rational claim to the use of property was the urgency of need (that is, he claimed that this was the only rational ground for recognizing an entitlement); in holding this view, it could be said, he was articulating a utilitarian theory of justice.[7] There is, however, more to a utilitarian calculation in the economic sphere than Godwin seems to have supposed: in distributing wealth a utilitarian, hoping to maximize pleasure by satisfying the most intensely felt needs, must keep in mind the need of the economic system for the accumulation of capital and for the replacement of worn plant and machinery. But provided they are careful not to undermine the market system of allocation itself by setting taxation so high that incentives are destroyed and the productive system is cut back from expansion and efficiency, utilitarian planners need have no qualms about following Godwin's reasoning and may redistribute wealth to the needy.

Although utilitarianism undoubtedly represents a great improvement on possessive individualism, because it is more concerned to offer a humane response to the needs of individuals, the superiority is bought at some cost in theoretical sophistication; for, as Rawls and Dworkin show, it requires us to deliberate in a way which does not attach sufficient weight to the family of moral concepts associated with entitlement. Utilitarians must consequently either accept the fact that the consequentialist approach is counter-intuitive and provide arguments to show why it should, nevertheless, be preferred over theories which take rights seriously, or state utilitarianism in a way which gives more weight to the concept of a right than Bentham seems to have allowed and provide a utilitarian theory of justice.

The first approach seems to be that of the utilitarian writers who follow Bentham. The only rights which he was prepared to recognize were those established by positive law, and he regarded the notion of natural rights as metaphysical nonsense. Even the obligations established by positive law were analysed by Bentham in a way which often seems to blur the difference between 'being obliged' and 'being under an obligation'.[8] Writers who have adopted the second approach follow J. S. Mill in thinking that there are no insurmountable difficulties in the way of the development of a utilitarian theory of justice. What they have hoped to provide is a plausible theory of entitlement, starting from the premise that the only relevant moral factor is the want-satisfactions which can be provided.

If one argues that all actions should be judged on their merits and assessed in terms of the amount of pleasure, pain or simply average utility which is likely to result, then it becomes extraordinarily difficult to show why, in particular cases, promises are binding or the innocent should not be punished. The issues relating to punishment present the most dramatic illustration, for we can conceive of situations in which the public good may be served by using an innocent victim as a scapegoat; a favourite example, much discussed by philosophers, envisages a situation in which a judge is confronted with an issue involving racial tensions, and failure to convict could lead angry citizens to take matters into their own hands by seeking vengeance through arson or murder. It is significant to note that a utilitarian case for punishing the innocent can be made progressively more plausible by loading the circumstances so that the consequences of not providing a scapegoat become worse and worse. If we restrict ourselves to utilitarian arguments, then, it cannot be shown that we ought to allow individuals to frustrate the achievement of desirable policy objectives in the name of individual rights.

In an effort to get clear of this kind of problem and to state the utilitarian position in a way which gives institutional commitments their full weight, some philosophers have posed their questions firmly at the macro rather than the micro level. Instead of asking 'Why should we not punish this or that person in these circumstances?' or 'Why should I keep this particular promise?', they have preferred to ask 'Why, in general, should we follow the rule that we ought not to punish the innocent?' or 'Why, in general, should we respect the rule that promises ought to be kept?' In each of these cases we are dealing with institutional arrangements — we are asking ourselves why it is important to follow a rule setting out what it is proper to do, and why it is necessary to commit ourselves to such a rule before we are confronted by the exigencies of social life. We are concerned here with the problem of showing why the rights established by our chosen rules should be taken seriously. The utilitarian answer to these questions is that if we follow rules by making a commitment to institutional practices, then this will tend, in the long run, to produce more advantage than would be the case if there were no prior commitment to follow the rule.[9]

Rule utilitarianism can be strengthened also by an appeal to the question: what if everyone did the same?[10] The idea is to impose on any utilitarian calculation the moral constraint of having to generalize the action. If the action cannot be generalized, so it is argued, then it should not be contemplated. For example, suppose we regard as desirable, from a utilitarian point of view, the rules which set out fair procedures regulating competition between candidates in democratic elections (we believe, then, that if the rules are followed more good than harm will result), it may still be the case that we can find utilitarian reasons for disregarding the rules in particular circumstances. Why should political calculators not rely on the fact that others will play by the rules while they secretly go about rigging their own chances by having no scruples at all? Like Nixon and his advisors, they may well profess a deep respect for democratic procedures and lawful behaviour but may feel, nevertheless, that in particular circumstances it would be best to maximize their own chances of retaining power. The generalization requirement is a device invented by philosophers for avoiding this kind of reasoning: by requiring our calculators to ask themselves 'What would happen if everyone were to break the rules of procedure during elections?' it is hoped that freeloading as a tactic can be avoided.

Unfortunately, the generalization constraint does not cut as deeply as many philosophers seem to believe, as our notions of 'like cases' and of 'doing the same' offer considerable flexibility as long as we allow fine distinctions to be made.[11] For example, those who contemplate ignoring democratic restraints during elections may treat their own case as unique with regard to such facts as their good intentions after they gain office and their competence to govern for the benefit of all; they may also genuinely believe that their rivals for office are dangerous idealists who would quickly bring the country to ruin. Nor can we discount wider considerations, such as emergencies (a war involvement, perhaps, which could be adversely affected by a change in government). Given this kind of specificity, utilitarian political leaders could comfortably reach the conclusion that anyone in exactly their circumstances should ignore the rights of other contestants as well as the rights of citizens when this would help to ensure that the best government is elected to office. The problem is that specific reference destroys the generalization requirement by allowing for a thousand qualifications. We would no longer be asking 'What would happen if all the candidates competing in the election were to ignore the constraints of the rules designed to ensure that the competition is fair?' but, because of our ability to apply specific qualifications to the general rule, 'What would happen if people situated in circumstances $C_a...C_z$ were to disregard the constraints of specific social rules?' In allowing for this kind of reference, the application of the principle collapses into a straightforward utilitarian calculation of particular cases.

It is not clear, then, that utilitarians can generate arguments for taking rights seriously. One suspects, however, that what rule utilitarian writers are struggling towards is an open recognition of the weight which should be placed on the claims of fairness in political argument. This is apparent from the fact that they misleadingly characterize the constraint which is supposed to result from the question 'What if everyone were to do the same?' as a worry about consequences: we conjure up in our minds an image of social chaos as the likely consequence of too many individuals playing fast and loose with social rules. But what generalization constraints in ethical argument are usually aimed at avoiding is freeloading; the intuitive appeal is to some conception of reciprocity, and the fundamental concern is with fairness. Utilitarian arguments are often subtle and ingenious, however, – full justice to the efforts of those who hope to take rights seriously without abandoning their commitment to consequentialism has not been done here.

Yet it would seem that those utilitarians who simply admit (with Bentham) the difficulty that teleological arguments have in accommodating notions of entitlement have the more straightforward approach, and they do make out a very strong case for their position. It is suggested that if we face up to the real issues when choices have to be made in circumstances in which it is plausible to suggest a conflict between utilitarian and other approaches in ethics, then utilitarianism emerges as the most reasonable approach to take. For example, when confronted with the charge that in some circumstances utilitarian arguments would support strategies such as the resort to torture or the conviction of the innocent, J. J. Smart responds by suggesting, first, that it is highly unlikely that utilitarian arguments could be found for supporting the resort to torture or a practice such as slavery; second, that when such a case could be plausibly made on utilitarian grounds the situation would have to be so unusual that other ethical principles would be of little use; third, that it is in precisely these circumstances that utilitarian considerations offer the best guidance. Anthony Quinton has also suggested that in some circumstances a strong utilitarian argument can be made for a resort to torture. Both these philosophers are prepared to challenge those who hope to dismiss utilitarianism by deducing what appear to be morally outrageous conclusions.[12] Their point is that where the deductions are in fact made the utilitarian conclusions no longer seem outrageous. It is, they tell us, only out of context that attempts at deriving a *reductio ad absurdum* from utilitarian premises seem to be compelling.

This response on the part of utilitarian philosophers only goes part of the way to meet the charges of their critics: the challenge to utilitarian ways of thinking presented by the hard cases thought up by critics need not be pressed to the point at which the position can be shown to generate unacceptable responses — all that needs to be illustrated by these cases is that utilitarian ways of thinking oversimplify the issues involved. For example, the central charge which Rawls makes against utilitarianism is that the approach leaves out of account significant moral considerations such as the notion of human dignity, the idea of desert and the claims of fairness when resolving the problem cases; he does not suppose that in the kinds of judgements they make utilitarians will be likely to depart very significantly from those of us whose ethical approach is much broader. His point is that even if utilitarians can find arguments to show that their position does not do grave violence to our intuitive judgements on most issues, this does not mean that there is not a more adequate theory available. The real test is not whether utilitarianism is defensible, for it clearly is, but whether it can claim to be better than other approaches in political philosophy. Thus, Rawls argues that the decisive objection to utilitarianism is that a better theory is available; and in this regard he tells us that his own approach more adequately balances our concern about the consequences of actions with our sense of justice. Of course, if we were required to choose between some form of utilitarianism and possessive individualism (which, as we have seen, violates our concern for the effect on others of free market systems), then most of us would be inclined to choose the former.[13] But this is not the choice with which we are faced, for Rawls has provided a fruitful synthesis of the two perspectives by focusing on our sense of fair play in a way which allows consequentialism a significant place within a deontological theory.

Radical Individualism

Dworkin and Rawls set out to provide a theory which takes rights seriously but which is not grounded in the assumptions of possessive individualism. They see no compelling reason why a rights-based theory should presume, for example, that individuals be treated as the owners of socially transmitted skills or as having a natural right to accumulate assets and to allocate these freely as they choose. These rights claims are derived from a specific theory which conceptualizes 'entitlement' in a narrow, unsatisfactory way (by treating liberty, conceived as the right to be left alone, as the primary social value). But there is no cogent reason why a deontological approach should be founded on such a commitment, and it is therefore sensible to search elsewhere, as Rawls and Dworkin do, for a more adequate point of departure from which to construct a theory of rights. While they concede that the concept of a right often presupposes some exercise of choice — as when we establish a claim by showing previous transactions and relationships between individuals which have been voluntarily entered into — they argue, nevertheless, that political rights and obligations cannot be identified in this way. Often what is at issue in political life is not whether agreements and authorizations can be identified, but whether individuals are being treated with equal concern and respect. Rawls and Dworkin, then, develop a theory of rights in which liberty as an ideal is subordinated to some principle of equity, and their approach is grounded in a commitment to the democratic ideal of mutual respect among citizens.

Rawls thinks it important to distinguish approaches which accord a conception of rights a proper place, as providing the basis for claims which enable individuals legitimately to frustrate the policy objectives of the collectivity. And in his quest for an adequate theory of rights he seems to have been tempted first by rule utilitarianism. Rawls abandoned the hope that a consequentialist approach could serve this purpose, however, concluding that all teleological approaches in ethics subordinate rights claims, in an unacceptable way, to some conception of the collective good.[14] Thus he writes, in comparing utilitarianism with his own rights-based theory:

> The last contrast that I shall mention now is that utilitarianism is a teleological theory whereas justice as fairness is not. By definition, then, the latter is a deontological theory, one that either does not specify the good independently from the right, or does not interpret the right as maximizing the good.

And he goes on to describe the contrast:

In utilitarianism the satisfaction of any desire has some value in itself which must be taken into account in deciding what is right. In calculating the greatest balance of satisfaction it does not matter, except indirectly, what the desires are for.

With regard to his own position he writes:

The principles of right, and so of justice, put limits on which satisfactions have value; they impose restrictions on what are reasonable conceptions of one's good. In drawing up plans and in deciding on aspirations men are to take these constraints into account. Hence in justice as fairness one does not take men's propensities and inclinations as given, whatever they are, and then seek the best way to fulfil them. Rather, their desires and aspirations are restricted from the outset by the principles of justice which specify the boundaries that men's system of ends must respect. We can express this by saying that in justice as fairness the concept of the right is prior to that of the good.[15]

This analytic distinction is of very great significance and provides the basis for the charge which Rawls and Dworkin direct at utilitarian writers — that they do not take rights seriously enough. If, for example, some polemicist claims to recognize the right to free speech but then qualifies his or her commitment by requiring that such a right should be ignored in circumstances in which a social goal may be frustrated or even those in which there may be great public inconvenience, then, as Dworkin puts it, his or her position is exhausted by the collective goal; the putative claim adds nothing and there is no point in recognizing it as right at all. Similarly, those who hold to a religious conception of the role of the state — such that they conceive it to be the duty of governments to uphold certain moral ideals and to encourage citizens to live up to these, even if this requires that they use the criminal law against non-conformists — can make no claim to take rights seriously, for they subordinate the claims of individuals to their religious conception of the point and purpose of social life. In general, Dworkin tells us:

The strength of a particular right within a particular theory is a function of the degree of disservice to the goals of the theory, beyond a mere disservice on the whole, that is necessary to justify refusing an act called for under the right.[16]

In terms of this criterion, then, act utilitarianism can hardly be said to take rights seriously, for the theory requires that rights claims always be considered subordinate to the goal of maximizing welfare; rule utilitarians, on the other hand, make much more of an effort to give rights an independent weight.

For Rawls the central difference between theories which are deontological and those which are not is the fact that the former are individualist, in the sense that they accord equal importance to the choices of all individuals. Utilitarians, it is true, are also prepared to regard people's choices as of equal worth but, as Rawls points out:

> from the standpoint of contract theory one cannot arrive at a principle of social choice merely by extending the principle of rational prudence to the system of desires constructed by an impartial spectator. To do this is not to take seriously the plurality and distinctness of individuals, nor to recognize as the basis of justice that to which men would consent.[17]

It is for this reason that he seeks a fresh start in political philosophy.

I should stress here that Rawls and Dworkin differ very much from Nozick in their assessment of what a theory must be like before it can be said to take rights seriously. According to the possessive individualist Nozick, as we have seen, the central distinction is between historical and teleological theories; for Dworkin and Rawls, by contrast, a theory which is deontological need not necessarily be historically orientated — all that is required is that those rights be recognized which have the effect of frustrating social goals when there is a conflict. A developed theory of rights must, of course, describe how they can be identified, and different theories would provide basic principles of justice which set out the terms in which relationships between people are to be conducted. Logically, however, a theory does not abuse the concept of a right as long as it is not subordinated to some overriding social goal. Thus, Dworkin would even allow that some rule-utilitarian approaches give sufficient weight to rights claims for it to be reasonable to describe them as compatible with a sense of what is involved when we make an assertion of a right.[18] Nozick's own theory, of course, qualifies as fully deontological and involves both an analysis of the logic of rights claims and a description of how one identifies rights. Nozick differs from Dworkin and Rawls in insisting that his method of identification is part of the logic of rights discourse; rights for him are identified historically when they point to some exercise of liberty, whereas for Dworkin and Rawls rights are identified by way of an appeal to a conception of equity based on fairness. Dworkin and Rawls claim that Nozick's method of identification is merely a feature of his own particular theory of rights — a most unsatisfactory one — and that it is a mistake to suppose that it is part of the logic of rights discourse; they argue that a strong conception of rights presupposes only that rights claims are not subordinated to any teleological goal, and that nothing about the method by means of which rights are to be identified can be deduced simply from conceptual analysis.

In developing a deontological theory to serve as an alternative to possessive individualism, Rawls and Dworkin take up the suggestion of H. L. A. Hart that the core idea which explains the undoubted appeal of the classical idea of a social contract is some conception of fairness. Hart justifies this claim by arguing that rights can be established not only by reference to some process of authorization, but also by way of an appeal to what he calls the 'mutuality of restrictions'. He writes: 'when a number of persons conduct any joint enterprise according to rules and thus restrict their liberty, those who have submitted to these restrictions when required have a right to a similar submission from those who have benefited by the submission.'[19] What seems to worry Hart is that the distribution of liberty becomes skewed unless the burdens of social co-operation are mutual. But other burdens besides loss of liberty may follow as a consequence of institutional arrangements, and it is therefore a matter of some importance whether or not Hart's appeal to fairness can be extended to cover these as well. Is it not the case, when our actions have consequences for the lives of others which are of a serious nature, that the relationship of causal connection establishes rights claims whether there has been a process of authorization or not?

The problem is illustrated most clearly by the example, much discussed in philosophy tutorials, of a drowning man who hopes that an individual passing by, whom he does not know personally and with whom he has had no previous relationship, will take some action to save his life. Can we say that he has a right to expect assistance? If entitlements are established by the very fact of dependency on others (of the kind illustrated in the example), then all efforts to distinguish entitlement considerations from those concerned purely with the consequences of actions will have been undermined. The difficulty is that if we accept as the ultimate determinant of rights an assessment of the consequences which will follow from actions, then everyone's claims will have to be established by a computation which discriminates between rights merely in terms of cost and benefit.[20] Once we allow that rights arise whenever one person's actions can be said to affect someone else, even where what we are talking about is an act of omission, we have a theory which is virtually indistinguishable from utilitarianism.

Dworkin worries about this problem but argues that it is not a fatal difficulty in the way of a deontological theory based on equity as a primary value (rather than on liberty). He tells us that what we need to take notice of is the special role that utilitarian arguments may play within a theory of rights. In this regard he distinguishes abstract rights from concrete rights:[21] an abstract right arises out of a fundamental political commitment (such as that all rights be adjudicated on the basis of utility, or that all rights be established by processes which do not violate natural freedom, or that rights be adjudicated in a way that treats all individuals with equal concern and respect); concrete rights, on the other hand, are the result of a process of adjudication in which some abstract principle (of the kind listed above) provides the reason for recognizing a specific claim made by an individual as having priority in situations in which there may be conflicts. Thus, in dealing with practical cases (where, for example, we are asked to decide whether a drowning man has a right to expect a passer-by to give up some of his or her time to save him) our prior commitments to fundamental principles will give rise to different resolutions. If, for example, our abstract commitment is to treat individuals with equal concern and respect, we could perhaps conclude, with regard to the problem of deciding what action a drowning man may legitimately require of someone passing, that where life can be saved at no great risk this fact itself would establish a right (the reason for this conclusion is purely utilitarian). The requirement of mutual respect does not, however, allow such a case to be solved on the basis of a calculation of what would produce the common good, for it does not allow us to conclude (as an abstract commitment to the utility principle would) that an insignificant person is under an obligation to attempt to save an important person even at great risk, but that the latter is not required to take any risks at all if the circumstances were reversed. If we consider the same problem in the light of Nozick's principle of natural freedom, on the other hand, we would have to allow that the drowning man has no right to aid. Possessive individualists may argue that it would be a good thing if a passer-by were to provide help, or that anyone passing who did not help should be regarded as having a bad character, but they cannot say, in the light of their fundamental principle, that the drowning man is entitled to insist, as a matter of right, that he be assisted. It matters a great deal, then, what our abstract principles are, for it is only by reference to them that the weight of utilitarian arguments supporting rights claims can be appreciated; it is also only in terms of them that we are able to identify specific rights.

Rawls and Dworkin's theory of rights, then, allows utilitarian arguments to be put and to have a significant bearing on the issue of whether or not there is a right involved in particular cases. It also allows us to develop arguments (which appeal to rights) supporting government initiatives to benefit poorer groups in society, even when these involve substantial interference with purely market forces. Dworkin goes so far as to suggest that an appeal to the principle of equal dignity and respect may allow, and indeed require, programmes which involve positive discrimination in favour of some minority groups. His arguments in this regard are worth looking at, briefly, for they illustrate how policy considerations may affect the way that we adjudicate rights.

Dworkin's views are made clear in his discussion of a number of recent court cases, in which the issue that the court was required to resolve was whether a claim to have a fundamental political right protected should be recognized. The first case Dworkin discusses occurred in 1974 and arose out of an action brought by an applicant to the Washington Law School, DeFunis. The Supreme Court of the United States was asked to find that the law school had violated DeFunis's right to equal treatment (protected under the Fourteenth Amendment) by refusing to admit him as a student.[22] DeFunis's point was a simple one: he could show that the law school was giving preferential treatment to applicants from minority groups such as Chicanos or blacks and that his own test scores and college grades were such that he would have been admitted to the law school had he been a member of a favoured section of the community. The question at issue was whether citizens have a right to be protected against such discrimination. DeFunis's case was complicated, as Dworkin points out, by the fact that the court had already ruled in 1941 (in the case of Sweat, who was refused admission to the University of Texas Law School)[23] that discrimination against a black American was a violation of the Fourteenth Amendment. The issue in 1974 was whether, and if so why, the discrimination against DeFunis should be thought to be different. A judgement which denied DeFunis the protection of the courts would, then, have challenged what in the liberal conception is usually regarded as a basic right to equal treatment.[24]

Summarizing drastically, and ignoring Dworkin's wider consideration of the many issues in political philosophy which are raised by this case, he asks, first, whether there is any basic right against a law school discriminating between candidates. Clearly, the answer here is that it makes little sense to say that there is no such right, for some discrimination must necessarily be used to govern admission (unless the process of selection is to be run as a lottery, so that considerations relating to merit and suitability are eliminated). If we accept this point, that some discriminations do not violate rights, then Dworkin asks whether there is anything about a racial criterion which marks it off as different from other forms of discrimination as, for example, intelligence tests, or class grades or the capacity to pay fees, and so on. Dworkin's answer to this question is that in some circumstances justice would be violated by such discrimination, and that this would be so even when selection based on race could be shown to serve some desirable social purpose (such as, for example, helping to maintain the peace). This would be the case, Dworkin tells us, where racial criteria were used to deny a group an equal share of resources, or where such discriminations denied citizens equality of respect. If, on the other hand, racial discrimination did not constitute a threat to a group or undermine their dignity, and if, moreover, the policy of discrimination were intended to promote justice by correcting anomalies in the distribution of resources between communities, then, he tells us, it should not be held to violate rights.[25] It is on the basis of this distinction that Dworkin believes that DeFunis's claim should be considered to be different from that of Sweat.

The second case Dworkin discusses, *Bakke vs University of California Medical School,* involved similar issues. The school set sixteen places aside for which only members of 'educationally and economically disadvantaged minorities' were to compete. Bakke complained that he had been denied a place in the medical school even though, as the California Medical School itself acknowledged, he would have been admitted as a student if it had not been for this affirmative action programme of positive discrimination in favour of minorities. What the court had to decide was whether affirmative actions of this kind — involving distinctively racial criteria — necessarily constituted a violation of an individual's right to be treated in accordance with the requirements of the Fourteenth Amendment to the United States Constitution (which requires that there be no discrimination on the basis of race).

Dworkin is clear that if one claims a right of this kind, one necessarily rules out of order any consideration of the good served by an affirmative programme. It is for this reason that he praises Bakke's lawyer, who had suggested that the issue of whether Bakke's position should be supported by the court should not be settled merely by way of an examination of whether or not the affirmative programme was good or bad public policy. Such a judgement is in any case, not one that ought to be a matter for a court to decide, for the competence of a judicial body does not qualify it to make judgements about policy. With regard to Bakke's case, then, the court's responsibility was to declare whether or not any constitutional right had been violated; it should not, therefore, have attempted to settle any matters relating to the desirability of the affirmative action programme adopted by the medical school.

Dworkin insists that Bakke had no case, for he could not establish that his rights had been violated. He would not have been able to establish this, we are told, unless it could be shown that affirmative action programmes were being used merely as an excuse to discriminate against a particular group (in this case the majority community to which Bakke belonged). In the circumstances, given the historical pattern of discrimination against blacks and other minorities, such a claim was not plausible. Moreover, there is sufficient substance to their belief that a form of discrimination was a necessary part of a programme to promote more equal opportunities for it to be clear that the university authorities were not acting in an arbitrary or malicious way; thus, even if it could be shown that 'positive discrimination' will never, in fact, prove successful in promoting greater social equity in the long run, it would still have to be conceded that they were acting in good faith. Dworkin is able, then, to advance again the argument that he applied to the *DeFunis v Odegaard* case to show that affirmative action programmes do not necessarily violate rights. As to whether such programmes are desirable, this, Dworkin tells us, is a matter for the university authorities, or perhaps the relevant legislative authority, to decide.

Rawls and Dworkin commit themselves to the proposition that individuals have a natural right to mutual concern and respect and take an intermediate position between utilitarianism and possessive individualism. In developing his position, Rawls utilizes Hart's observation that a special rights-conferring situation arises when individuals are involved in practices which demand a mutuality of restrictions as the basis for a theory of political obligation. He is able to argue that the burdens involved in social co-operation are such that distributive questions about what it is that citizens may claim as of right in a democracy are also questions about what it is fair to expect of them. Thus, he develops a theory of justice in order to demarcate those expectations of civility which it would be rational to demand, and in this way he subordinates any notion of entitlement based on liberty to the requirements of political justice.

7
Rawls's Conception of Justice

In this chapter I review Rawls's main argument for his general conception of justice. I want, in particular, to illustrate his mode of reasoning and its presuppositions. I shall do this by considering one serious criticism of his argument — that Rawls has not allowed for the fact that his negotiators might agree to adopt a strategy of gambling on future possibilities in the hope that they would gain more than is offered under the principles which Rawls argues they would accept. I suggest that Rawls's contract approach can be defended, and that his own account of the best strategy available to his negotiators (the claim that they would seek to maximize their worst expectations) is the most plausible.

Rawls's Use of the Contract Device

Rawls, who is very much influenced by Rousseau's approach to democratic theory, uses the idea of a social contract to explicate what a commitment to the ideal of reciprocity entails in social life. The central idea upon which he bases his theory is that when a number of people conduct any joint enterprise, and particularly when they participate within institutions, those who submit to the burdens and restrictions imposed by their willing co-operation have a right to similar submissions from all those who benefited from their compliance.[1] If we accepted as the basic democratic ideal this notion of reciprocal relations, what principles of justice would this commit us to in regulating our lives together? Rawls sets up this question for analysis, and his use of the idea of a contract between negotiators is meant to serve as a heuristic device to provide us with a sharpened intuitive understanding of the claim to reciprocity which he accepts as fundamental.

It should be noted that there would not be much point in taking rights seriously (that is, according to the Rawlsian interpretation, respecting the claims of others to reciprocity) if we did not have to solicit compliance and co-operation from others. Of course, governments in practice do not usually take the rights of their subjects into account, and effective rule can take place even where only a few combine together to monopolize force. Within the community of the exploiters themselves, however, there will necessarily be a continuing dialogue in which sacrifices, risks and privileges are balanced against some notion of what is is fair to expect, which is shared between them. When dialogue of this kind is restricted to a few, and large sections of society are left out of account because they lack the power to make their claim to equal treatment effective, we may say that the system is not democratic, because the survival of the governing class depends, ultimately, on its ability to enforce compliance on the part of those whose rights are not being respected. The philosophical task, as Rawls sees it, is to show how social relations can be fair, for this would provide a standard in terms of which we may demarcate between legitimate democratic demands which can be imposed on citizens and those which are not so. In talking about 'justice' as a form of reciprocity, then, Rawls is at the same time providing a theory in terms of which the legitimacy of rights claims can be established.[2]

Although it is not easy to find cases in which bargaining between people has been on a totally reciprocal basis, Rawls argues that it is useful to construct such a situation imaginatively and to speculate about what rational negotiators (in such a situation) might agree to. He calls the hypothetical circumstances which he regards as setting up conditions for a fully equitable negotiation the 'original position'. By supposing that negotiators are required to deal with one another from a basis of equality in bargaining strength, and using the technique of rational reconstruction, Rawls is able to articulate principles (which he suggests would be agreed to by the negotiators) to serve as criteria of rational and non-coercive relations. He thinks that if we could show which principles would be accepted by negotiators who have no socially predetermined advantages, then we would have defined critical standards which could provide a moral basis for dialogue in more realistic political circumstances. Those who refused to accept these principles as a guide in their relations with others could be said to be taking advantage of their superior power to negotiate by forcing agreement to (or compliance with) arrangements which are biased in favour of their own particular interests. This would clearly be an undemocratic commitment and would necessarily stand condemned in terms of the justificatory theory. The hypothetical contract in the original position serves, then, as a kind of regulatory process, for it helps us to see which claims are prejudiced. As Rawls puts it:

> The idea of the original position is to set up a fair procedure so that any principle agreed to will be just. The aim is to use the notion of pure procedural justice as a basis for a theory. Somehow we must nullify the effects of specific contingencies which put men at odds and tempt them to exploit social and natural circumstances to their own advantage.[3]

Rawls first asks us to suppose individuals so situated that they have no notions about what their position in any future society is going to be and no knowledge of their own special talents and abilities from which any competitive advantages they enjoy may be deduced; he then requires that we speculate about how they would choose if asked to negotiate the principles which are to regulate their future life together.

Now, it can be seen that once negotiators were asked to reach an agreement from a position of complete ignorance of their life circumstances, they would be most reluctant to endorse principles which allowed for inequalities, for such a commitment would place them at severe risk. The negotiators would not know where or how they were going to be placed socially, and so they could not anticipate being amongst the privileged; nor could they assume that they would not be severely prejudiced if society were to distribute benefits in a way which favoured a few. For this reason Rawls argues that they would adopt what he calls a 'maximin strategy' — this would require them to agree only to those principles which could be shown to maximize their circumstances if their worst expectations about their social position were realized. According to Rawls, then, they would reason as though their future role in life were to be allocated by their worst enemy.

Of course, if a demand for equality cost nothing in terms of a loss of efficiency, there would be no political problem and no need for a cautious strategy. We could choose not to allow inequalities knowing that no sacrifice of general welfare would follow. On these assumptions, then, the more equality there were, the greater would be the efficiency;

hence, any commitment to maximize utility would also be a commitment to greater equality. The 'real world' situation is not likely to be so accommodating to egalitarians, however, and this is certainly the case where capitalism is the dominant mode of resource allocation. In any event, our negotiators in the state of nature cannot afford to assume that there will be no trade-off between equality and productivity (given that we accept that it would be rational for them to adopt a strategy designed to maximize their worst expectations) and they must, therefore, choose principles which reflect the fact that they may well have to sacrifice equality in order to maximize utility. Consequently, they will, as already noted, be most reluctant to endorse a form of utility maximization principle without some severe qualifications to protect the claims of equality.

Would they be equally reluctant to choose the possessive individualist solution — what Nozick calls the principle of natural freedom: from each as they choose, to each as they are chosen?[4] I shall leave the consideration of Nozick's suggested principle for the next chapter. Here I wish to note Rawls's own claim that a rational response, trading-off the maximization of utility in order to preserve equality, is available to the negotiators in the original position. He tells us that negotiators would compromise with utilitarianism at the point at which further equality begins to affect the general utilities available to those who fall into the least privileged group in a community.[5] Rawls is suggesting that it is not rational to insist on complete equality as long as the utilities available to everyone can be maximized by allowing some forms of social inequality. Nevertheless, he argues that it would not be rational for the negotiators to accept principles which allowed utilities to be maximized without any regard for how they were to be distributed or for the burdens placed on particular groups and individuals (who may be affected in negative ways by programmes which, taken as a whole, would be beneficial rather than harmful). The suggested compromise has been formulated by Rawls as the 'general conception of justice', which, as we have seen, requires that social goods be distributed equally unless an unequal distribution is to the advantage of those who are worst off.[6]

Rawls claims that the compromise between the goal of utility maximization and the claims of equality reflected in his general conception of justice would be agreed to as long as the negotiators had no guarantee that they would not be among the least advantaged group. This is because the principle is the most cautious available; it is a principle which would recommend itself to anyone who knew in advance that he or she would be carrying the heaviest burden. Rawls argues that everyone negotiating from the original position would seek to ensure in advance that they and the groups that they represented in future generations were protected, in case it turned out that they stood to gain least under the arrangements adopted. All of them, according to this line of reasoning, would ensure in advance that privileges were tolerated only when it is reasonable to suppose that they would work to the advantage of everyone. The principle they chose, would necessarily treat everyone with equal concern. Institutional burdens which fall on some more harshly than on others can only be justified, then, if the claims of the least advantaged groups are respected.

It is worth emphasizing, yet again, that the point of using the original position model is to elucidate the rational basis for negotiating when the outcome will not be determined by what Rawls describes as a threat advantage. If there is total equality in the bargaining situation, individuals who negotiate are forced to base their offers on considerations which will appeal to the others, and this is why they can only find common ground by suggesting solutions which are fair. However, when the basis for compromise is loaded by the fact that one or other of the parties is to have a crucial monopoly over some resource, then rational negotiators will be willing to accept something less than reciprocal burdens. The situation will be invasive (in Macpherson's sense) for those who have a capacity to monopolize can set terms for future co-operation which enables them to extract some of the powers of others; such biased principles foreclose on the ability of the weak to have an equal voice in determining the basis of future relationships. By postulating negotiators in a situation of complete equality, then, Rawls is able to develop a strategy analysis to show those principles which should be respected by everyone committed to the democratic ideal of treating citizens with equal respect.

The Gambling Problem

Is Rawls right to suggest that free negotiators would choose a 'maximin strategy', and that they would refuse to subject themselves to the hazards of market competition even if this could be shown by economic theory to be likely to promote the common good?

Brian Barry has argued that Rawls's claim that negotiators in the original position described would maximize their worst expectations by adopting a cautious policy is not justifiable. There is, Barry suggests, nothing to show that it is irrational to gamble.[7] We do, as a matter of common practice, put all of our eggs into one basket; furthermore, this is often a rational strategy for us to pursue. A society which did not require that some burdens and benefits be allocated by means of a gamble would be hard to find. The point is that some decisions (about transport, for example) which commit citizens to risks if they are unlucky or careless (those involved in accidents) but benefit others who are more fortunate (those who travel without mishap) do not seem unfair or irrational. Thus, provided we start from a position of initial equality, as suggested by the original position, it may be more rational to gamble than to maximize our worst expectations in the cautious way suggested by Rawls. Negotiators who agreed to gamble their places in a future society on their chance of doing well out of a lottery might decide, for example, that general utilities, as decided by the majority of a community, should be maximized. This choice would be a rational one even when it was known that the maximization of utilities would involve disproportionate sacrifices on the part of a few to benefit the majority (as is the case in the area of road transportation). Everyone could rationally agree to forgo his or her own selfish perspectives if they were deemed expendable in the light of a public decision to maximize utilities in general. There is nothing irrational about accepting the risks of such a gamble, providing that everyone has an equal chance of benefiting.

Depending on one's taste for gambling, there are no firm or obvious criteria by means of which we can rule out as irrational even more daring innovations. Suppose it were suggested that the future society be divided into castes, under which system some would be greatly privileged and others obliged to undertake all the unpleasant tasks in return for a mere subsistence. It may be that the benefits of privilege are so enticing that rational individuals would be prepared to gamble a birthright away. Whether or not such a strategy can be regarded as rational depends on a judgement of the circumstances in which it is made, in the light of values. Consider a world, for example, in which everyone needed some crucial drug but there was not enough to go around. If it would be better to have some rather than none at all, negotiators would be tempted to argue for a fair distribution based on equal shares; however, if the usefulness of the drug depended on the acquisition of a certain amount (supposing, for example, that a cure were not possible unless a certain minimum quantity were taken), then there would be no point in negotiating for equal shares if each of the portions turned out to fall below the required minimum. The tendency to aim for an unequal distribution is marked when resources are very scarce and the amount required for effective use substantial. In the light of this consideration we must suppose, if we are to make a case for Rawls's general conception of justice, that our negotiators would be contemplating living in a society in which at least subsistence level has been reached by everyone — otherwise the negotiators would be more rational to accept some form of a gamble strategy. Of course, what should count as subsistence level would also vary with values, and it is difficult to know how a rational choice could be made from a position in which the negotiators were ignorant about the kind of life that they valued. For example, those who thought that it was necessary to be really wealthy in order to benefit from material possessions, and that affluence below a certain minimum merely led to a dull lifestyle, would be tempted by some form of gambling strategy. On the other hand, those who were disposed towards so-called bourgeois mediocrity, valuing the standard of life which could be achieved by Mr and Mrs Average, would be more cautious about endorsing a social system in which the chance of prosperity for a few, who would be able to benefit as a privileged elite, was balanced by a substantial risk of falling below this level. The point is that the inclination for risk-taking reflects values and cannot be ruled out as irrational.[8]

Rawls himself acknowledges that gambling may be a rational strategy as long as everyone can be said to have an equal chance of benefiting and is subject to the same risks. Because of the requirement in the original position that there be a veil of ignorance, it is open to the negotiators to to calculate as though they were about to enter into a lottery for their position in a future society. They could assume, in the absence of information, that they each stood an equal chance to gain or to lose. But while Rawls allows that gambling strategies may be rational within the original position, he argues that the negotiators would be disinclined to take risks.[9]

In dismissing gambling strategies, Rawls asks us to consider certain psychological considerations which he believes are important. In the first place, there are the attitudes which the negotiators are likely to bring to their task. Rawls points out that they are being asked to act as agents and to make choices which will not only bind themselves but also the people who entrusted their interest into their care; and that they will be aware, also, of their responsibility to future generations, who will have to live with the compromises they reach in framing the social contract. Rawls suggests, in this regard, that individuals who have to make choices on behalf of others for whom they genuinely care will not be likely to take risks, even though they might be prepared to gamble for themselves alone: the suggestion is that cautious strategies would recommend themselves as more responsible in the circumstances.[10]

Taken in itself, however, this observation is less than adequate as a justification for rejecting the gambling strategy, because it does not show such a strategy to be irrational, and Rawls himself acknowledges this. However, he argues that his appeal to the caution of responsible agents will have force when we take into account the fact that the best bet, from a position of ignorance, is to endorse principles which maximize average expectations (this offers the best chance of winning, with the least risk). A decision to maximize average expectations allows inequalities to be tolerated in the future society, provided that it can be shown that the general standard of the average citizen will be improved as a consequence. Rawls argues that cautious negotiators, although tempted by the best bet, will prefer the general conception solution he suggests, because it has the advantage of allowing the same goal to be realized (the establishment of incentives to increase efficiency) without subjecting future generations to risk. There is, then, no need for the negotiators to assume equal probabilities in the absence of information (a risky assumption), for they are able to avoid a gamble of this kind and can still opt for a solution which allows for utilities to be maximized through an incentive system by choosing the general conception of justice.[11]

A more important psychological consideration, which Rawls makes much of as a means of dismissing the idea that a gambling strategy would be adopted in the original position, relates to what he calls the strains of implementation. The negotiators will know that the principle chosen in the original position will have to be accepted in real life, and Rawls argues that they will, therefore, be very much aware that some principles would be more difficult for people to accept than others. A good example of Rawls's reasoning along these lines is his claim that because the negotiators understand what it is to be religious, and because they anticipate that they themselves may have religious convictions, they will be most reluctant to see any departure from religious toleration; they know that they would not be able to abide by laws prohibiting religious practices if they turned out to be believers.[12] More generally, he applies the same line of reasoning to the gambling problem, suggesting that similar considerations, relating to what the negotiators judge to be the likely strains of implementation, would be relevant wherever a principle allocates a distribution of burdens in social life. If (to take an extreme example) we consider the institution of slavery, it can immediately be seen that it is very difficult for the slave not to feel resentful about his or her place after social positions are allocated. How is the slave master going to convince the slave that the burdens imposed upon him or her are justifiable? Rawls suggests that wherever inequalities are introduced, there will be a psychological strain resulting from resentment and envy; and he suggests that our knowledge of this explains why the negotiators would choose the general conception of justice solution he offers in preference to one which involved a gamble. They would realize that because the general conception solution focused on maximizing each individual's well-being and did not allow some to suffer for the good of others, it assumed less capacity on the part of those who are hard done by for identifying with the interests of others. This is because the worst-off would know that their own special circumstances in life could not be improved by any conceivable change — apart from the requirement that someone else occupy the least advantaged position. Thus, the only emotion that they would be likely to feel in the face of the inequalities imposed socially would be envy — and this, Rawls argues, should not be taken as a rational reason for changing a distribution. They would not be likely to feel resentment, for there would be nobody whom they could charge with living at their expense, and there would be nothing anyone could do which would help them to better their circumstances. On the other hand, if any other principle were adopted, including the principle of complete equality, resentment would be a rational response (assuming that we are dealing with a world in which there is a trade-off between equality and efficiency).[13]

There is a good deal to be said in support of Rawls's psycho-social assumptions, and especially his claims about the importance of cognitive factors like the sense of fair play in the growth of moral sentiments. However, it is not appropriate for him to appeal to his theory as though it would be accepted by every negotiator within the original position (for this is what he assumed in developing his argument about the strains of implementation, which, as we have seen, is a crucial part of his response to those who would advocate a gambling strategy). The problem here is that, unlike other scientific theories and factual claims which may be taken for granted by the negotiators, there is no general consensus among researchers in the area of psychology about the correctness of Rawls's views of strain. Many psychologists would argue that people's attitudes towards inequalities need not be influenced by judgements of the kind that Rawls postulates, and that he exaggerates the cognitive factor in moral development. Indeed, if we are to allow the negotiators some understanding of the processes of socialization, which we surely must do if we are to allow them psychological knowledge in the original position, then they would probably be inclined to question Rawls's assessment of the causal significance of cognition as opposed to other influences. If people can be taught to accept inequalities as morally acceptable — as, for example, some suggest that young girls learn to tolerate the advantages afforded their brothers without any perceived strains — then it may be that our sense of what is fair is culture-relative. If this is the case (and I have my doubts, for I follow Rawls in believing that people are not socialized into accepting inequalities without significant psychological strain), then we could be socialized into accepting inequalities which are greater than those which would be tolerated under Rawls's general conception principle. Thus, unless Rawls can show convincingly that resentment will always follow what he regards as unfair allocations, regardless of socialization, the force of his appeal to potential psychological strain as a reason for preferring his recommended principle of justice over those which involve a gamble would be lost.

Even though Rawls's conjectured model of the socialization process and his claims about psychological strain are plausible, it must be conceded that he is not in a position to argue that his theories have been sufficiently demonstrated to insist on consensus. It follows that his central argument against the negotiators' adopting as a principle of justice one that relies on the rationality of a gamble strategy in the original position, because it rests on his psychological claims that it will be difficult for people to accept such a principle when it turns out that they are to be losers, begs the question at issue. If, for example, the principle of average utility were chosen in the original position, then the negotiators could rely on the alleged fact that it could be made viable as a regulative principle through public endorsement sustained by socialization processes. Rawls is not entitled to assume that the negotiators would agree that this kind of indoctrination is impossible.[14]

It is open to Rawls to put his case in a different way. He could argue that the negotiators are faced by two mutually exclusive conjectures about the human condition: the first assumes that human beings are capable of respecting regulative principles, even when these impose severe burdens on them personally; and the second assumes that people will be resentful of advantages enjoyed by others unless they can see some contingent benefit for themselves. Given this choice of assumptions, it may be suggested that the negotiators should choose to be cautious and that they should, consequently, assume that people would be resentful if the principles chosen impose too heavy a burden.

What we come back to here in assessing Rawls's views about psychological strain is that he will not accept any principle which cannot be shown to be fair. He is saying that if a principle is not fair, it will not be accepted easily in practice, and that the negotiators will know this and will, consequently, treat the anticipated strain of commitment as a reason for avoiding principles which impose a risk. I have suggested that Rawls's claim is too controversial to serve as part of an argument within the original position. Rawls's position, because it relies on establishing a link between political emotions and reason, nevertheless, has an advantage over other psychological assumptions in that it relies less on the impact of socialization. Cautious negotiators would, then, be attracted to his point of view because he makes only pessimistic assumptions about human nature and does not take it for granted that we can be taught to accept any principles as reflecting 'justice'.

Rawls's argument can also be rescued by treating 'reciprocity' and 'fairness' as basic moral conceptions. I mean by this that if a proposal can be shown to be fair, this is sufficient reason for rejecting any claim that it violates rights; conversely, if a proposal is shown to be unfair, this is sufficient reason to condemn it from the moral point of view, for it violates people's rights. It is implied here that what is basic to the morality of a democrat is a commitment to treat each individual as having a fundamental right to be considered equal to all others. Each person's interests must be given the same consideration; the onus is on anyone who would act in ways which appear to be in conflict with this fundamental requirement to show why this should be so. Given these commitments, we can suggest that it is perfectly legitimate for Rawls to rest his case not on psychological claims about the likely passions which will be aroused by various principles, but on the observation that gambling strategies manifestly commit the negotiators to accepting principles which impose unfair burdens. We can concede that gambling is a good and appropriate strategy in most situations involving choice under conditions of uncertainty. However, within the context of Rawls's original position the purpose of the negotiation, from the point of view of the theory, is to find principles which reflect our intuitive sense of fair play — and in this regard we must be careful not to take the hypothetical negotiation as more than a heuristic tool.

Rawls's imagined contract, then, is intended to provide a way of testing our intuitive judgements about what is fair; and for this purpose we are to imagine the negotiators rationally discussing their disagreements in the context of the original position. By using the heuristic device of the original position, and by employing the technique he calls 'reflective equilibrium' (which requires that we test any suggested principles against our intuitive moral responses by trying to reach a satisfactory accommodation between the requirements of theory and our instinctive reactions), Rawls is able to explicate what a commitment to reciprocity entails. The imagined contract, then, provides a way of shaping our intuitive judgements into a coherent theory. The aim is somehow to characterize the capacity we have for reaching judgements about institutional arrangements in a theoretically adequate way. We are to imagine that the negotiators discuss critically their list of possible principles; we are to suppose that they want to see how each can be accommodated within a theory of the 'just', and that they will try to show how to bestow a weighting on each of them in their moral deliberations. Rawls tells us that if we are to suppose ourselves negotiating in this way within the original position, then we will, on reflection, come to see how some of our judgements (the ones we are inclined to make before we acknowledge any commitment to co-ordinating principles of justice) are incongruous with those at which we arrive when guided by our chosen principles. As he puts it:

When a person is presented with an intuitively appealing account of his sense of justice (one, say, which embodies various reasonable and natural presumptions), he may well revise his judgments to confrom to its principles even though the theory does not fit his existing judgments exactly....From the standpoint of moral philosophy, the best account of a person's sense of justice is the one which matches his judgments in reflective equilibrium. As we have seen, this state is one reached after a person has weighed various proposed conceptions and he has either revised his judgments to accord with one of them or held fast to his initial convictions (and the corresponding conception).[15]

His aim is to show that the principles he recommends — those that satisfy a conception of justice as fairness — provide a better match for our considered judgements on reflection than any plausible alternatives which might be suggested.

Bearing these points in mind, and considering the various principles which might tempt negotiators to adopt a gamble strategy, we can see that whenever we come to apply such a principle our task will be mostly one of adjudication; there will be a given distribution of burdens and benefits (which includes, of course, the burden of risk-bearing) needing adjustment or endorsement. In some cases it will be appropriate to respond to those who are unfortunate enough to carry the more significant burdens by pointing out that everyone accepted the same reasonable and fair risk; in most cases of social dispute, however, it cannot be shown that privilege is the result of some necessary and fair gamble in which everyone had a fair chance. The point here is that in most cases of social conflict, where the implications of following a principle which allows for substantial inequality may be resented, the burdens and privileges cannot be shown to have resulted from an equally shared risk. But unless this can be shown, 'fair gamble' justifications of institutional arrangements gain their plausibility through deception. Thus, although our negotiators may find that gamble solutions to the problem of choice are rational under conditions of uncertainty in which there is equal ignorance, they may, nevertheless, reject the possibility of gambling in the original position. This is because they may see, on reflection, that a principle which assumes a 'fair gamble' as part of its rationale cannot serve as a viable principle of justice and that such a principle violates our sense of fair play when applied in circumstances in which individuals have not been equally exposed to risks. The negotiators will, then, rule out gambling as a response to the problem of choice confronting them.

I should note with regard to this suggestion that gambling can be seen as an inappropriate solution to the problem of choice in the original position, that Rawls is unhappy with the argument. He writes:

The contract doctrine is purely hypothetical: if a conception of justice would be agreed to in the original position, its principles are the right ones to apply. It is no objection that such an understanding has never been or ever will be entered into.[16]

However, as we have seen, when he comes to show why the general conception will be chosen before other principles which involve a gamble, his reasoning is based on the claim that the negotiators will see that it is fair as a compromise and that any other solutions would impose burdens which would be resented. But why should gamble solutions be regarded as unfair? The answer here lies in the fact that in real life there is no social contract gamble. On reflection, then, it is an objection to some principles (those which assume a gamble) that 'such an understanding has never been nor ever will be entered into' — for had there been a social contract in which everyone took an equal risk, then the gamble would be fair and there would be no good cause for resentment. Rawls seems to have missed this point, even though his own arguments about psychological strain assume that unless gambles are perceived to be realistic, the resultant inequalities will be resented. Rawls, then, in expounding the advantage of his general conception (it will be readily accepted because it represents a fair compromise) effectively outlaws gambling strategies from the original position because the principles chosen in the light of such a strategy will be vitiated when applied as principles of justice unless an actual gamble imposing an equal risk on all takes place. It is perceived unfairness which leads to psychological strain, and it is this possibility, in turn, which Rawls provides as the most compelling consideration favouring his general conception of justice over alternative solutions.

The point I make here can be illustrated by our responses to a number of policy problems. Take the issue of health risk, for example. Whether we like it or not, some health risk attaches to all members of society. Most of us try to meet this hazard through medical insurance, but we also require that governments do what they can to minimize hazards. Of course, a lot more could be done in the area of health care than is actually carried out by governments today. Furthermore, if we appeal to Rawls's general conception of justice, we should surely see that those who have lost their health are, in fact, the least privileged group in society. It follows that unless far more is done to provide greater protection, and unless the maximum aid is given to those who suffer illness or accident, the situation will not square with the criterion suggested by Rawls's conception of democracy.

Taken without qualification, this consideration represents a *reductio ad absurdum* of Rawls's maximin strategy; for if this is really the implication of a consistent application of his general conception, hardly anyone would be willing to take his recommendations seriously. In fact, the example merely illustrates what we have already observed, that almost all societies have to allow certain burdens to be allocated by means of a gamble. In this case, however, as in cases involving accidents, we can point out that everyone suffers approximately the same sort of risk; in other words, the claim that there is a real chance that everyone may suffer illness or accident is not totally spurious. There is not complete equality here, of course, for not everyone actually suffers the same degree of risk. It is clear, for example, that the rich are often better protected than the poor, and country people enjoy better health than those who work in cities (or so it might be claimed). Furthermore, there are groups for whom there are specific risks which are not shared by everyone equally. In terms of the general conception of justice, they would have a claim to special compensation if burdens could be shown to be unfair. Usually cases of this kind involve risks resulting from dangerous work, and it is widely recognized that there should be compensation for those who are involved in occupations which are particularly risky. In these days of city pollution it is also coming to be realized that some sections of society have special claims resulting from features of the environment such as noise and poison.

It is not my purpose to suggest that proper compensation has been paid to those who suffer special burdens in liberal societies. What I do suggest is that Rawls's general conception of justice requires reforms that are designed to make the claim of equal burden a reality. Risks can only be tolerated when they are shown to be fair.

8
Rawls and his Critics

In this chapter I review two different challenges to Rawls's conception of justice and consider possible responses. First, I examine Robert Nozick's claim that his own chosen principle of natural freedom ('from each as they choose, to each as they are chosen' is his way of summarizing the main idea) should be preferred to Rawls's general conception as a basic principle of justice. Then I turn to Joel Feinberg's claim that there is no rational way in which conflicting moral judgements about basic rights can be resolved. This, he tells us, is because our sense of the applicability of principles to specific circumstances will depend on an intuitive sense of their comparative relevance, and this may differ between individuals.[1]

Robert Nozick's Response to Rawls

In his recent *Anarchy, State and Utopia* Robert Nozick has recommended a principle of justice which he believes to be more adequate than Rawls's general conception. This latter conception, Nozick argues, is flawed because it involves a commitment to a particular end-state pattern (the maximization of the position of the worst-off). He claims that any principle which embodies such a commitment must be rejected as reflecting an inadequate conception of justice because its implementation would inevitably require a violation of rights.

It is worth considering the example Nozick provides to illustrate his claims about the poverty of theories based on end-state commitments.

We are asked to review the case of a certain Wilt Chamberlain who is greatly in demand as a basketball player, thanks to his very special athletic talent; we are also to imagine, that Wilt, who realizes that he is a very big attraction, demands that everyone who watches him play provide him with twenty-five cents over and above the normal price of a ticket. We may suppose, for the purpose of the example, that everyone starts off with equal amounts of money (distribution D1). If spectators choose to spend an extra twenty-five cents in order to watch Wilt play (that is, they choose freely to give money to Wilt), this leads to a situation of social inequality (let us call it distribution D2), as Wilt becomes a rich man as a result of his popularity as a player. The question at issue is whether in justice we should allow that this process, by means of which some spectators choose to transfer a small part of their holdings to Wilt, is justifiable. In this regard Nozick writes:

There is *no* question about whether each of the people was entitled to the control over the resources that they held in D1; because that was the distribution (your favorite) that (for the purpose of the argument) we assumed was acceptable. Each of these persons *chose* to give twenty-five cents of their money to Chamberlain .... If D1 was a just distribution and people voluntarily moved from it to D2, transferring parts of their shares they were given under D1 (what was it for if not to do something with?), isn't D2 also just?[2]

It is clear from this example and Nozick's discussion (which I have quoted) that he is committed to viewing the claims which we are morally entitled to make against one another in terms of the processes by means of which they are established without any consideration of the consequences. To make an acceptable rights claim, according to this view, one must be able to point to historical sequences in terms of which the rights are said to have become established. It is, then, necessary to show the processes of acquisition, the authorizations, the transfers and so on which produce the result. Provided an acceptable story establishing entitlements is put forward, the theory holds that the consequential distribution must be regarded as justifiable. This kind of emphasis is said to be morally true to our conception of rights claims because it prevents any possible exploitation of one person's effort by others. Two different core requirements seem to characterize Nozick's position, for he tells us that we can justify a claim if we are able to show how it is grounded in the choices freely made by others, or if what we claim as a right can be shown to be the result of our own efforts and skill. When either of these claims can be met (as in Chamberlain's case) no one can complain of an injustice.

A central feature of Nozick's account of 'entitlement' is that it leaves very little room for an appeal to notions such as 'fairness' and 'reciprocity'. For Nozick this is the great strength of his conception, which gives the principle of natural freedom a marked superiority over the general conception of justice suggested by Rawls. Nozick takes the trouble, for example, to review H. L. A. Hart's suggestion (quoted above, page 141) that where individuals restrict their liberty in order to co-operate with others in a mutually advantageous enterprise they have a natural right to expect similar submissions on the part of those who benefit. Nozick tells us that this view is intuitively implausible and provides the following example to illustrate his point:

Suppose some of the people in your neighbourhood (there are 364 other adults) have found a public address system and decide to institute a system of public entertainment. They post a list of names, one for each day, yours among them. On his assigned day (one can easily switch days) a person is to run the public address system, play records over it, give news bulletins, tell amusing stories he has heard, and so on. After 138 days on which each person has done his part, your day arrives. Are you obliged to take your turn?...As it stands, surely not.[3]

As is the case with many of Nozick's arguments which proceed by way of provocative examples, this challenge to the Rawlsian position is deceptively powerful: the case he provides as a challenge is misleading. What Nozick fails to take account of are the wider circumstances (what Rawls calls the 'background conditions') in terms of which the initial collective choice to institute the system of public entertainment has been made. In Nozick's example such conditions are violated, for it is surely *unfair* for a few eager neighbours to make the 'collective decision' on behalf of everyone else. Before the institutional arrangement of the public entertainment roster which they have proposed and put into effect could be regarded as having established obligations, it would have to be shown that the interests of each participant had been treated with equal respect; thus, the situation would have been very different had the neighbours held a referendum, taking everyone's responses to the practice equally into account. I would argue that in some circumstances in which democratic consultation of an appropriate kind has taken place a minority which disagrees with a practice which is agreed to by a majority may be morally bound to perform the duties imposed. Even if Nozick refuses to concede this, however, he should surely recognize that the 'fairness' of procedural arrangements is a relevant consideration which can invalidate a rights claim: whatever else we might say about institutions, we can at least claim that if they are unfair, they violate rights.

Nozick's challenge to the Rawlsian view by way of an appeal to our intuitive responses is not successful. He does, however, attempt to provide an alternative account of the way in which appeals to fairness can be successful in moral argument, which he recommends as more adequate then Rawls's analysis. The appeal to fairness is most appropriate, he tells us, when we have a situation in which there is a scarce resource and more than one claimant. Consider the case of several farmers, each with land alongside a river and each hoping to utilize the water constructively for irrigation: if those who are upstream take too much of the available water (supposing this to be scarce), then the others might complain that such action was unfair. The problem here, as Marx pointed out some time ago, is that labour power is not the only source of value — we require access to many resources before our labour can become productive. The problem is that there is no obvious right to appropriate in circumstances where resources are scarce, for those who claim the right to use materials to manufacture what they choose may not be able to leave enough over to satisfy the claims which others may like to make. How can we resolve such a dilemma without resort to some other distributive principle than the natural law of freedom upon which Nozick relies?

Nozick sets out to provide an answer to this problem. What he suggests is that the processes of free choice which normally establish entitlements may legitimately be ignored when it can be shown that innocent parties are adversely affected. Thus, he argues that although an entitlement claim must usually be validated by proof that certain promises or authorizations have been made, the obligation which arises may only come into effect where further conditions are also satisfied. Nozick tells us that what has to be shown specifically is that no third party is made 'worse off'. This is normally the only condition (apart from the grounding of the entitlement itself) which is needed, in Nozick's view, to validate an obligation.[4] His conception of what is to count as 'worse off' in this context is, however, a very narrow one, and he makes two points in this regard.

The first point is that we are not entitled to question the consequences of market competition itself. Thus, if A chooses to marry B rather than C, D or E, these last have no legitimate cause for complaint, even though they may be 'worse off' because A (a very desirable partner) is no longer available, unless they can show that the harm which they object to has resulted from some feature of the situation apart from the competition itself. Nozick writes:

> The 'worse-off' proviso, does not include the worsening due to more limited opportunities to appropriate...and it does not include how I 'worsen' a seller's position if I appropriate materials to make some of what he is selling, and then enter into competition with him.[5]

Thus, although a large-scale capitalist corporation which squeezes a smaller firm out of the market makes it 'worse off' it does not do this in a way that infringes Nozick's proviso. The only case which violates the requirement, in Nozick's view, seems to be the one epitomized by the situation in which there is only one water hole in the desert; it is those circumstances in which depriving others of a scarce resource gives an unfair advantage in market competition that Nozick seems to be most concerned about.

The second point that he makes is that we are not entitled to complain that we would be better off if allocations were not based on the principle of natural freedom.[6] According to Nozick's account, then, we are not to take into consideration the objections of those who think that they are more disadvantaged under capitalism than they would be under some other system, as comparisons of this kind focus on utilitarian considerations which should not be used to question an entitlement (as an appeal to fairness might). Nozick argues that we must keep clear his distinction between the grounds for an entitlement and its validation: utilitarian arguments may be deployed not to challenge the basis for an entitlement but only, in conjunction with an appeal to fairness, to question its validity. So, according to Nozick, if we suggest that market processes themselves are less beneficial than other systems of allocation, our arguments are beside the point; the grounding of an entitlement is a matter of rights and cannot be challenged by any utilitarian considerations. As for the validity of an entitlement, this may depend on further considerations, for when utilitarian considerations are combined with an appeal to fairness a case can be made for showing that an entitlement claim (grounded on consents, authorizations and so on) should, nevertheless, be invalidated. In brief, then, one can never establish an entitlement by appealing to fairness, according to Nozick, but one can invalidate such a claim.

Problems with Nozick's Conception of Justice

Nozick's treatment of the weight which should be accorded to 'fairness' as a consideration when we deliberate about rights is not acceptable.

What if we complain that we would be better off under a social system based on Rawls's general conception of justice? Nozick's responses to the utilitarian challenge will not do here, for in addition to a utilitarian argument (to the effect that free market competition makes us worse off than we might be under some other system), there is an appeal to fairness. Surely, then, we may ask Nozick to invalidate all the entitlements established through a process of unbridled market competition: can we not ask whether market systems are themselves fair, in the way that Rawls does? If we look more closely at Nozick's assertion that we are not entitled to question the consequences of market competition itself, we find, again, that the claims of fairness are more pressing than he allows for. The problem is that while we may accept his premise that individuals are entitled to a return commensurate with effort and − although this is more doubtful − achievement (because it is fair that the efforts of those who work hard should not be exploited to provide benefits for those who free-load), his second claim that we should be entitled to what others choose to give in free market competition is much more controversial (for we would want to know whether the competition was equal).

It is not sufficient for Nozick to try to avoid the difficulties involved here by providing loaded examples. Thus, he should not be allowed to place much weight on his observation that were someone to worsen my circumstances by marrying a person I love, then an appeal to justice would not be an appropriate response. Rawls himself argues that fairness requires us to recognize liberty of this kind, where it is compatible with the like liberty of all; and in any case there are so many other moral considerations involved here that it is misleading to use the example as a test to expose our intuitive responses, especially when the focus of the discussion is exclusively the problem of 'entitlement'. Nozick must, then, show why he thinks that we are not entitled to question the propriety of allowing benefits to flow according to market forces.

What Nozick seems to rely on, in justifying his claim that his principle ought to be preferred to Rawls's general conception of justice, is the notion that the value of a person's contribution must be seen as equivalent to 'what he can get for the product in free market competition'. Given this assumption, it does seem fair that we be paid a return commensurate with the value of our contribution. Once we concede that we are not entitled to take from those whose achievement is considerable in order to give to those whose achievement is marginal, and if we concede further that achievement is to be measured by whether others are prepared freely to dispose of some of their holdings to purchase that contribution, then all of Nozick's conclusions follow; by his account, it is unnecessary to require that people set fair prices for what they offer, for according to his theory of value, the fair price turns out to be 'what producers can get on the market' (this is what their contribution is worth).

But how plausible is all this? Nozick seems to be relying on his economic theory to justify his claims about 'justice'. He has built a conception of 'fairness' into his account of entitlement by way of a theory of value. But there are competing theories of value which, if valid or more adequate than that suggested by Nozick, enable us to challenge his conception of entitlement itself. I think here particularly of Marx's view that we can distinguish processes at work in terms of which the price of a commodity will, in the long term, prove to be a function of the capacity of manufacturers to supply. Marx assumes, of course, that the price of commodities will fluctuate in the market with supply — that is, that the demand is not insatiable. Thus, according to him, we start with a high price, when there is a scarce supply. This encourages producers to enter into competition to manufacture (as long as they can produce at a cost which is below the market price), and as more and more manufacturers enter the market, the demand for the commodity slackens (because the commodity is no longer scarce), so production can only be sustained by lowering the price. Marx argues that manufacturers will not go on producing a commodity if they cannot sell it for more than it cost them to produce, so it is likely that the market price will tend to gravitate towards the point at which it is more or less equivalent to the cost of production. This, Marx claims, is the 'real' or 'natural' value of the commodity. Liberal economists, as Nozick himself makes clear, share some of these insights with Marx.

If we allow, as it is only sensible to do, that the cost of production (however measured) will in some situations be different from the market price, then we may question Nozick's suggested principle of justice; for 'what one chooses to give' will correspond to the cost of production (the effort expended), whereas what one is entitled to receive will correspond to the price ('what others choose to give'). It also follows that if we allow for structural scarcity by suggesting that some offerings on the market cannot be easily or quickly replaced through reproduction, then the relationship between effort and reward, measured as the market price (as Nozick suggests), will not be acceptable because market forces in such circumstances of scarcity will not tend towards a fair equilibrium. The problem here is that the mechanisms at work (the encouragement of more producers) do not apply, and there is, consequently, no resulting equivalence between the market price and the 'real value' (measured in terms of the cost of production). As long as some have a monopoly, in the sense that what they produce is not easily reproducible, the processes normally generated through market competition do not apply, and 'real value' (in the Marxist sense) will not materialize as the price.[7]

What Nozick seems to overlook in his discussion is that it is one thing to justify exchange and quite another to show that the price at which exchanges are transacted is fair: is a producer entitled to charge what the market will bear? Why should we assume this to be so? The problem here, as I have already indicated, is that we cannot move, without further argument, from a first premise establishing entitlements based on a claim to the fruits of one's own labour (the appeal here is to fairness) to the assumption that our entitlement should be measured by market forces, for once monopolies in skills and resources are established, the price of a product or service will not necessarily reflect the amount of labour expended. Both doctors and garbage collectors do work which is necessary for the health of the nation; but though the contribution of garbage collectors may be seen to be more important, it is unlikely that they will be able to exchange their services for the same fee as doctors because almost everyone is capable of shifting garbage, whereas only a few have been initiated into the secrets of the medical profession. Similarly, in terms of Marx's analysis, once some private owners control the means of production, they will be in a position to contract with those who must necessarily sell their labour power in a way which enables the owners to extract a surplus. Marx was not prepared to emphasize the point that this situation was unfair (because he regarded moral gestures as more or less pointless, and because he reasoned that the natural price of labour power — reflecting the cost of producing labourers — was being paid). He did argue forcefully, however, that labourers were very much worse off under a system of market exchange than they would be under some other system.

Nozick seems to be aware that the distinction drawn here between the cost of production and the market price poses problems for his theory of 'justice', and he takes trouble to dismiss cost-of-production theories of value and, in particular, Marx's view of 'socially necessary labour time'. He does, however, make a number of irrelevant points. For example, all the standard objections which he lists ('found natural objects (valued above the labour necessary to get them); rare goods (letters from Napoleon) that cannot be reproduced in unlimited quantities....')[8] are exceptions noted and taken account of by Marx. Marx's theory only applies to the value of commodities which, by definition, are capable of being reproduced and have a use value. Thus, the idea that what one produces must be wanted by someone before it can be said to have value is not an *ad hoc* restriction but an essential assumption which has to be made before one can apply the labour theory of value. Nozick writes:

suppose someone works for 563 hours on something of some very *slight* utility (and there is no way to make it more efficiently). This satisfies the necessary condition for value that the object have *some* utility. Is its value now determined by the *amount* of labour, yielding the consequence that it is incredibly valuable?[9]

What Nozick does not seem to take account of here is that the production of such a commodity will not be worth the effort unless it can be exchanged for other commodities (or a money equivalent) which embodies a similar labour effort — that is, 563 hours. Thus, if it can be exchanged at all (if it is worth producing and is a product 'capable of satisfying the wants of others', a matter proved by the act of exchange itself), then its value in the long run must be determined by the amount of labour which it is necessary to expend in order to produce the commodity. Nozick goes on to argue:

What is socially necessary, and how much of it is, will be determined by what happens on the market!! There is no longer any labour theory of value; the central notion of socially necessary labour time is itself defined in terms of the processes and exchange ratios of a competitive market![10]

This is not so. Only what is socially useful is established by what people want (and is reflected by market demand); the 'socially necessary labour time', although relevant to the issue of use (for people may not want a commodity if the cost of production is too high) is determined quite independently of market forces and depends on the level of technology and the labour effort needed. Marx explains the processes of exchange using his labour theory of value. He argues that it is precisely because more efficient modes of production give a competitive advantage to those able to produce at a cost below the social average that they are able to derive higher profits (because they are able to exchange what they produce at a price which reflects the labour time involved in the former but still prevalent methods of production); his claim is that the cost of production ultimately determines the dynamic of market competition.

One does not have to be a Marxist to question Nozick's assumptions. As soon as we agree that scarcity has a part to play in determining market price, we can see how, through no fault of their own, some producers (farmers notoriously) may be badly effected by fluctuations in supply (due, often, to unforeseeable circumstances), whereas others (due entirely to luck rather than to foresight) will come to gain tremendously. To allow 'desert' to be determined in this way by fortune is counter-intuitive and violates our sense of what is fair.

It is worth noting that Locke, from whom Nozick derives much of his inspiration, had much more regard for the claims of fairness than his modern disciple. As is well known, he qualified his defence of the right to accumulate property by recognizing certain provisos which were clearly intended to reflect the requirements of natural justice and to protect the interests of those adversely affected by unrestricted processes of appropriation and exchange. These limitations applied in the state of nature and required that before one could justify claims to control resources there must be no spoilage or wastage; enough and as good left over for others; and an entitlement only to that with which one has mixed one's labour.

Macpherson suggests that it was Locke's purpose in the *Second Treatise* to argue that these provisos, which foreclose on some of the possibilities for appropriation and exchange in the state of nature, can legitimately be ignored in civil society.[11] He reads Locke as providing a utilitarian argument: if certain arrangements (Locke had in mind the recognition of money, private holdings of capital and free market exchange) can be shown to give rise to an end-state which benefits everyone in general, then the state of nature provisos may justifiably be held not to apply.

This utilitarian argument has, of course, been seriously under challenge since the publication of Rawls's work, for he forcefully asserts that before institutional arrangements of the kind Locke recommends can be acceptable they must be shown to confer benefits in a way which can be regarded as fair. Nozick, in his attempt to save Locke from this challenge, argues that Rawls's objections are beside the point, for his principle of natural freedom applies just as much in the state of civil society as it does in the state of nature; his only proviso is a very weak requirement, which allows virtually no weight to be placed either on utilitarian considerations or on an appeal to our sense of fair play. I have suggested that Nozick's defence of Locke in this regard is not persuasive.

One way of showing that Nozick's 'worsening the situation of others' proviso is too weak is to look more closely at the way in which appeals to fairness operate within our moral deliberations about entitlement. To do this it is necessary to provide an example which may serve to highlight those features of the situation which are relevant.

The case which best serves this purpose is that in which members of a slave work detail negotiate with one another. Such a case is especially suitable for our purpose because in this situation we are not faced with complications resulting from inequalities (I trust that the slaves are equally without resources, and that each has to rely entirely on his or her own endeavours). The example also has the advantage of establishing circumstances in which it is meaningful to assume that individuals are entitled to their own capacities, as they owe nothing to society for them; and it enables us to consider this assumption in the light of a further relevant feature — that the prisoners have to work as members of a gang of workers who are required to negotiate their share of the joint product earned by the group. We imagine, then, a camp very like that described by Solzhenitsyn in *One Day in the Life of Ivan Denisovich*, and we are to consider the kinds of entitlement claims which prisoners would be likely to make against one another in various circumstances.

If no constraints are imposed by the camp superintendents, and the food allotment is provided regardless of the work which is accomplished, then this is a situation very much like that illustrated by Nozick when he considers the way in which a group of people would be likely to divide up a pie. Provided the food appears miraculously or there is no demonstrable relationship between the labour contributed each day by individuals and the amount of food available, it would be quite arbitrary to base entitlement on any principle other than that of equal shares. (I assume here, of course, that we are dealing with self-interested rational egoists, and that a humanitarian appeal to need as a criterion will not be considered as having any weight).

Let us now suppose that all of the circumstances of the situation are the same, except that the superintendents require that a specified amount of work be accomplished by the gang as a whole before any food is provided. It would now be rational, allowing for some necessary qualifications to accommodate the possibility of sickness and accident, to require that each prisoner contribute an equal share of the work if he or she are to qualify for an entitlement to an equal share of the food. (We can simplify the situation here by assuming that each prisoner is forced to work on some easily quantifiable task like digging holes or making straw mats)? Thus, the work requirement laid down by the superintendents is divided by the number of able prisoners and each is responsible for contributing an equal share.

We must note that although the prisoners in any actual prison would be likely to choose procedures for allocating rights which give the stronger, healthier workers a chance to obtain more food, it would not be *just* for them to do so. Each prisoner at this stage would have a claim to at least an equal share, and the weaker ones would resist the idea that the entitlements to food be allocated competitively in terms of their work contribution measured at the end of the day. If this were the situation, the stronger and faster workers would be able to prevent those who are slow from getting an equal share, for they would be in a position to claim more food on the strength of their greater contribution within the time allowed. But as soon as the consequences of a procedure establishing entitlements can be shown to affect the circumstances of some in this way (by not leaving as good for others), then Nozick's proviso about leaving people worse off comes into play. If one is to appropriate a share by one's own effort, this will only be just when the consequences do not cut back on the opportunities available to others.

Nozick's proviso operates here as a principle of justice which can be appealed to in order to monitor the entitlements which individuals claim by appealing to the principle of natural freedom. Competitive procedures with results which vitiate the principle cannot be tolerated because they cannot be shown to be just. If we think in terms of validating conditions, as Nozick recommends, we must allow that when the consequences of an institutional practice can be shown to affect some people adversely, making them worse off than they would be otherwise, these circumstances can invalidate the claimed entitlement.

Nozick, as we have seen, does not deny that an appeal to fairness of the kind that we have been considering would have validity. He does, however, argue that the real world is rather different, in that industry is productive of its own rewards. The situation in real life, Nozick tells us, is more like the case which would arise in the slave camp if the food were provided by the superintendents in proportion to the amount of work contributed by each slave because it is often possible, in real life, to specify not only those whose efforts make a difference to the total amount there is to divide, but also to identify how much each individual contributes through his or her activities. If the circumstances of the slave work details were more like those which Nozick believes to be applicable in the real world, the activities of the faster workers in accomplishing their tasks and establishing their entitlement to food would not cut back on the opportunities available to the slower workers, for the latter would be free to make the most of their talents as best they could on the same terms.

But the model is not an accurate representation, for in the actual division of labour in the real world our allocated roles do often cut back on the opportunities available to others — not everyone who wants to play in the orchestra is accepted, and not everyone who does play can be the conductor — and it is not possible for everyone to contribute as much or as well as the next person, even if he or she is capable of doing so. Suppose, for example, that a special camp were set up to accommodate philosophers who were critical of the labour theory of value (it would have to be a very big camp!). Let us suppose, further, that prisoners had to work in teams on complicated tasks which involved a division of labour; that each team were given an amount of food in proportion to its accomplishments each day as compared with those of other teams; and that none of the philosophers in the camp could boast any useful capacity apart from his skill as a logician. Our philosophers would now have to negotiate with each other in circumstances which provide a reasonable model of the real world in which we are forced to debate about entitlement.

In the situation outlined, there would be an obvious need for some of these very talented individuals to acquire useful skills, which they would attempt to do by specializing their job roles. It would also be agreed that the members who displayed the most aptitude for particular tasks and those who were younger and stronger be trained for the more important roles because, given the fact that each group must compete with others, everyone would have an interest in seeing the best workers in the skilled areas. We should note, however, that most of the members of each group would be capable themselves of acquiring whatever skills were needed, and they would not wish to see a situation in which they were disadvantaged within their group. They would, therefore, insist on a costing which only allowed for differentials based on the labour theory of value. Thus, although skilled work is usually more productive than unskilled work, especially if machines are used, the entitlement of each worker would have to be quantified in terms of labour time if the group were to respect the proviso that none of their members be made worse off. Workers who demanded more for the privilege of doing skilled work would violate the 'worsening the circumstances of others' proviso, because the unskilled workers would be better off had they been allowed to do the skilled work on the agreement that they are paid no more than an equal share. The only differentials rewarding extra effort and achievement above the social average which would be tolerated by the group would be those based on the labour theory of value (awarding more to those whose contributions are above the social average), and those which, for some reason or another, could be shown to work to the advantage of the least privileged.

I have assumed throughout this discussion that all of our philosophers (or at least a large number of them) have the capacity to be trained in the various tasks which are required to be done, and that innate ability, although not equal between individuals, is widely spread throughout the group. Nozick's argument for market entitlement, in contrast, assumes that skills often reflect very marked differences in innate capacity and not simply in training. This is why his Wilt Chamberlain example is such a persuasive one for his case. The man clearly has an ability to do something which no one else can easily accomplish, and it is because of this capacity, it is plausible to suppose, that he is so much in demand as a player: he has a monopoly, in the sense that only he can accomplish the task. We should not, however, allow Nozick to generalize from this case because most of the differentials established through unbridled market competition are not based on any unique capacity attributable to individuals but arise, rather, from socially imposed monopolies resulting from the division of labour and the special rules regulating property rights. Enough people are capable of being trained as scientists, doctors and lawyers (not to mention managers and directors) to make nonsense of Nozick's assumptions. It is true, of course, that in competitive social systems there is an effort to select only the most capable candidates for training; but this in itself should not make us think that the privilege of doing something more interesting and demanding should also entitle the more competent to a greater return for their efforts.

What Nozick fails to see is that Rawls's 'fairness' requirement operates as a critical principle in terms of which social processes establishing rights have to be monitored. Even if one were to agree that the value to society of a person's contribution should be measured by the demand for it, it still does not follow that the person who contributes is entitled to a return which is equivalent to the market price. To say this assumes that those who learn skills owe nothing to the wider society for the monopoly.

Other arguments have, of course, been advanced to show why we should tolerate the privileges established through market competition. These have usually pointed to the beneficial consequences that are alleged to follow from this form of institutional arrangement. What should be clear from my discussion is that some such claim is required, and that it is not sufficient for Nozick to rest his assertions about entitlement on an assumption that individuals owe nothing to the rest of society for the special advantages which their trained capacities (or their control of social resources) provides them in the competition for the benefits which flow from co-operative production.

The Place of Intuition in Moral Argument

Joel Feinberg has put forward the opinion (which also seems to be shared by Brian Barry) that moral judgements about the salience of basic principles in establishing rights claims cannot be settled in the abstract. He tells us that this is because the weight of their application in specific circumstances is a matter for intuitive judgement.[12] Once we have carefully examined all the ramifications of a problem and are clear about the principles and other considerations (such as those of utility) which may be said to apply, then, so it is argued, we can do nothing more than to rely on our intuitive sense of what is right or just in the circumstances. Furthermore, when there are conflicts over how to resolve hard cases, there is no rational way of reconciling divergent judgements. The central task for philosophers in the moral area, then, must be to clarify. Through analysis we can become aware of the actual issues upon which there is disagreement, and we can learn not to confuse misunderstandings or conflicts over the facts of cases with disputes which arise because we intuitively assess the salience of principles differently. Many philosophers believe that if we proceed in this way, we will find that actual differences in intuitive judgements between individuals are not frequent.

Rawls responds to this position by suggesting that 'the only way therefore to dispute intuitionism is to set forth the recognizably ethical criteria that account for the weights which, in our considered judgements, we think appropriate to give the plurality of principles.'[13] For example, when we are asked to choose between equality and efficiency as ideals, Rawls is clear that what provides the key (explaining the weight we would ascribe to these considerations in specific cases) is some notion of fairness. It is on the basis of this insight that he adopts a contract approach in political theory, for his 'original position', as we have seen, provides the background conditions in terms of which his negotiators are to make their choices, and in this way it ensures that they will be concerned with what is fair. Rawls gives notice that his conception of the priority of competing principles which can be postulated (that is, his theory of justice) will be such that it will not allow the sacrifices of some to be outweighed by the advantages enjoyed by others, nor will it permit any other social goal to be imposed at the expense of individuals; efficiency and equality may only be balanced in a way which is fair, Rawls tells us, and his contract device is designed specifically to ensure this.

Rawls's problem is to convince us that 'fairness', as reflected by the circumstances of his original position, provides a set of principles which we can recognize as accounting for the priority which we do, in fact, accord to competing considerations in making intuitive judgements. In my own case I find that Rawls is indeed right, for when I reflect on the judgements I am inclined to make I find that the balance which I generally reach reflects some underlying concern for what I regard as fair in the circumstances. It may well be that my responses are not unusual, and that there are many others whose intuitions reflect a similar concern for what is fair. However, as R. M. Hare puts it in his review of Rawls's work: 'the fact that Rawls is a fairly typical man of his times and society, and will therefore have many adherents, does not make this a good way of doing philosophy.'[14]

This may be so; but the criticism misses the point of Rawls's enterprise, for he justifies his appeal to 'fairness' by claiming not that such a position will be popular in these times (which it is not), but that it is only by reference to 'fairness' that we can best account for the judgements that most of us make. His point (directed at the pluralist intuitionist position) is that, as theorists, we have a responsibility to account for our judgements, and that moral theories can be ranked according to their success in providing such coherence. Thus, Rawls tells us, utilitarianism is an internally coherent theory which requires us to reach certain conclusions in moral argument that reflect a concern to promote good consequences; however, as we have seen, when we follow the utilitarian line of reasoning we often reach conclusions which conflict with our basic intuitive sense of priorities. It is the match between the judgements inspired by a theory and those produced by intuition that Rawls relies on for finding a test of whether a theory is adequate or not; it is because utilitarians are forced, by the logic dictated by their theory, to reason in a way which leaves out of account considerations which many of us find to be of central importance that he regards the approach as unacceptable. Rawls is not asking that we list our principles in advance of application, setting some rank between them so that they are in what he calls a lexical order; but he does require that we provide a theory which accounts for the way we are most happy to balance the claims of each against the others when we are dealing with specific problems.

This is a feature of Rawls's theory of ethical reasoning which is taken up by Dworkin. Unlike Rawls, whose inclination is to reason from an abstract explication of a conception of justice to its application when dealing with specific policy problems, Dworkin's theory emerges from an analysis of specific cases and moves towards the articulation of abstract principles. Indeed, his focus throughout is on legal reasoning, and his favourite examples are taken from Law Reports. What Dworkin notices about the behaviour of judges is that they are not content, when dealing with hard cases, to rely on intuition as a justification for their decisions. They find it necessary not only to co-ordinate their decisions, so that they do not contradict other cases which might be thought to be similar, but also to account for the way in which competing considerations are balanced in terms of some overriding political theory. In this regard Dworkin suggests that a good theory of jurisprudence (and of political philosophy) is one which can best accommodate (account for) the judgements which courts are inclined to make on specific issues; and a good judgement is one which can be squared with other judgements, based on recognizably ethical criteria (usually a principle), which can be shown to have informed the judge's reasoning.

With regard to critics like Feinberg, who contend that we cannot usefully account for our intuitions in the way recommended, Dworkin suggests that their objection rests on the mistaken notion that moral reasoning must somehow be an analogue of scientific reasoning.[15] Dworkin tells us that the intuitionist assumes that moral judgements about values should be treated as the observations of scientists are treated — as potential falsifiers in empiricist theories. If they conflict with what may be deduced from a theory, then this forces a decision, for the theory must be adapted to accommodate the anomaly or it must be regarded as having been falsified. Dworkin suggests that because intuitionists find that in the sphere of morals falsification of this kind — according to this view, the application of scientific reasoning — produce no common viewpoint between philosophers (because their intuitive core judgements regarding their values are not public in the way that scientific observations are), they mistakenly conclude that there is no rational way to proceed towards the resolution of disputes, and that we are stuck with an irreducible pluralism. However, this model of the nature of moral reasoning is, Dworkin reassures us, quite

178 RADICAL INDIVIDUALISM

mistaken: intuitions are not observations in any scientific sense, and we can, therefore, decide to ignore them without being irrational. Indeed, he tells us that it is precisely this ability to play fast and loose with our intuitions that distinguishes ethical reasoning from science: scientists may not ignore observations just because they falsify their theories, whereas the ethical philosopher may do precisely this with his or her intuition about the good or the right. Thus, a utilitarian writer may well agree, on the basis of an intuitive judgement, that 'we ought to do unto others as we would be done by' but may, nevertheless, ignore this rule when it is shown that in a given set of circumstances more good than harm would follow from this. There is no contradiction involved here, according to Dworkin, for an intuitive judgement cannot have the force in moral deliberation that an observation may claim in science.

But if intuitive judgements do not provide the regulative standard by means of which truth is to be distinguished from falsehood in ethical argument, they are, nevertheless, given a firm place within the methodology of both Rawls and Dworkin, for both make intuition the foundation of their moral theories. What they claim, as Dworkin puts it, is that:

men and women have a responsibility to fit the particular judgments on which they act into a coherent program of action, or, at least, that officials who exercise power over other men have that sort of responsibility.

And he goes on:

decisions taken in the name of justice must never outstrip an official's ability to account for these decisions in a theory of justice, even when such a theory must compromise on some of his intuitions. It demands that we act on principle rather than on faith. Its engine is a doctrine of responsibility that requires men to integrate their intuitions and subordinate some of these, when necessary, to that responsibility.[16]

Dworkin's model of responsible and principled argument is asserted not merely as a normative recommendation about what we should be aiming towards in political and moral discussion, but also as a description of what actually takes place in many instances. It is Dworkin's belief that political arguments characteristically involve attempts to provide coherence, and that they are not abandoned at the point at which intuition is consulted. He suggests that whether we recognize it or not, we distinguish between good and bad political arguments by making some assessment of the reasons which are provided for giving principles a particular weight in a given set of circumstances.

On my interpretation of Rawls's and Dworkin's approach, then, 'fairness' is assumed to be an absolute moral requirement in political dialogue. We can demand of political arguments, when they attempt to justify by appealing to justice and are not merely disputes over the efficiency of policy programmes, that they show proposed policies to have consequences which are fair.

Those who are unhappy about the theory of rights which Rawls derives from his commitment to reciprocity as a basic democratic ideal may challenge his position by providing an alternative theory which can more adequately co-ordinate our basic intuitions, or by reaching conclusions different from those of Rawls by way of a deduction from the commitment to treat persons as equals. We have already examined two alternative approaches: Nozick's theory, which assumes a basic right to liberty without showing that the implications of this are fair, and utilitarianism. In both these cases we have seen that the theories entail perspectives which violate our intuitive judgements about what would be appropriate in some circumstances; and I have suggested that they, consequently, provide a less adequate co-ordinating frame of reference than that which is offered to us by Rawls's general conception of justice. With regard to the suggestion that someone might wish to question Rawls's account of the rights which are entailed in his theory of justice (whilst conceding Rawls's point about the crucial role of 'fairness' as a co-ordinating concept), I would suggest that such an approach is a challenge, and that attempts along these lines are worth exploring. In this regard I consider (in the next chapter) the argument of Richard Miller, who makes such an attempt from a Marxist perspective. I also explore Dworkin's attempt to challenge positivist conceptions of law in Chapter 10 and, in Chapter 11, his conception of civil disobedience, which he defends as more adequate than that provided by Rawls.

9
Approaches to Democratic Theory

In this chapter I wish to explore three approaches to democratic theory, and to compare them with each other. I take Nozick as representative of the possessive individualist approach, Rawls as reflecting a liberal democratic perspective and Macpherson as representing a radical approach. I will suggest that a comparative analysis exposes weaknesses in liberal theory and that Macpherson's radical perspective can be defended.

Nozick's Theory of Democracy

In the Lockean tradition (which, following Macpherson, I have called possessive individualism) we are concerned with origins: we are interested to know how (by what processes) political association came about or *could have* come about. The focus of Lockean philosophers is the transformation problem: how did mankind pass from a situation in which there was no political authority (no associations) to one in which we recognize some authority claims as legitimate? This focus on processes and on origins reflects the fact that once we assume that persons have rights which do not arise out of association with others but are held to be prior to such political involvement, it is difficult to show how any political authority could emerge without transgressing these rights. By requiring an explanation of origins, Lockean writers set up a test for distinguishing between acceptable and unacceptable institutional demands: only those which can conceivably be said to respect individual rights are tolerable. Lockean theorists require, therefore, that apologists show how a political authority's claim to regulate the behaviour of citizens could have arisen from the state of nature without transgressing their rights. Unless a plausible story can be constructed to show how the political realm could have emerged out of the non-political by processes which respect everyone's natural entitlements, we are (as Lockeans) unable to acknowledge legitimacy.

In assessing the Lockean contract approach it is important to stress that a hypothetical history of the transformation from the state of nature to civil society does not necessarily reflect the real origins of existing institutions. Most of us admit that the real history of mankind has been barbarous and that so-called civilization has often involved conquest and enslavement of one form or another. Hypothetical histories designed to show what can and what cannot be justified in the light of a commitment to the notion that individuals have rights should not be taken, then, as descriptions of what actually happened. The point of such hypothetical reconstructions of the origins of civil society is to show how a given set of institutions could have come into being in a way which did not violate rights. The legitimate functions of the state are proscribed, for Lockeans, by the possibility of providing some acceptable outline of origins. Unless an acceptable story is forthcoming, we have to assume that our rights are being violated by the coercive instrumentality.

In presenting a restatement of Lockean theory Nozick argues that if we could show how a given set of institutions could, in principle, have evolved without violating rights, then we would have provided some reason for valuing them more highly than those that embody processes which could not have emerged without transgressing the rights of individuals. A central issue for him is whether or not institutional arrangements embody processes which clearly violate rights. In this regard he seems to think that if we could provide a hypothetical history demonstrating how an institution might have evolved from the exercise of free choice by rational individuals, then we would have shown that the processes constituted in terms of that institution are acceptable. Given the premises with which they begin, and considering the stringent requirements that they set themselves, it is not surprising that Locke and Nozick should argue that the only legitimate function of the state is to protect rights. What does surprise is the difficulty they have in justifying even this limited role for government.

There are five stages by means of which Nozick believes a state

(limited to the function of protecting rights) could emerge out of the state of nature without violating anyone's rights.
(1) Individuals seek to protect themselves by joining agencies. (They cannot afford not to join them, even if they realize that these organizations, because they specialize in coercion, may be dangerous to everyone.)
(2) People want to join the most powerful agency for greater protection and shift membership to the most competent. (This process can lead to a situation of near monopoly as powerful agencies acquire control of geographical areas.)
(3) Agencies are concerned with the rights of non-members. (This is justified, Nozick tells us, even though it allows free-loading by those who do not join the agency.)
(4) The agencies protect members against risks which arise when other individuals try to take the law into their own hands to protect their rights, for they require that those who police for themselves follow certain procedures. (This imposition on others is justified, Nozick tells us, because individuals have a natural right to protect themselves against risk.)
(5) The ultra-minimal state develops as a result of these processes, leading eventually to the minimal state as the agency emerges with a *de facto* monopoly.

Nozick's claim is that at no stage in his deduction are new rights created. As he puts it:

> the *de facto* monopoly grows by an invisible-hand process and *by morally permissible means,* without anyone's rights being violated and without any claims being made to a special right that others do not possess. And requiring the client of the *de facto* monopoly to pay for the protection of those they prohibit from self-help enforcement against them, far from being immoral, is morally required by the principle of compensation....[1]

Even if Nozick's strategy analysis is correct in detail and we agree that citizens would make the kinds of choice he suggests, all that he shows is that a commitment to take the possessive individualist notion of natural rights seriously does not entail anarchism. He is still faced by the fact that his hypothetical history is not real history — so that any actual state, even if it restricted itself to police work, as Nozick requires, would be enforcing the spoils of robbery and plunder. Even if we allow, as Nozick does, for some principles of rectification, so that the property of those whose holdings we know to be derived from plunder are confiscated and redistributed to compensate those who have been abused in the past, are we to tolerate a state exercising such a positive role to enforce justice?[2] By what criteria are we to determine the rights and wrongs of history? These questions are not directed, of course, at the conceptual claims which Nozick makes about the notion of a right; nor are they a challenge to his view that liberal society can be shown to embody processes which do no violence to rights. What I do suggest, however, is that if we are to take his conception seriously, then it is difficult to see how to give it practical application. Other conceptions at least have the advantage that they do not commit us to a review of history. In general, however, I am prepared to concede this part of Nozick's argument, for I find anarchism an entirely unacceptable conclusion, and the limited policing role which Nozick is prepared to allow a political instrumentality falls far short of what I would wish to see. (The negative conclusion which Nozick believes is justified by his argument is much more controversial: why should we accept his claim that 'The minimal state is the most extensive state that can be justified. Any state more extensive violates people's rights'?)[3]

An important weakness of Nozick's approach is that he fails to address himself sufficiently to the fundamental problem of democratic theory: how are citizens (or shareholders) to control the state (or protective agency)? It is not sufficient merely to claim that any actions on the part of this agency that go beyond protection are illegitimate, for we must show how this restrictive mandate can be guaranteed. The possessive individualist must supply us with some definite institutional proposals, and he or she must model political processes which are likely to provide protection against the protectors.

As Nozick is silent on the subject (apart from casual remarks about 'the usual protections'),[4] I must be excused for indulging in some speculations. First, we can see that Nozick must oppose majority-rule solutions: if we are to suppose that all members of the citizen body have an equal voice, what is to prevent them from demanding that the rich pay the costs (as in the United Nations)? What is to prevent them from demanding that those with significant holdings give some of their assets to the majority of poorer members? If, on the other hand, we allow that those with significant wealth have greater control, so that their common interest in private property rights sustains a consensus on the minimal use of state power (as Macpherson interprets Locke),[5] what is to prevent them from using this coercive instrumentality (now in their hands) to entrench their advantages in market competition? What is to prevent gangsterism when you start from a situation in which those with the most control coercion? It would seem that Nozick must be suspicious of majority rule and wary of oligarchy. It is, then, difficult to see how any solution can be found to the democratic problem of control, once we accept his initial assumption that political procedures must not give rise to circumstances in which people are likely to use the state for anything more than the protection of an assumed natural right.

It may be suggested that these considerations are unfairly directed, and that Nozick does not have to provide an answer to save his argument. All he sets out to do, after all, is to show what activities on the part of a government can be justified, given certain Lockean assumptions about the rights of citizens.[6] Nozick should not, then, be criticized for failing to answer the very different question relating to how the state can best be controlled so that there is no abuse of the monopoly of coercion. We need to do him the courtesy of distinguishing between his political philosophy and his theory of democracy. He is concerned, for the most part, with philosophical problems associated with entitlement and not with modelling the most desirable set of political institutions.[7] Thus, even if no institution can be thought up which has a chance of providing citizens with a reasonable defence against possible abuse, and even if it can be shown that his protective agencies would not behave in the way suggested by his strategy analysis (because they would be tempted to abuse their monopoly of coercive power), these considerations do not mean that Nozick's arguments are without point. He has still shown, to his own satisfaction at least, what governments ought not to be doing if they respect Lockean rights. To challenge his argument we would have to demonstrate that considerations of the possible abuse of power on the part of those who control the minimal state (protection agency) would affect the calculation individuals are likely to make about allowing such an agency to acquire a monopoly. But, as Nozick shows, individuals have no way of promoting their collective interests in this area.[8]

In the light of these democratic considerations we can, however, accuse Nozick of Utopian speculation, for he discusses problems in the abstract and provides no concrete solution (not even a model) to show how we can eliminate exploitation and abuse in the real world. To make his speculations relevant to the circumstances of actual societies, we have to presume that human nature is such that except for a small minority people everywhere are disposed to respect the rights of others, even at some cost to their personal interests. It would seem that Nozick does make some assumption of this kind, but his position is not clearly stated. Furthermore, his position is complicated by the fact that sufficient numbers of people in the state of nature are said to ignore the entitlements of others to make it necessary for those who fear abuse to enter into an agreement to help protect each other. But Nozick gives no convincing reason for supposing that the robbers would not also form gangs to protect their plundering activities from harassment by the agencies; nor does he show why the forces of righteousness would prevail in the long term. The evidence of history surely calls Nozick's optimism in question, for it may be quite seriously argued that civilized society began when warrior gangs of hunting tribes began to enslave settled communities by protecting them from other plunderers and exacting in return for this service a not insignificant proportion of their produce and labour. Like Al Capone in Chicago, the nobility of traditional society lived off the productive efforts of those it both terrorized and protected.

Rawls and Democratic Theory

Theorists who conceive of entitlement in terms of 'fairness' have thought it necessary for political instrumentalities to provide some check on purely market relationships in order to prevent any massive accumulation of social resources in the hands of a few; they have also required that the state be used as a transfer agency, redistributing resources confiscated from the rich among those who are not so lucky. In this regard they have thought it important for governments to establish a social minimum, so that even the least privileged have some guarantee that they cannot fall below a cut-off point, and for social services to be established which provide for essentials such as health needs, accident compensation and pensions. By providing free education and career training for poorer members of the community who wish to better themselves, and by offering legal aid and advice in case of need, welfare agencies help to promote a fair society. Rawls argues that welfare of this kind can correct the market in a way compatible with the general conception of justice; he suggests that by taxing the rich, especially those who acquire their wealth through inheritance, and by compensating with grants of aid individuals who suffer from the disadvantage of a poor start in life, a measure of social equality can be sustained even in systems in which the market generally determines resource allocations.[9]

This sort of corrective solution to the injustices which arise through market competition relies very heavily on assumptions about the use of political power. What Rawlsian liberals have to show is how political protections can generate processes effectively to ameliorate or prevent the occurrence of the unjust inequalities which they concede will be the likely consequence of unbridled market competition. They must also show how a political instrumentality, powerful enough to initiate and administer the redistributions thought necessary to promote justice, may itself be controlled so that it is used only for this purpose. The task of providing this kind of democratic theory is not an easy one, for once inequalities are tolerated (which would be the case under even a managed capitalist system), political dangers immediately arise. This is partly because the rich are notoriously active politically and, because they are able to use their resources to advantage, often influential; the needy and weak members of society, by contrast, are usually unable to exert influence in the corridors of power. Like Nozick, then, Rawls requires further arguments to supplement his philosophical exposition of 'justice', for he must provide a solution to the democratic problem of how elites are to be controlled so as to ensure that they do what is fair. Unlike Nozick, his worry is not that leaders will abuse the political instrumentality, however, but that the governing elite will be too weak to force the rich to give enough to meet the requirements of justice.

Would the democratic problem of controlling elites be perceived by Rawls's hypothetical negotiators as standing in the way of their possible agreement to accept the general principle of justice as a fundamental commitment? Even if we assume that the negotiators might believe that persons of good will should be disposed to accept the general conception of justice as their guiding principle, we must still suppose that they would have good reason not to agree to it because they would be reluctant to tolerate the inequalities in the real world which (on liberal economic assumptions) would be justifiable in terms of Rawls's principle. Their anxiety would not be the product of envy or of the fact that they placed a greater value on equality than is reflected in the general conception of justice; rather, their concern would be a political one, for they would be wary of the danger of abuse which could follow if the rich (tolerated under the principle) started meddling politically to their own advantage. Like Hobbes's negotiators, who recognize an obligation *in foro interno* but not *in foro externo*, Rawls's representatives would be aware of the fact that what they lacked was a necessary political security; they would, then, reject Rawls's solution and seek a principle which placed more weight on equality and less on the maximization of utility.

Rawls is undoubtedly aware of these difficulties. In his book (although not in the earlier article 'Justice as Fairness') he is clear that the negotiators in the original position would demand the entrenchment of certain political safeguards. It is for this reason he argues, that they would make a commitment to the priority amongst values of liberty and would express the general conception as two separate principles, of which the first would be:

Each person is to have the most extensive total system of equal basic liberties compatible with a similar system of liberty for all.

and the second:

Social and economic inequalities are to be arranged so that they are both:

a) to the greatest benefit of the least advantaged, consistent with the just savings principle, and

b) attached to offices and positions open to all under conditions of fair equal opportunity.[10]

He argues that the first principle, which is concerned to secure equality in the amount of political influence which each citizen can expect, should take priority over the second, which allows for inequalities in other values such as wealth and status. In this way Rawls seeks to provide some guarantees for those who are nervous that political power will be abused when inequalities in wealth and status are tolerated.

Rawls also seeks to persuade the reckless that there is a need for political caution because it may sometimes seem to be the case that social and economic gains can be made by giving away fundamental political liberties. Taken in itself (that is, before it is expressed as two separate principles), the general conception of justice does not rule out the possibility of one-party rule through the restriction of widely accepted liberal freedoms to oppose government. As Rawls puts the problem:

Now it is possible, at least theoretically, that by giving up some of their fundamental liberties men are sufficiently compensated by the resulting social and economic gains. The general conception of justice imposes no restrictions on what sorts of inequalities are permissible; it only requires that everyone's position be improved....It is this kind of exchange which the two principles as stated rule out; being arranged in serial order they do not permit exchanges between basic liberties and economic and social gains.[11]

Because he recognizes that circumstances could arise in which it might seem rational to barter political freedom for economic gain,

Rawls allows that freedom has little value in societies which are very poor. In his view, the considerations which are persuasive in establishing the special place of liberty among our values only become relevant after a certain level of affluence has been reached. Rawls is clear, nevertheless, that once the requisite level has been reached, political liberties should be retained even at the cost of a great reduction in efficiency. His assumption here, which has a good deal of force, is that a strategy of abandoning democratic rights is much too risky to contemplate. This is another reason, then, why the negotiators in the original position would be inclined to put Rawls's two principles in what he calls a lexical order; they would hope to pre-empt short-sighted responses on the part of well-intentioned majorities.

By establishing the lexical order of the two principles, Rawls's negotiators hope to allow for inequalities in the economic sphere so as to increase the total number of goods available to everyone without jeopardizing political equality. Rawls supposes that his idea of entrenching political rights provides a way of preventing social inequalities from presenting a serious threat.

Two further points about Rawls's idea of establishing his principles in lexical order are worth noting. First, it is not merely inequalities of wealth that can seriously undermine the protections offered under the first principle entrenching political rights, for a wide range of social factors is recognized as having an influence on the effective functioning of liberal political processes.[12] The problems here are sometimes deep-rooted, for groups with intensely felt interests may become identified as a permanent minority. This would be the case when such groups had special conflicting interests (for example, farmers in a society in which most people live in cities) or when an historical legacy provided the basis for community ties such as language, religion, and race. Any adequate appreciation of the relationship which should exist between Rawls's two principles must, then, take these considerations into account.

The second point is that it is not easy to defend a majority-rule solution to the democratic problem of providing a mechanism for controlling the governing elite, unless the power of future majorities is seriously qualified. Certainly, Rawls's negotiators could not adopt the idea of majority rule as their guiding principle, for they would be aware that the choices of the majority might prove prejudicial to the claims of a minority. The negotiators would each anticipate being in a minority on some issues and they would, therefore, hesitate before accepting a rule which did not provide them with an assurance that their right to persuade others and their equal chance of winning a majority over to their way of thinking would not be jeopardized. This means that they would wish to see certain freedoms (to speak, to publish, to assemble and so on) placed beyond the control of any majority.[13] This is one of the reasons why Rawls is so insistent that his principles would be placed in order of lexical priority — it would only be rational for the negotiators to accept a majority-rule solution to the democratic problem if their rights were protected.

Radical Perspectives and Rawls's Liberalism

It is worth noting that there is a serious point at issue between liberal and radical writers regarding the political consequences of an unequal distribution of social resources. Richard Miller, for example, has argued that there is no way in which one can legitimately deduce Rawls's commitment to the lexical priority of his first principle of justice from the perspective of rational negotiators situated in the original position. To illustrate this point, he suggests that a Marxist, being someone with sociological assumptions which are very different from those of Rawls, may be inclined to assert the priority of the second principle, especially if we include amongst the political liberties the right to private ownership of property.[14]

Miller's point must be well taken, for the deduction of the priority rule clearly depends, as I have shown, on sociological assumptions about the worth of liberty in circumstances in which inequalities exist. Miller is, however, somewhat misleading in his statement of the differences between Rawls and his left-wing critics, for what is surprising about the latter's position is the strength of his concern for equality in political life. Rawls would have us maximize the capacity of the poorer groups to make use of their political freedom, and he seems at times to imply that the inequalities allowed by his second principle should not exceed the point at which the effective value of equal political liberty, protected by his first principle, comes to be undermined. He writes:

Historically one of the main defects of constitutional government has been the failure to insure the fair value of political liberty. The necessary corrective steps have not been taken, indeed, they never seem to have been seriously entertained. Disparities in the distribution of property and wealth that far exceed what is compatible with political equality have generally been tolerated by the legal system. Public resources have not been devoted to maintaining the institutions required for the fair value of political liberty.[15]

It would seem that Rawls is too pragmatic to argue for complete equality, for this is a Utopian goal which, in any case, is not required by his general conception of justice. But he is too wary of the possible abuse of power when people control unequal resources to allow that basic political liberties should be made unequal for whatever reason. Indeed, he requires, where social inequalities begin to undermine the fair value of political liberties, that some process of redistribution be instigated. Rawls's position, as Dworkin has shown, also allows for positive discrimination so that it would be legitimate for the state to encourage a redistribution of resources to strengthen the political voice of minority communities.

Miller's view of the hypothetical Marxist may also be questioned, for he exaggerates the points of disagreement which may arise over Rawls's idea of entrenching political rights. Far from resisting such a suggestion, a Marxist is likely to require even more stringent priority rules before the risks of inequality contemplated by the application of Rawls's second principle come into force. Rawls's insistence on full and effective political equality would surely be seen as a step in the direction of more equality, not less; his is an egalitarian principle which limits the application of the general conception of justice. Whatever other inequalities may be tolerated as being just, our negotiators would at least have the security of knowing that there would be a chance to protect themselves through political participation in any future society. The hypothetical Marxist and the liberal Rawls clearly disagree over their assessments of the capacity which liberal democracies have shown to provide the working class with a defence against exploitation, but Miller is wrong to imply that there is a sharp conflict of opinion. Indeed, many Marxists would go a long way with conventional pluralist assumptions about the effectiveness — and, consequently, the importance — of political rights. They do not claim that political equality can provide a corrective to the contradictions which they believe to be generated by the processes of capitalism, but they do not think that they need conclude that rights are worthless because of this.

Macpherson, for example (along with other Marxists like Ernest Mandel), willingly concedes that liberal political institutions have contributed greatly, and continue to contribute, to the welfare of the working classes, and he is a strong advocate of a free society, in contrast to those who consider political freedom to be of little or no significance. However, as we have seen, he hopes to persuade liberals to correct their perspectives, for he does not think that they should be allowed to assume that political equality takes precedence over the demand for social equality. It matters a great deal to Macpherson whether we are struggling to realize democracy under capitalism or whether we choose the path of socialism. Even under free-enterprise systems of allocations, Macpherson tells us, the influence of the workers would be very much weaker if they had not acquired a good deal of political power as a result of franchise reform. Workers have been able to organize themselves (mostly through the establishment of trade unions) to take a fully competitive place within the institutions of liberal society, and although this has never modified the more basic social inequalities contingent on market resource allocation, it has been of great significance. Indeed, Macpherson tells us that it is precisely because workers have had some leverage with which to better their circumstances that the harsher effects of the market economy have been kept within tolerable limits.

As to the reasons why free elections have not led to a situation in which the majority rejects capitalism (as Engels and Marx predicted would be the case), Macpherson speculates that the role of political parties is partly to blame. He tells us that the role of the parties has served as a mechanism ensuring that only moderate programmes are put forward with any serious chance of gaining sufficient support to be implemented. Although he allows that the role of parties differs significantly between democracies and that it is influenced by a wide range of sociological and historical factors, he argues that the moderating influence of the parties has been a feature of all liberal democracies, even of those systems (such as those of France and Italy) in which communist parties have been able to play an important part. The reason for this, Macpherson tells us, differs according to whether the system is based primarily on competition between major parties, who alternate in office, or on governments formed as a result of an alliance between collaborating parties. In two-party systems each of the parties moves towards the middle ground of the political spectrum, projecting itself as the representative of national as opposed to class interests. Where more than two parties are in serious competition governments must usually be formed by means of a coalition which necessarily excludes extremist groups on both the left and the right. Macpherson tells us that a similar process of coalition formation takes place in those two-party systems in which the parties represent a broad spectrum of interest groups rather than a class, as is the case in the United States.[16]

In addition to the role of parties (which blurs class conflict), another factor that encourages moderation in political life is the very success of the labour movements in most liberal societies. The extension of the franchise to workers in the nineteenth century actually served to prevent the victory of the radical left in most liberal systems. This is partly because the demands of political competition ensured that the leaders of the most significant working-class movements were cautious reformists rather than revolutionaries seeking to destroy capitalism.

It would not be out of place to take account of one significant change in the ground rules of capitalism which Macpherson has not himself made much of, even though it illustrates fairly clearly some of the points that he makes about the interaction between political and economic sources of power in liberal systems. The revision I have in mind results from the fact that the political strength of workers, a product of franchise reform, enabled them to entrench the right to strike as one of the fundamental features of modern liberal society. This recognition of a new economic right represents a change in the property relations of capitalism, for it allows workers not only to withdraw their own labour but also to prevent others from working during a strike, to prevent employers from dismissing the strikers and to prevent the owners from gaining access to stockpiles of produce when this would undermine the impact of the strike. These changes are the most substantial victories which workers have been able to achieve politically. It is largely because this change gave workers a reasonable chance to better their circumstances within liberal society that the framework of market allocation has not been more threatened by the democratic participation of the people. Once armed with some leverage in the economic sphere, workers have seen as their best strategy a threat to withdraw their labour and to force huge capital-intensive plants to remain idle.

In his most recent work Macpherson speculates that there are possibilities for incremental social changes towards socialism (of a kind not anticipated by Marx or by Mill in the nineteenth century). He lists three features of the advanced capitalist period which, taken together with the democratic rights which already exist (always assuming that they will not be abandoned by a Fascist reaction to crisis), may conceivably exert sufficient pressure to bring about a shift towards a more humane society. The signs of change are, first, that people are beginning to see that unlimited economic expansion is affecting the quality of life and are consequently, demanding that governments take action to protect natural resources in order to prevent ecological damage and to ensure that we are afforded scope for living in a reasonably healthy environment. Second, citizens, especially industrial workers, are beginning to explore new modes of democratic participation, and they often take direct action to put pressure on political leaders. Third, people are becoming aware of the central contradiction of capitalism — that it requires consumers, yet produces inequalities of a kind that are not conducive to a continuous expansion of the purchasing power of the majority — which is manifesting itself in frequent recessions of near-crisis proportions.

In Macpherson's vision of the future these factors may work themselves out to a point at which significant disruption of the world economy combines with the political demand on the part of majorities for more and more welfare programmes to threaten the very process of market allocation itself. Although the situation in most liberal societies is still one in which on the whole governments interfere to monitor the wage demands of workers in the name of efficiency (capitalism); although they are often persuaded by the claims of expediency to ignore the claims of justice, they are coming to be held responsible for the consequences of the market system. Macpherson predicts that working-class movements throughout the world will subject market allocations to greater pressure in the name of justice, and that they will, consequently, force an erosion of market allocation by demanding more and more political review.[17] He argues that the contradiction between sound public policy and the allocations determined by free enterprise are such that capitalism may even be rejected eventually. He does not claim that those with power will voluntarily give away their privileges (as one commentator interprets his position),[18] but that strikes in the name of justice by powerful working-class groups, in combination with other disruptive responses by the frustrated poor (such as terrorism and riots), will turn liberal societies into societies of near-anarchy. It is this process which will eventually bring substantial changes to the property relations which now characterize liberal economies.

Macpherson, then, does not deny Rawls's point about the importance of elections and political freedoms. He readily agrees that political power is more diffuse in countries which can boast free elections than in those without them. What he questions about the liberal pluralist perspective is the assumption that political influence (which, he agrees, is now partly in the hands of working-class groups) is so very significant in the overall balance of power. That this is not obviously the case can be seen from the fact that while most of us would concede that trade unions have considerable political influence in countries like Australia and the United Kingdom, we would at the same time note that industrial power is a much more potent weapon in the struggle to better the circumstances of the working people. In a reference to the work of Robert Dahl (also discussed, but with enthusiasm, by Rawls)[19] Macpherson concedes that the former's preoccupation with power sets him off on a discussion of the right sort of problem. He takes Dahl to task, however, for not going far enough along the right track. Dahl seems to assume that as long as franchise reforms make a polity inclusive, and as long as civil liberties are protected, this is all that needs to be done. He does not, of course, think that social injustice has disappeared, or that it will do so in liberal systems; nor does he try to justify market resource allocation. But Dahl fails to ask whether the arrangements characteristic of capitalist economic systems are inimical to the democratic commitment. Furthermore, his description of what he calls 'polyarchy' is clearly based on the sharp distinction which he draws between social and political sources of power. Dahl is concerned primarily with the latter and chooses to treat economic relations as outside the range of his concern as a democratic theorist. Macpherson is unhappy about this way of restricting our focus. He believes that democrats should challenge inequalities of power, whether these be in economic or in political life; and, as he sees it, this implies that democrats should oppose capitalism. What we have to realize, he tells us, is that although governments in liberal systems are clearly important, it is still the case that many social allocations of significance are not determined by political processes. This means that the importance of the political sphere of influence within the overall pattern of social power, while clearly significant, is not primary.

Macpherson tells us that if we are to make progress in democratic theory, then we must begin to see the problem of power in a different way from liberal pluralists. (I quoted earlier his basic statement of the criterion of democracy as 'that equally effective right of individuals to live as fully as they may wish'.) What we have to see, in his view, is that we can only exercise our capacities, making the most of ourselves, if there is freedom from certain impediments, both social and political, which mankind already has the capacity (although not, it seems, the power) to alter. Macpherson believes that the circumstances of the times are increasingly forcing us to concern ourselves less with purely market conceptions and more with a reconsideration of our human potential to develop our capacities. Although he concedes that at present our vision is focused, for the most part, purely on the pragmatic struggle to ensure that we can earn a living, he believes that in the assumed circumstances of greatly increased productivity, the crucial question will no longer be how to provide a sufficient flow of the material means of life: it will be a question of getting the quality and kinds of things wanted for a full life, and beyond that, of the quality of life itself.[20]

Class and Political Power in Liberal Society

It may be useful to summarize the three positions outlined in point form.

POSSESSIVE INDIVIDUALISM
(a) Market processes do not lead to injustice because everyone receives his or her due according to the principle 'from each as they choose, to each as they are chosen'.
(b) The state should not be used as an instrument to redistribute wealth.
(c) Democratic processes, because they provide a significant resource for the poorer classes who are likely to demand welfare, are a danger.
(d) Serious checks should be placed on the majority-rule principle to ensure the role of the state is minimal.

RAWLSIAN INDIVIDUALISM
(a) Market systems can lead to inequalities which are unjust.
(b) Democratic processes are necessary to ensure that the state is used to provide welfare (this is needed to correct the unjust distributions established through market allocations).
(c) The value of political liberty can be maintained by government action to restrict the influence of the rich and to increase the competence of the poor.

RADICAL DEMOCRACY
(a) Market systems lead to inequalities which are unjust.
(b) Democratic processes enable the poor to promote justice politically.
(c) There is a contradiction, in liberal systems, between the demand for justice, which the poor can register through democratic channels, and the requirements for economic efficiency under capitalism. These systems are constantly in crisis, therefore, as the demand for welfare leads to economic recession, which leads, in turn, to a call for the withdrawal of welfare, which allows injustice to emerge, which, in turn, leads to a renewal of the call for more welfare.

There is not much one can say about the possessive individualist model, apart from the points already made: its fundamental concept of justice is unacceptable, and its ideal of the state as a protection agency is Utopian.

Rawlsian individualism, on the other hand, offers a far more challenging defence of liberal democratic institutions. This is because Rawls attempts to marry liberal economic theory with a real concern for justice (correctly conceived as an egalitarian commitment). He holds strongly to the view that market systems in the economic sphere can provide a better means of encouraging production and initiative than other forms of resource allocation, and he seems to have conceived it as the best strategy, in caring about the circumstances of the poorest groups in society, to try to give them a share of the affluence generated by capitalism. He argues that any massive accumulation of social resources in the hands of a few monopolies can be prevented by means of a system of progressive taxation, and especially by estate levies, which help continually to redistribute wealth more widely. Despite these correctives, Rawls suggests that the advantages which economic theorists believe to accrue as a result of market allocation may be retained.

It comes as no surprise that this kind of liberal theory reflects the crisis of our present predicament. The citizens of many formerly stable liberal systems now show a dangerous volatility in their political loyalties; according to whether they demand justice or efficiency, they swing to labour leaders who offer more welfare only to swing back to conservatives who hope to sustain the capitalist system. They do this, it seems, when they find that labour governments flounder in economic difficulties as a result of too high an expenditure on welfare. But the marketeers of the liberal conservative establishment, who present to the public an image of competence and responsibility, are unable to provide salvation at an acceptable cost, for it is quickly discovered that the consequences of their policies are such that they threaten workers with the dole and greatly reduced handouts. As the organized labour movement realizes this, it begins to confront the self-proclaimed guardians and protectors of the capitalist system. The chaos and strife which follows industrial unrest brings, in turn, a demand for the labour politicians – they at least understand the workers. The central contradiction of capitalism today arises, then, precisely because of the political strength of the labour movement, whose demand for justice undermines the functioning of capitalism.

As long as the economic system is based on an incentive requirement which is unjust, it will not be possible to correct for anomalies without precipating a crisis. This follows because where there is too much political interference in the economy the market will tend to react unfavourably and the resulting crisis (reflected in rising unemployment and inflation) will be likely to force the political retreat of the labour movement. It is not likely to retreat in total disarray, however, and the problem which liberal theorists have yet to face up to is that the victories of reformist labour governments are not easily dismantled. Thus, politicians are required, if they hope to be elected, to advocate welfare programmes on the one hand and cuts in government spending on the other. Even if free market advocates are correct in their assessment of what is needed for economic stimulation under capitalism, they are wrong to think that such policies could be put into effect without the coercion of the working class. It is just this contradiction that will eventually destroy liberal systems as we know them.

10
A Radical Conception of Law

If one believes, as radical individualists do, that 'justice' conceived as 'fairness' is a fundamental consideration which should guide our discussions of social and political issues, then one is likely to be attracted by an attitude to law which is very different from legal positivism. If one believes, moreover, that the basic political institutions of liberal societies are vitiated by the characteristic prevalence of private interests rather than concern for the public good, and that this is the result of the class basis of power, then one's inclination to appeal to 'justice' as the basis of authority will be reinforced. In this chapter and the one which follows I will be concerned to explore the implications which claims of this kind have for our conception of law. I shall suggest that what is characteristic of most liberal arguments about the nature of law are confusions about the conceptions of authority upon which their jurisprudence has been founded. For the most part liberals have attempted to describe institutions in a matter-of-fact way. We are required, even before discussing issues of political morality, to get clear in our minds precisely what the given legal and moral requirements in a community are. It is only when we are clear about these facts, it is suggested, that we can begin the process of assessment and evaluation. Bad law, according to this view, is still law, and it matters a good deal that this is, allegedly, the case.

As I show, particularly in the following chapter, this quest for an objective description of legal and moral duties (the positive morality and the actual law recognized in a community) can lead theorists to make serious errors of judgement. I shall recommend an alternative, radical conception of law as more compatible with democratic ideals than the liberal position analysed. My argument relies very much on the lead provided by Ronald Dworkin, who has shown how the radical individualist orientation outlined in earlier chapters has implications within the field of jurisprudence.

This chapter will serve to prepare the way for the objectives outlined above. I will be concerned primarily to analyse an attitude to authority which has been fundamental within liberal political theory. The view I have in mind can be traced back to Thomas Hobbes, who was the first great political writer to link authority with the need for a method of reaching decisions which are public (in the sense that everyone is bound by them). I shall call this position the *auctor* view[1] and will take Professor H. L. A. Hart, whose *The Concept of Law* provides perhaps the most able defence of this view,[2] as a modern exponent for detailed discussion. I begin with an exposition of the *auctor* view as it emerges in Hart's work.

Authority

It is well known that Hart has a great respect for the utilitarians Jeremy Bentham and John Austin. He is in full agreement with their desire to expose the law to the critical scrutiny of a utilitarian assessment. But although an admirer of this aspiration, Hart is a stern critic of the conceptual limitations of their attempt to develop a positivist theory of law. In particular, he launches a formidable attack against what we may call their 'gunman account' of political and legal obligation. This conception focuses on the coercive nature of legal rules and identifies what the law requires by reference to the likelihood of a sanction: where there is no threat, there is no law. Hart argues that the 'gunman account' is too crude to provide an adequate basis for jurisprudence. The problems, put briefly, are that it misrepresents the way in which behaviour in society is regulated, in so far as it ignores the extent to which people voluntarily do what they are told because they think it is right (that is, because they recognize authority); it fails to account for the way in which we speak about obligations, in that it confuses 'being obliged' with 'being under an obligation'. These difficulties, Hart tells us, require that we provide some account of the normative element in authority, for we need to postulate something like Hans Kelsen's *Grundnorm* if we are to make sense of bureaucratic behaviour.[3]

Hart is most unhappy with talk about norms, however, for he thinks that this misleadingly implies some connection between law and morality. While he recognizes the fact that in connection with most institutional practices people, and particularly officials, defer to and acknowledge authority, he points out that they do this for a number of different and often conflicting reasons, or even without reflection. Talk about norms is confusing, Hart tells us, because it conjures up the notion of moral approval and blurs the different reasons why people recognize authority. He goes so far as to claim: 'There is indeed no reason why those who accept the authority of the system (legal) should not examine their conscience and decide that, morally, they ought not to accept it, yet for a variety of reasons continue to do so.'[4] Those who pay taxes to totalitarian governments or petition officials in the name of social justice are presumably in this position. Their actions clearly show that they acknowledge the special status of those who impose the tax or who are asked to change the laws. This, in some sense at least, is a recognition of the authority of the officials and the government by whom they are appointed.

The argument which Hart poses so forcefully in his *The Concept of Law*, in opposition to those who wish to account for the authority of law in terms of the postulate that communities share a political morality, rests in part on his claim that authority, and indeed even legitimacy, are not necessarily concepts which operate against a background of moral theory. Evidence for what we might call a neutral conception of authority can be found, he argues, by observing practices such as games. We can observe that a scorer in cricket has no authority to declare a player out, and that in chess it is not possible to move a piece which exposes the king to attack. These kinds of example are interesting because they show that authority is often acknowledged without reference to standards we would normally call moral; also, they indicate that the concept may be explicable in terms of a system of rules. The rules of chess or cricket are not moral, but they nevertheless define a practice in terms of which 'rights', 'obligations' and 'privileges' are allocated. It is a short step from this observation to the claim that the bothersome fact that people often obey an authority voluntarily can be explained in terms of some rule or system of rules which they recognize and follow. The occurrence of authority within the framework of games and other practices indicates that the concept may best be understood in relation to the rules which govern these kinds of activity.

The above account is too simple to do justice to Hart's position, for in his view not all rules can give rise to authority. Indeed, it may be argued that where rules defining rights and duties are generally recognized there is no need for authority at all. Children can invent games for themselves; they can even agree to be bound by the rules and can often play without much trouble. It is only when disputes arise or are likely to arise that there is any need for authority. We do not need to appoint an umpire when we play tennis socially, although it is usual for players to agree to be bound by the judgement of a third party when competition is particularly fierce or when reputations are at stake.

In his discussion of legal authority Hart shows that only a very simple community could survive without an authority (in the sense of adjudicator). He points out in this regard that it is often necessary to set up procedures for settling doubts about what the rules of a community are. This can be done either by reference to some text, recognized by all as authoritative, or by accepting that the declarations and judgements of some appointed official will be final. A second reason why an authority is needed is that we often find it expedient to make changes to the rules which govern practices in social life. Children can change the rules of their particular version of hopscotch as they hop along, but it is much more difficult for a community to adapt its rules in a similarly informal way. Procedures are required in terms of which it is recognized that rules will be promulgated; it is necessary, then, for most communities to recognize an authority which has the power to make and change the rules. Further, it is often the case that a community finds it necessary to appoint some person or body to determine whether or not there has been a violation of the rules and whose judgement is final.

These considerations enable Hart to give an account of legal authority along the following lines. We can say that when people accept rules as a guide for conduct it is often necessary for them to recognize rules about rules, and it is these secondary rules (I use Hart's terminology) which establish authority, for they determine how the other rules may be ascertained, introduced, eliminated or varied. These secondary rules also determine how violations of the rules can be conclusively ascertained, and they normally stipulate what punishments may be imposed on offenders. Most rule-governed practices involve recognition of secondary rules of this kind, and we can say, therefore, that wherever conduct in any reasonably complex community is regulated by rules, there must be some recognition of authority. This, Hart tells us, is part of what is meant by a system of rules.

We are now in a position to see why Hart is able to claim that the recognition of legal authority in no way implies a conceptual link between morality and law. For Hart, all that is involved in the notion of legal authority is that 'rules of recognition specifying the criteria of legal validity and its rules of change and adjudication must be effectively accepted as common public standards of official behaviour by its officials'.[5] Naturally, if we are to talk about the existence of a legal system, it is necessary that 'those rules of behaviour which are valid according to the system's ultimate criteria must be generally obeyed'. But this obedience can result from any motive including fear; what is authoritative is determined by the rules and is not adequately accounted for either by reference to the motives for obedience or by prediction about what is likely to happen.

According to Hart, then, authority is important for at least two reasons. First, we need an author for the rules which define our social relations (secondary rules must specify who is authorized to make rules). Second, we need clarity about the scope of rules and judgements which can settle finally whether or not there has been a violation of the rules. In both these areas authority provides finality. Once it has been settled that a rule has been validly *auctored* in terms of the secondary rules, no further questions about its authority can arise. Of course, some person or agency has to decide whether any particular rule has the right pedigree, and this is one of the reasons why courts are sometimes held to be quasi-legislatures. In terms of Hart's account, courts have no authority to overrule a legislature, provided that the pedigree of a rule is clear; they do themselves become *auctors*, however, when they settle questions about the scope of particular rules. This legislative activity of courts is restricted to that penumbral area of vagueness left by what Hart calls the 'open texture' of rules. The notion of authority involved here requires that we think of an authority as an *auctor* — that is, as a figure or a body which makes declarations that either establish standards or serve as an adjudication where there are disputes. Authorities, in this sense, will be effective if their decisions are accepted simply because it is *they* who have declared and not because their judgements are wise or correct; an authority in the *auctor* conception operates, then, within a system of rules which specifies who has the right to make declarations which are binding on all.

The *auctor* view of authority outlined, using Hart's work as an example, is very strikingly Hobbesian. The central problem for Hobbes is to determine when one person's choices may be limited by those of another. It is because he believes that the subjective nature of evaluation could, if unchecked, lead to a war between everyman and everyman that he urges the creation of Leviathan. Hobbes is concerned to limit the area of human freedom for the paradoxical reason that it is only in this way that the certainty with which individuals can predict, and so plan their lives, can be increased.

Hobbes is right to see that the *auctor* conception of authority involves a form of absolutism: it involves the denial of the right of individuals to evaluate the reasons which may be given in support of judgements about our obligations (which is not to deny them the right to criticize the choices which the *auctor* makes). The difficulties with Hobbes's position arise because his premises are not acceptable; there is, however, nothing logically wrong with his argument. If value relativism did present a threat to our lives and the security of our property in the way that Hobbes supposes, given that we regard these as important, then the suggestions that we forgo any natural right we may have to make individual judgements and to act on these, and that we accept the will of an *auctor* as binding (provided, of course, that others do the same), become persuasive. Luckily, not all of us view the world from Hobbes's pessimistic perspectives; far from finding value relativism intolerable, we may even welcome disagreements. Few believe today that free choice, even when unbridled, will necessarily lead to anarchy of the kind that Hobbes fears, and most of us are prepared, consequently, to treat Hobbes's worst fears as groundless.

But while the Hobbesian argument for the *auctor* conception of authority is not persuasive, his analysis is coherent. In particular, he has no difficulty in relating authority, in the *auctor* sense, to the claims of moral standards and principles traditionally respected as natural law. He tells us, in this regard, that where the *auctor* is silent, one has to fall back on natural law (everyone, including judges, is bound by natural law unless and until the 'declarer' has provided a clear guide to the contrary). Unlike Hart, for example (who, as we have seen, believes that if the *auctor* is silent, then the judges have discretion to declare), Hobbes goes so far as to say that the claims of natural law are so compelling that each successive sovereign must be treated as unique, and that it must be assumed that he or she will support natural law unless there is an explicit declaration against the standard. Hobbes goes on to argue that no sovereign can be bound by the decisions of a predecessor, and that it must be assumed by lawyers and judges that each respects natural justice. Hobbes is able to take this position only because his reasoning elevates the *auctor* above morality (the exception occurs, as might be expected, when the sovereign actually threatens the life of his or her subjects).

Other theorists who accept the *auctor* conception of authority are not prepared to follow Hobbes's lead at this point; consequently, they have had difficulty in accounting for the part which extra-legal standards play in the processes of legal argument and deliberation. The problem is to keep separate the roles of legislator (who has authority to *auctor* establishing law) and adjudicator (who is authorized to make declarations about what the law requires). In most cases courts are concerned with adjudication, and the role of the judge is to declare what the court takes to be the will of the legislative authority. In some circumstances, however, it may not be clear precisely what is intended by a rule, and here a judge may often have to assume a legislative role, for in declaring what the law requires he or she determines the meaning which is to be placed on the *auctor's* words — its application to particular circumstances. Posivists tell us that in hard cases, in which what is intended by a rule in a particular application is unclear, a judge is bound by no legal considerations and thus assumes an *auctor* role.

This particular view of law, and the account of discretion which it entails, has been challenged by Dworkin, who claims that it rests on a particular conception of discretion which, once it has been exposed by means of conceptual analysis, will be rejected by democrats. The root of the problem here lies in the connection between authority and discretion, for the two concepts are closely related, and one cannot give an account of the one without at the same time committing oneself to a conception of the other. This follows, as Dworkin tells us, from the fact that when we talk about discretion we need to take into account the 'background of understood information against which it is used', He tells us that 'discretion, like the hole in a doughnut, does not exist except as an area left open by a surrounding belt of restrictions'. It is at home in such contexts as 'when someone is in general charged with making decisions subject to standards set by a particular context'. Dworkin tells us that we use the term discretion in at least three different ways, which are worth distinguishing and bearing in mind: we use it when we are referring to the fact that officials are required to use their own judgement and are not restricted specifically by their instructions (sense 1), when we wish to make clear that an official's decisions are final (sense 2) and when we wish to indicate that an official is not bound by standards (sense 3). Illustrating the differences between these three senses, Dworkin tells us that in the third sense outlined we say that a sergeant has discretion who has been told to pick any five men for patrol he chooses or that a judge at a dog show has discretion to judge airedales before boxers if the rules do not stipulate an order of events. We use this sense not to comment on the vagueness or difficulty of the standards, or on who has the final word in applying them, but on their range and the decisions they purport to control. If the sergeant is told to take the five most experienced men, he does not have discretion in the strong sense because that order purports to govern his decision. The boxing referee who must decide which fighter has been the more aggressive does not have discretion, in the strong sense, for the same reason.[6]

My interest in the conceptual links between authority and discretion relates to the fact that the two are easily confused. The fact that the boxing referee has discretion, in the sense that his decision as to who is the most aggressive fighter will be accepted as final (sense 2), does not mean that he has authority to come to any decision he likes (sense 3). But positivists often talk as though finality implied a freedom to choose of the kind reflected in Dworkin's sense 3. Richard Peters, for example, writes in a well-known article: 'The term "authority" is essential to those contexts where a pronouncement, decision or command must be accepted because some person, conforming to specifications laid down by the normative system, has made or gives it — where there is a recognised 'auctor'.[7] This is the Hobbesian conception of authority and is linked with Dworkin's sense 3 discretion, in which finality is not bounded by standards. In fact, we seldom find that officials are authorized to exercise discretion in this sense, and yet positivist writers often define law in this way (as in the slogans 'law is the command of the sovereign' and 'law is what the courts say it is'). Claims of this kind are only plausible where we can show discretion in the strong sense 3 distinguished by Dworkin. But courts surely do not have such unbounded discretion; nor, for that matter, do legislative bodies, for there are limits to what will be acceptable as law — unless we accept Hobbes's arguments for an absolute sovereign. In fact, even when this strong sense of discretion is acknowledged in practice (and, as I say, this is not very common), the contextual background usually limits the area narrowly, as in Dworkin's example of the judge who has discretion to judge airedales before boxers at the dog show. The strong sense of discretion which applies in this case does not extend to the more important task of evaluating the dogs, and we should be careful, when analysing this kind of case, to keep the senses of discretion involved distinct. The distinctions are particularly relevant when we are discussing judicial discretion, for positivists who argue that judges have discretion in the strong sense (who claim, that is, that moral standards do not apply) often moderate the impact of this view — which, taken in itself, appears to be unacceptable — by allowing that judges also have a moral (as distinct from a legal) duty to act responsibly. The *auctor* view, then, seems to be acceptable only as long as we are satisfied that judges will act in ways of which we approve. Indeed, it would seem that positivists really want things both ways, for they want to analyse judicial discretion in the strong *auctor* sense, and yet they also want to claim that moral standards are relevant.

Authority seems to be linked with standards, purposes and principles, which form the background to institutional life; whereas discretion is linked with questions relating to the procedures for decision-making: 'Who is to decide?', 'Is the decision final?' are questions typically about discretion rather than authority, but 'What is the point of deference to X's judgement?', 'In terms of what standards ought the decision to be made?' are typically concerned with authority. In the case of discretion in the strong sense 3, what is significant is the act of decision itself: 'Choose any five men.' We may appropriately blur authority and discretion in these cases (as Hobbes does); this should not be done when we are dealing with discretion in sense 1 and 2, however, because standards and purposes hover in the background — 'Choose your most experienced and reliable men' involves judgement to be sure, but it does not establish who is reliable and experienced simply by virtue of the sergeant's choice (we are free to tell him that be has made the wrong decision).

I mention the conceptual connections between authority and discretion because, as I have said, they are often confused by those who hold *auctor* views about authority. As Dworkin shows in his criticism of the assumptions of positivist jurisprudence, as long as we are talking about the discretion of courts (and even of parliaments), and as long as we resist attributing discretion in sense 3 to these institutions (that is, as long as we resist the Hobbesian argument for absolutism), we must recognise that standards and values will restrict the area of discretion by bringing a moral dimension into discusions about the scope of authority. Hobbes evades this consequence because he provides arguments to show that *finality of decision* is an overriding value; he is able to do this, however, only because he deals exclusively with discretion in the strong sense 3. In Hobbes's *Leviathan* individuals are prepared to recognise that the sovereign's authority entails discretion in the strong sense 3 because they value peace above all else, and also because they accept that any diminution of the sovereign's discretion could lead to conflict and even to social anarchy. Their obligation is nullified, however, if the sovereign proves incapable of providing security. But *Leviathan* is no exception, for all our institutions have point and purpose, and this is precisely why individuals are often prepared to accept rules as obligatory. We cannot, then, comprehend human institutions simply by listing the rules. This applies even to games, which are not the analytical consstructs which Professor Hart sometimes encourages us to suppose. Can we claim that someone who knows the rules of chess understands the game? Surely not. For we only comprehend what the rules are about when we understand that they are to govern our play — there is a difference between knowing *how* we may move the chessmen and knowing *why* we ought to move them. People who thought chess was a complicated kind of aptitude test, for example, would hardly enjoy the game; they would treat every gambit as a special kind of challenge (a test to expose their caution or aggression, for example), and even if they had mated their opponent, they would not know whether they had fared well or badly. They certainly would not think they had won.

These points are important, for it is clear that Hart's *auctor* account of authority in terms of a system of rules fails to provide for important limitations which our different conceptions of the point and purpose of any particular practice places on those who wield authority. Why ought courts to recognize that they are bound by the rules enacted by a legislature? Presumably because we do not extend to courts the authority to make rules or to disregard the principle of legislative supremacy, except under very special circumstances. But if courts are bound by the limitations of their authority, why not hold that legislatures are similarly bound? If we are to think clearly in this area, we must bear in mind that discussion about what the law requires cannot be divorced from the wider debate about the nature of the democratic commitment. We cannot settle by way of precise definition the relations between legislative and judicial branches of government, and any adequate theory of jurisprudence must include also a theory of the democratic commitment.

It is because we are usually so closely in agreement about the point and purpose of authority in the context of games that they provide such good examples for the *auctor* view of law. In most games the point of granting authority is to get a decision in cases there there is likely to be disagreement. The ball is either in or out, and someone must decide if the game is to go on and the score to be counted. In this sense the umpire's decision is said to be final, and this is so even when (as is the case sometimes when we watch replays on television) we know that a particular decision is wrong. The need for finality and authority are, however, often tenuously linked even in this context, for we also require umpires to be fair and accurate. If he or she persistently makes mistakes the point of having an adjudicator is lost. In the context of games, therefore, we are often uncertain about whether discretion is being used in sense 1 or sense 3. Although games could probably be played even if officials were extremely bad at making the kind of decision we expect of them, this may not be the case in other areas of life, where the discretion granted involves more serious issues, for we would be more reluctant to allow that anyone has discretion in sense 3. In such contexts it becomes imperative that officials exercise authority responsibly, and it would be wrong of them to assume the kind of arbitrary power reflected in the strong sense 3 of discretion; we must, therefore, be extremely wary of political theories (such as the *auctor* view of the nature of law) which are premised on the assumption that what is significant in political life is that some officials confer finality on an issue.

Radical and Liberal Conceptions of Law

It is important to see how conceptions of authority are linked with theories about the nature of law. In this regard it is worth noting that Hart's reason for developing his neutral account of legal authority, as analogous to the conception of authority often found in games, is precisely that he believes that this will promote clear thinking in a way which best allows us to bring into action a critical liberal framework. Hart seeks a way of establishing what the law is which is free from ambiguities, so that it can be more easily exposed to critical scrutiny. It is for this reason that he treats authority as morally neutral. If Hart embraces Hobbes's *auctor* view, it is not because he is authoritarian but because he has no moral respect for authority *per se*. This attitude is, of course, also reflected in the work of the classical utilitarians, and until quite recently some form of positivism has been widely accepted by most lawyers and philosophers of law as the most sensible approach. What positivists are concerned with is the establishment of the objectivity of law, and they believe that this can best be accomplished by keeping political and moral arguments out of the legal arena. They claim also that their approach clarifies issues in moral argument because facts about our legal duties must be significant when we are deliberating about our moral duties (they are relevant because it makes a difference to the *morality* of what we do — so, at least, it is argued). If we decide to ignore rules and regulations promulgated by a political authority, no matter how respectable our reasons might be, it still remains a fact, it is claimed, that we are ignoring our legal duties. Positivists argue that it does not promote clear thinking, nor is it theoretically useful, to pretend that legal duties which are ignored are somehow not there. It is suggested that unless we keep separate the questions 'What ought I to do?' and 'What does the law require me to do?' we are liable to confuse many situations in which policy choices have to be made.[8]

In recent years positivism has been challenged, and theorists like Dworkin have developed an alternative approach to discussions about law which reflects the more accurate appreciation of the relations between authority and discretion which we have discussed above. According to this account, which can be characterized as a secularized natural law approach, the question of legality is of such crucial significance that we cannot possibly presume to judge our duties without bringing to bear a wide range of political and moral considerations (although, as I show in the next chapter, these often counsel an attitude towards promulgated rules which is not very different from that of conventional jurisprudence). However, when issues of democratic importance are at stake, as in situations in which citizens claim that they have an entitlement which conflicts with what government officials are prepared to concede, it is crucial that the ideals which provide the point and purpose for social co-operation should inform any public decision about what the law requires. The question of legal duty, then, should never be settled in this kind of case unless there is agreement over these considerations. Moral values and political principles are seen to be relevant to our legal calculations, and we cannot presume to formulate the law (what we believe that citizens owe as a duty to society) without considering our idealized conception of the nature of political association. What is distinctive about this kind of view, which is offered as an alternative to positivism, is that the *auctor* conception of authority is said to be unacceptable in political life: those in political and legal office need adequately to justify their decisions before we can accept their declarations as authoritative.

The debate about law and its relation to democratic theory has been brought more sharply into focus in modern times by documents which embody internationally recognized standards of humanity, principles and political ideals. I refer to agreements like the Geneva Convention, the Declaration of Human Rights embodied in the United Nations Charter and the precedents set by the Nuremberg Tribunal. The liberal positivists argue that the ideals of political civility reflected in these declarations and commitments are not properly part of the debate about legal duties within nation states. In their view, we should first decide the law before considering our wider duties in the light of any commitment we might, as democrats, make to these ideals. Natural law theorists, on the other hand, are greatly impressed by these documents because they articulate standards which are widely shared by people of good will. Furthermore, the nations who have signed these declarations have made their commitments clear. In this regard Americans have been able to point to the additional fact that some of these standards are protected by the Constitution of the United States. It is partly for this reason that the principle of judicial review has become an accepted part of the institutional practice in that country. The United States is not, of course, the only country where there is an entrenched Bill of Rights, but it is with regard to that country particularly that there has been a major debate about the role that such protections should play within the political practice of a democracy. Although there is not settled opinion about the role of moral standards within the American system, the Supreme Court has been forced, nevertheless, to interpret the import of these rights. This has meant that positivists in the United States have had to recognize that a political and moral dimension is relevant to the deabte about the nature and function of the law.

Because the American Supreme Court has played a significant role in the debate, natural law conceptions do seem to be more obviously applicable as descriptions of the way in which lawyers and judges have thought about the law in that country. Ironically, however, most lawyers and legal theorists have held to their positivist conceptions, which they have sometimes defended by suggesting that law can be satisfactorily defined as 'what the courts say it is'. The idea here is that the Supreme Court is granted the right of final review; that is, its interpretation of the Constitution puts an end to any debate there may be about what the law requires in controversial cases. Positivists tell us that the basis for interpretation must, of course, be traceable to what is specified in the written document, and that as a matter of policy the court ought to narrow its area of discretion, for it has no authority to rewrite the national commitment. The finality of the court's judgement does mean, however, that we can get clear advice from lawyers, for they can acquire the skill necessary to predict judgements; in this way, then, 'what the law requires' emerges and is placed beyond dispute.

Radical democrats have been unhappy with this statement of the peculiarities of American legal practice. Their suggestion is that courts may well be wrong in interpreting the national commitment, and that in forming their opinions they will, in any case, have to draw on principles and ideals which are claimed to be part of the democratic commitment. The process here is said to be one of persuasion and reasoned argument, and it is in this sense that the debate about what the law requires is said to be open-ended, for radical democrats tell us not to accept that any court can have the final word: it may be wrong about the law. In terms of this conception, then, judgement is often a matter of supporting arguments through the citation of ideals and principles which are embodied in national commitments like international agreements or reflected in the precedents set by prestigious tribunals and courts. What the radical lawyer insists on is that this aspect of the debate about law be recognized, and that we should acknowledge that wider standards have a proper place in legal debate.[9] We should also recognize that what the courts say does not necessarily put an an end to the matter, and that persons of good will and serious democratic commitment may still find reason to question the propriety of argued judgements. There are correct answers to questions about law, but we cannot rely on anyone to come up with them.

11
Disobedience and the Rule of Law

It is important to see how the two views about the nature of law outlined in the last chapter play their parts within the debate about the democratic commitment. The legal positivist orientation encourages an emphasis on the moral significance of institutional facts. The claim that facts about the law are relevant to policy choices fits in with prevailing liberal accounts of the democratic commitment: if the institutional system, as constituted by the rules in terms of which political claims are regulated, allows for procedures whereby citizens can lawfully influence government, then, provided also there is no discrimination against certain sections of the population, the system is held to be democratic and there is a presumed political obligation to respect the law. When liberal theorists talk about democracy in this way, they mean primarily that politics is conducted within a framework of legality which guarantees fair competition for the right to govern.[1] Accordingly, when faced with any constitution we may ask, 'Is the basic framework such that political equality is respected?' When this requirement is met, even if one disagrees with the law (that is, if one believes that it is clearly unjust or bad), in terms of the justificatory theory one has a political duty of obedience which arises out of the very nature of the institutions.

Clearly, the liberal argument here depends on the assumption that one can describe one's legal duties in an objective way. We must be able to say, 'This institutional system, as constituted by the following rules of procedure N to N_1, is democratic.' Where this is the case rules promulgated in terms of these democratic procedures carry a special moral obligation because in a democracy *they are the law*. The obligation here follows not from any condition inherent in the legal system but, rather, from a theory of democracy. In the case of liberal apologetics such a theory usually takes the form of utilitarian arguments or, in some cases, involves an appeal to the notion of a social contract.

John Rawls has provided the most adequate alternative model by developing a theory of justice which generates principles which are then used to assess given institutional structures. Actually, Rawls's position on the nature of political obligation is complex, for he argues that the grounds for an obligation are not that institutions are just but that we have a natural duty to support and uphold such institutions. Thus, we reason in two stages: first, we ask whether a particular set of institutions is just and, second, we derive our sense of duty by reference to natural law. It is, however, significant that even in Rawls's theory justice is something external to legality, and we are required to assess institutional systems separately — apart, that is, from any assessment we might make of particular laws. His position here is not dissimilar to that of rule utilitarians, who wish to discuss the utility of practices such as promising or punishing apart from any assessment of the consequences which might be thought to follow from breaking particular promises or punishing individuals in specific circumstances. For Rawls a set of institutional rules may be perfectly just, yet particular rules may be unjust. It is a central claim, thought to be of great significance within liberal theories of democracy, that fundamentally fair institutional processes can in some circumstances give rise to undesirable consequences. Rawls and other liberals such as Sidney Hook believe that it is a gross mistake, characteristic of much radical political theory, to slide over this paradox in discussing the problem of political obligation; they argue that we have a moral obligation to obey an unjust law in a democracy. This duty may, however, give way in certain special circumstances in which civil disobedience is appropriate.[2]

The radical individualist orientation which I characterized in Chapter 10 as embracing a natural law perspective denies that one can reduce the democratic commitment to a purely formal recognition of the authority of the rules which are promulgated in accordance with a desirable set of procedures. On this account, social and political justice are so closely interrelated that the question of obligation cannot be settled by looking at the nature of institutions; it must take into account a wider perspective which has as its base some conception of the primary purpose of political co-operation. Mere promulgation which ignores these underlying purposes, no matter how fair the procedures, can never give rise to an obligation.

Obligation and Civility – the Liberal View

It is not surprising that liberal and radical conceptions of law have given rise to sharply conflicting descriptions of the nature of democratic civility. In this section I will be concerned to outline the liberal positivist viewpoint. I shall compare and defend the radical individualist conception of civility in the following section.

For the liberal, as we have seen, the crucial question in relation to democratic systems is not *whether* one may oppose government but *how*: it is the law which proscribes and entitles in this area.[3] Citizens have the right to act politically, so that they may play an effective and equal role in the political competition which characterizes liberal forms of government. There are, of course, some serious problems relating to the issue of the extent to which citizens' rights should be protected by the courts: does the right of free speech entitle citizens to shout 'Fire!' in a crowded cinema, or may the government restrict the right when there is a clear and imminent danger? Does the right to dissent protect those whose actions are not altogether orderly and peaceful? What if the disorder which accompanies a demonstration is provoked by a hostile audience? These questions have been relevant to the kind of case which the American Supreme Court has had to adjudicate in recent years. Despite these penumbral issues, however, the framework of liberal legality rests on very clear assumptions about the nature of democratic civility and, ideally, excludes the possibility of political advantage. With regard to basic civil rights, the requirement is absolute equality. The liberal commitment is to a system in which all citizens, rich and poor, workers and president, stand equal before the law. In this regard a liberal commitment to democratic order must tolerate dissent and the give and take of conflict politics. But the law has a duty to arbitrate so that there should be no privileged citizens, for no one must be able to abrogate the rights which others might claim.

It is, of course, primarily governments which are seen to be bridled by the framework of legality. Political leaders are notoriously tempted to treat their opponents without due process. Police officers too are often tempted, in the firm belief that their suspects are guilty, to treat them as though they had no right to procedural protections. However, these orientations are strongly condemned by liberal writers, who are never slow to remind us that the great miracle of democratic systems is that they require officers of the state to account for their actions before the law. Officials in a democracy in which the 'rule of law' is respected may take action against citizens only in ways sanctioned by the procedural rules. In the political area the limitations on government and police action may be very extensive: officers of the law, for example, usually have a duty to protect protesters even when they are hostile to the views which the latter propagate; they are also limited in the methods they may use to gather evidence of criminal activity and are required to charge people whom they have apprehended or to release them within a given period. In these and countless other ways the state is itself answerable to the law.

For liberals (and, indeed, all reasonable people) the requirement that political authority be subservient to law is of very great significance. The political implications of this claim were well illustrated by the debate over the involvement of the United States in Vietnam. Some prominent legal scholars (Dworkin, for example), as well as many of those who were active politically in opposing the American involvement, argued that the fighting of an undeclared war and the use of selective conscription as a means of recruitment was in breach of the rights of citizens as these are recognized in and protected by the Constitution.[4] The claim was at least debatable, for among other legal considerations which were cited it was shown that the war was not properly declared in the way required by the Constitution (the Senate had never been asked to ratify the presidential decision to commit the United States to the war). The Constitution also clearly states that the government may not discriminate between citizens without reasonable grounds, and it was argued by many observers at the time that the way in which the draft was administered placed an undue burden on some groups.

It is worth emphasizing, in this context, that the Supreme Court was not asked to declare whether or not the United States was justifiably involved in Vietnam. This would have constituted a political question, more properly settled by other branches of government. The Court was asked, rather, to declare how such an involvement could lawfully be undertaken in terms of the procedures and principles which constitute the American system. By pretending that it had no authority in this area, when it was clearly required to decide in terms of the principle of judicial review, the Supreme Court avoided not only a legal but also a moral duty. The reason for hesitation here (that congressional debate of an issue over which there were marked differences of opinion would have taken time and could have interfered with the efficient conduct of the war to which the nation was already committed) was of a political nature. Thus, by using it as an excuse for not tackling the legal issues, the Court was itself effectively settling the political dispute in favour of the war. In this respect, then, the judges were party to the presidential abnegation of the 'rule of law'.

In retrospect this whole episode may well be reviewed as a blatant and hypocritical retreat from standards of civility which are almost universally shared by the people of the United States, whatever their political persuasion. There are few, indeed, who would argue that a government may retreat from requirements embodied in the Constitution. Even if one were to claim that a government could justifiably act in breach of constitutional norms in times of imminent danger to the community, it would be difficult to show that a distant Asian war actually represented such a threat.

The purpose of raising the Vietnam controversy here is to illustrate how a commitment to the rule of law may be said to place a government under obligation to citizens. Many would regard this case as rather too controversial to serve as a useful example for study; those, for example, who were in favour of the American commitment to the war may resent my claim that the involvement was both undemocratic and illegal. This kind of questioning is not in itself undesirable, however, for part of my purpose has been to show that the issues surrounding the notion of the 'rule of law' are often extremely significant politically. It matters a great deal how we think about these questions.

If we leave the matter of government obligation to act within the framework of legality and consider the relationship between citizens and the law, we face some difficult issues. The problem is that no matter how strictly we may wish to view the requirement that governments act lawfully, hardly anyone is prepared to argue that ordinary citizens have such an absolute duty. One important consideration to bear in mind here is that citizens are not in the same position as governments with regard to the possibility of changing the law. Some people in the community are at a clear disadvantage in political resources even when political rights are protected, and this makes it questionable whether we can argue by analogy that the duties of citizenship with respect to the law are similar to those of a government. Initiating political changes in a democracy often takes time and expertise as well as a capacity to influence. It also requires the ability to gain access to the media, so that one can communicate with a large number of citizens. If prominent personalities like Bertrand Russell have found it difficult to obtain a hearing for their points of view, especially when they have been competing with government departments,[5] the position must be far worse for those who are not already famous, especially if their issue is not a popular one. When governments break the law they are generally trying to evade available channels for changing the law, but when citizens break the law it is often because they have been frustrated in their attempts to put their case in an effective way.

Liberal theorists, for the most part, recognize the difficulties which citizens face when they attempt to act politically, and it is for this reason that they accept that in their efforts to achieve political objectives citizens often have much better reasons for breaking the law than do governments. Liberal theories of democratic civility, therefore, generally attempt to allow for a certain amount of civil disobedience on the part of citizens. Rawls, for example, has recognized that in some circumstances citizens may well be justified in breaking the law, and he has even gone so far as to argue that acts of disobedience may have a positive role to play within a democratic system: they can sometimes gain publicity for points of view which might otherwise be ignored. Liberals are, nevertheless, concerned to distinguish *civil* disobedience from other forms of disruptive behaviour, and they have been eager to spell out the requirements of democratic civility as these apply in cases in which citizens may be contemplating disobedience. They insist, in particular, that in a democracy we all have a duty to accept certain restraints, and that it is the recognition of these which makes for the difference between civil disobedience and other forms of law-breaking.

The notion of civil disobedience, then, is a peculiarly liberal conception. Only those who are fully convinced that there is something morally special about a given set of institutions and who conceptualize the democratic commitment in terms of a respect for procedural solutions (in the way I have outlined as typically liberal) are likely to talk about civil disobedience, as opposed to just plain disobedience. The core idea is that law-breaking can sometimes serve as a mechanism of last resort by which citizens who are very seriously disadvantaged with regard to conventional political channels and who feel intensely about issues can gain access to the media in order to demonstrate their concern to the wider public in a manner dramatic enough to make an impact.

We can best explore the liberal conception of civility in this area of law-breaking by considering what forms of disobedience would not be regarded by liberals as civil.[6]

CIVIL DISOBEDIENCE IS NOT RESISTANCE OR REVOLT
Those committed to democratic civility need to be distinguished, it is

argued, from those whose disobedience is simply a manifestation of revolt against a government or a law. The features of the situation which are thought to be important here can best be highlighted by considering whether civil disobedience is possible in systems which are not liberal democracies. For example, Gandhi's passive resistance in India or the bus boycotts which took place in Johannesburg, South Africa, resulted from circumstances which had prompted large numbers of people to adopt an attitude of defiance. These campaigns of resistance were aimed, however, at achieving specific political or economic goals. Similarly, the riots in the Polish docks during the Christmas of 1971, which contributed to the downfall of Gomulka, or the riots in Johannesburg's Soweto in 1976 are also cases of revolt provoked by grievances. In this kind of case a population is terrorized to such a degree that the only resources available to it are either riot, as an expression of extreme anger, or the withdrawal of co-operation, as a manifestation of controlled resentment at an injustice. What makes many liberals hesitate to call these cases acts of civil disobedience is the attitude of those involved in disruptions of the system of government. Liberals distinguish civility from defiance when an attempt is made to take a more effective part in political processes which are respected in themselves. The civil disobedient wishes not to see the system changed but merely to gain publicity in order to put a point of view to the public. Disobedience, according to the liberal view, is a way of showing that dissidents are prepared to make personal sacrifices to this end and not a means of forcing a desired policy on others through violence or a disruptive refusal to co-operate. Liberals argue, in this regard, that those who disobey the law in a democracy should never try to avoid punishment but should, rather, choose to accept whatever suffering is involved as an additional means of showing that they really care.

CIVIL DISOBEDIENCE IS NOT DISRUPTION

Most instances of passive resistance are directed at bringing society to a standstill. The idea is to withdraw co-operation until certain demands are met. Thus the intention is to use the power to disrupt (through strikes, for example) in order to ensure a particular outcome. A well-known case of this kind of tactic was the Stop the Tour Campaign, directed at isolating South Africans from international sporting activities. The intention, in the United Kingdom and other countries, was to make it outrageously expensive and politically difficult for governments to allow South African sportsmen to tour; a minority which, for very justifiable reasons, was concerned about the plight of people in a distant country aimed to impose its will on the majority. Activists in the United Kingdom and, to some extent, in Australia succeeded in forcing a change in policy relating to South Africa through disruptive pressure.

According to Sidney Hook — and his views on this point are typical — disruptive activity of the kind adopted by the Stop the Tour campaigners is not civil because it does not adequately defer to majority rule as the basic principle of representative government.[7] In Hook's view, if the disobedients are to act in a way which can be regarded as civil, they should only break the law in a manner which does not put a stop to the lawful activities of other citizens. (In the case of the Stop the Tour Campaign it would have been tolerably civil for the disobedients to hold a sit-in on the field while play was not in progress, or to trespass in order to publicize their concern, but the tactic of disrupting games in progress showed little regard for what liberals regard as democratic civility.)

CIVIL DISOBEDIENCE IS NOT CONSCIENTIOUS OBJECTION

In a liberal society one of the fundamental virtues of citizenship is tolerance: governments are required to leave individuals free to pursue their value commitments in their own way as long as this is compatible with the liberty of others. As a consequence, there are often people who, when confronted by specific laws, find that in terms of their own values (their conscience) it would be wrong for them to comply with the requirements. If they disobey for this kind of reason, we talk about conscientious objection. What distinguishes this kind of disobedience from civil disobedience, according to the liberal view, is that it often has no political purpose. They argue that unless disobedience is part of a strategy of persuasion, it is misleading to classify such an act as civil, according to the democratic conception of the term.

CIVIL DISOBEDIENCE IS NOT THE AVOIDANCE OF WHAT THE LAW REQUIRES

Clearly, the ordinary criminal who is trying to get away with some deal outside the law is not a civil disobedient. There are cases, however (such as that of draft-resisters in Australia and the United States, who used their ability to avoid apprehension by the police as a dramatic way of publicizing their opposition to the recent war in Vietnam), which are much more controversial and difficult to dismiss as merely criminal. Liberals, although they agree that the point of civil disobedience is publicity, do not approve of law-dodging as a method of achieving that objective.

They argue that in a democracy acts of disobedience should be not expressions of defiance but appeals to the sense of humanity and justice of fellow citizens, and that one cannot discredit the police and still claim to be civil. If citizens evade lawful authority by hiding, it is argued, they are like tax-evaders, for they frustrate the law to no purpose which can be regarded as being in the public good. The added publicity to be gained by remaining at large, it is suggested, does not justify the contempt with which this kind of activity treats the lawful authorities; disobedients who resist arrest end up as mere criminals, according to this conception of civility.

CIVIL DISOBEDIENCE IS NOT TESTING THE LAW
It is sometimes the case, when disobedients are taken to court, that the law is deemed not to have been broken after all. Blacks arrested for entering segregated premises in America's southern states were able to defend themselves eventually before the Supreme Court, and their view that discriminatory statutes in the United States were illegal was upheld. Some writers prefer to treat this kind of case as distinct from acts of civil disobedience, for they maintain that before we can talk about disobedience there must be some purposeful intent to ignore clearly perceived legal duties. I am not sure how widespread this view is, and in any case it would seem to me that the distinction between testing the law and breaking it is a fine one. (I mention this distinction, however, because, as I shall show, some radical writers contend that much civil disobedience involves a legal challenge based on an appeal to rights.)

Taking all these five considerations together, we can see that the idea of civil disobedience is a very conservative conception. In this regard we may note some further characteristics of the liberal position on law-breaking. It is suggested, for example, that in a democracy there is a general duty always to be considerate of the rights of other citizens. Clearly, in terms of this conception, violence can never play a legitimate part in a campaign of civil disobedience. Liberals are, of course, worried by far more than threats to the person, for they argue that property rights ought to be respected;[8] they are also concerned that innocent parties to a dispute should be free to go about their business without being unduly disturbed by the disobedience of others. Thus, for example, if students in a university are protesting about civil rights, they ought not to make such a nuisance of themselves on campus that members of the university who are not involved cannot get on with their work. There are degrees of nuisance involved here, of course, and precisely where the line ought to be drawn in particular cases is a matter of judgement; almost all demonstrations, however, involve some disruption of the lives of people who are not involved. Liberal theorists disagree among themselves about what is a tolerable level of nuisance, but they are all agreed that those involved in acts of civil disobedience should try as far as is possible to minimize the consequences of their actions for others.[9]

A Radical Conception of Civil Disobedience

Thus far I have described the liberal conception of civility. I have shown how liberals require of law-breakers that they act responsibly and that they reflect by their restraint a very definite respect for the rule of law and for the rights of other citizens. Disobedients, according to the liberal conception, must often think as utilitarians, for they are to ask themselves 'What will happen if...?' questions: will other people become so outraged that they also break the law? Will those who have to enforce the law be brought into disrepute? Will the contemplated action frustrate the democratic right of the majority to rule? Will other people's rights to the enjoyment of their property and to liberty be violated? Will disobedience achieve the goal of communicating effectively, or will the tactic prove counter-productive? Radical individualists, by contrast, have not been as concerned with this kind of question, for they do not conceive of the democratic commitment as requiring that they accept the authority of procedural rules. For them civility is primarily a capacity to think and to act in a principled way. In terms of this view, disobedience in a democratic society constitutes a kind of challenge: those who break the law out of concern for political rights are seen as making an appeal to courts, to the wider public and particularly to the professional observers (the journalists and other commentators whose responsibility it is to review behaviour and to assess it in the light of what are taken to be the fundamental principles and standards of the political order). When such an appeal can be made in a principled way, or when actions can be justified in the light of widely accepted humanitarian standards, the actions of the disobedients must be regarded as civil — and this must often be the case even when they are disruptive or threaten the less fundamental rights of other citizens (such as the right to play rugby against visiting teams, the right to read in the library or the right not to have one's property damaged).

What radical writers require is that more consideration be given to the reasons why people involve themselves in disruptive and violent behaviour. It is in this spirit that they require us to review the manifestations of violence which often accompany demonstrations. Clearly, actions which place others in serious danger will not normally fall within the realm of civility. We must not, however, suppose that violence on the part of demonstrators will never be justifiable. In the first place, the range of violent activities allows for many different responses and need not endanger the physical well-being of others (for example, one could disrupt a sporting activity by shining a reflected light in a player's eye or by blowing a whistle at an inappropriate time); in the second place, violent responses on the part of demonstrators should always be reviewed in the light of all the circumstances which might be thought relevant. If, for example, Bernadette Devlin had reason to suppose that the Ulster Constabulary was going to behave in a violent way, disregarding the rights of the Catholic community, then she would have been justified had she encouraged people to resist when it attempted to enter areas which were under the control of Catholics.

In general I would argue that the problem of political violence cannot be handled as though it involved only issues of entitlement. We need to separate the question of whether a political protest in the name of justice is justifiable from a consideration of whether the means used to draw attention to the cause is reasonable. The use of violent methods such as terror bombing, assault and assassinations can only be justifiable, I suggest, if such resorts to violence can be shown to have a definite prospect of achieving democratic political goals, and then only if an assessment of the likely consequences shows such a strategy to be the best available, but it can never be justified when it serves merely as a symbolic gesture. Thus, I would suggest that terrorism cannot be justified as part of a political protest, although it may be acceptable as part of a revolutionary struggle. How much disruptive violence is justifiable in any given set of circumstances is, however, a matter of judgement and each case must be reviewed in the light of the available information.

According to radical writers, it is entirely inappropriate to treat political demonstrators involved in violent incidents in the same way as ordinary felons. They argue that the liberal way of conceptualizing this kind of problem fails to recognize adequately the stupidity of treating the politically conscientious as merely criminal. The problem here can be traced to the positivist view of law adopted by so many liberal writers, for they often mistakenly regard the motives and reasons in terms of which protestors might justify their acts of violence and law-breaking as irrelevant to the issue of whether disobedients should be treated as criminals. When a person appears before a court to argue that there are considerations which make it impossible for him or her to recognize a particular legal provision as binding, most liberals require that lawyers make every effort to distinguish the issues of law from those of principle and policy. In terms of their theory, the court must decide whether the rule in question has been correctly framed (is it properly 'law'?), and must ask whether the citizen is guilty of ignoring a duty under it. Wider considerations of political conscience and morals are said to be extraneous and should, therefore, be set aside by the court as irrelevant. The authority of the court, it is alleged, is limited to matters of law and does not include jurisdiction over questions relating to public policy or humanity. In terms of the alternative radical view of law, however, the court must consider the merits of the arguments which could be put by a defendant to justify an act of political violence or disobedience; it must also take into account the facts which the citizen had at his or her disposal at the time of the alleged act and must judge whether the action was responsible in the light of this. In other words, radical writers require that courts recognize the cogency of appeals to the democratic commitment when these can be put forward as an appropriate defence; according to this view, authority in a democracy can never extend beyond the appeal to justice. It is worth noting that cases in which citizens break the law out of a sense of justice have a corollary when courts are faced by a special kind of moral wickedness not anticipated by the law. The kind of problem I have in mind here is illustrated by the case of a woman who effectively got rid of her husband during the Nazi period in Germany by reporting that he was disloyal to Hitler in private conversation. Her motive appears to have been that she wished to continue her relationship with a Gestapo officer, and she was able to achieve this end quite within the law by acting as an informer. The husband was sent to a concentration camp and returned after the war seeking retribution from the courts. The positivist response to this kind of difficulty is well stated by Hart, who writes:

It may be conceded that German informers, who for selfish ends procured the punishment of others under monstrous laws, did what morality forbade; yet morality may also demand that the state should punish only those who, in doing evil, did what the state at the time forbade. This is the principle of *nulla poena sine lege*. If inroads have to be made on this principle in order to avert something held to be a greater evil than its sacrifice, it is vital that the issues at stake should be clearly identified. A case of retroactive punishment should not be made to look like an ordinary case of punishment for an act illegal at the time. At least it can be said for the simple positivist doctrine that the morally iniquitous rules may still be law, that this offers no disguise for the choice between evils which in extreme circumstances may have to be made.[10]

But how much light does the positivist framework throw on this kind of case? If we ask the courts to punish people for doing those things which they are entitled to do (or even encouraged to do) under law, we are asking a great deal and must have some powerful arguments to deploy. The positivist would have it that in these circumstances we must choose between the claims of legality and the claims of morality. In the case of the woman discussed above legal calculations, presumably based in part on the principle *nulla poena sine lege*, tell us that the accused is not guilty of transgressing any requirements which she could have been expected to acknowledge. Moral calculations, on the other hand, tell us that the accused is guilty of very great wickedness and that she brought great suffering to others. The question at issue is whether the accused should be punished. If the plea for punishment is going to be persuasive, then we will have to claim (even if we accept positivist assumptions) that the rules of law which applied at the time were so wicked that individuals could have been expected to resist, or at least to evade them as far as was possible in the circumstances. Unless we are prepared to make this claim we would have to justify our plea for punishment by recognizing that the husband has a right to revenge, and we would then have to balance this alleged right against the principle that no one should be punished unless he or she transgresses the law. But the desire for revenge, even though it may be powerful and fully justified (as in the case discussed above), is not a sufficient reason for punishing anyone. The case for punishment must fall squarely, then, on the claim that in certain circumstances we expect people to disregard, and sometimes to actively evade, the rules of a political system, even when these have been correctly framed by a legislature.

Whether we are prepared to call these rules 'law' is a matter of convenience and ideology rather than of substance. I would, however, suggest that if we withhold the designation 'law' from rules which do not give rise to obligations, we correctly highlight the important issues which arise when we are faced by the kind of problem left by the Nazi regime. The fact is that in some circumstances we are prepared to punish people for adopting a positivist attitude, and we do this because we wish to deter people from collaborating and exploiting situations when wicked men come to power. We (those of us, that is, who recognize that in certain circumstances people ought to disregard validly promulgated rules, even those of a democratic political system) expect citizens to have their wits about them and not to follow blindly. Thus, we hold them responsible in a way which takes into account wider considerations of political morality. This more flexible way of viewing such problems was advanced — and, as we have already mentioned, adopted as a defence — by those Americans who appealed to the Nuremberg precedents in cases involving opposition to the Vietnam war and resistance to conscription. One claim made in the courts was that acts against humanity are an individual responsibility, and that citizens have a duty to refuse co-operation when a state is involved in any enterprise which is in conflict with internationally recognized standards.[11]

Of course, liberal positivists would be most reluctant to allow this kind of sentiment to influence an American court. If we take as a point of reference the question of the alleged precedent set at Nuremberg, they could argue about the status of international law as law, or about the status of the Nuremberg Tribunal as a court which is competent to set standards with legal force in America. Another typical (and perhaps more interesting) line of argument effectively rules the Nuremberg precedent out of order in legal debate, on the grounds that it is impractical.[12] The argument here rests on the claim that no American court would admit that the Nuremberg principles apply: it is suggested that no national court would wish to rule that its government was acting illegally and without moral scruple in the conduct of a war, for by doing so it would undermine the foundation of its own authority. The reflexive character of the judgement required by defendants who appealed to the Nuremberg precedent (who wished the court to rule on its own moral standing) made it unlikely, as a matter of fact, that an appeal of this kind would succeed, as the court would have had to announce, in effect, that it was governed by a supreme law higher than, and in conflict with, the law it was bound to enforce.

The argument here makes sense purely as a piece of speculation on the part of a lawyer interested in what courts are likely to do. As a legal argument, however, and especially as an argument about the nature of legality in a democracy, the positivist claim is totally unconvincing. The question at issue is whether standards of a political kind should be seen to place limitations on government authority. When courts are asked to uphold standards, such as those established at Nuremberg or those embodied in the United Nations Charter, they are asked to make a public commitment to ideals of civility. They are not required to undermine their own legal authority. The case is properly seen as one in which they have been requested to assert their legal authority in the face of the abuse of civilized standards on the part of a government. It is pure evasion to argue that because courts are likely to shirk this duty and hypocritically to serve the interests of government that they have no such obligation. Seen in this light, the notion that 'law is what the courts are likely to say that it is' is indeed a politically pernicious doctrine, and one which has provided a rationalization for the actions of those many members of the legal profession who have had too little integrity to stand up for civility.

It should be clear that what distinguishes the radical commitment to democratic civility from the caution of positivism is a very different conception of authority: the positivists value, above all, the clarity which is the product of clearly recognizable rules in terms of which law may be distinguished; the radical, by contrast, finds that this kind of commitment to procedural solutions is blind to the real basis of democratic civility and requires us to operate with a politically informed and principled conception of the forms and limits of democratic civility.

It is only necessary now for me to add one last word of caution in order to pre-empt possible misunderstanding. In my remarks about what I take to be the weakness of the legal positivist orientation in confronting governments which depart from democratic standards, I do not wish to imply that individuals who have sincerely adopted such an attitude to law are themselves morally iniquitous. This would be absurd, for theorists have advanced some extremely compelling reasons why a firm distinction be made between law and political morality. One of the strongest arguments for positivism has in itself embodied a sincerely held political judgement which is directly in conflict with my own. The argument I have in mind asserts that the positivists' orientation provides the most adequate intellectual defence against the abuse of power by a government. The central claim is that when we are faced by evil government

What really is most needed in order to make men clear-sighted in confronting the official abuse of power, is that they should preserve the sense that the certification of something as legally valid is not conclusive of obedience, and that, however great the aura of majesty or authority which the official system may have, its demands must in the end be submitted to moral scrutiny.[13]

In the light of my discussion above, this political claim may well be questioned. I suggest that what is important in a democracy is to keep alive a dialogue about the nature of our legal obligations which refers to standards and ideals that are clearly moral and political. I can find no grounds for thinking that those who claim that legal obligations are a special kind of political obligation will be more likely to think the certification of something as legally valid is conclusive of the question of obedience. Once it is accepted that officials can and often do abuse power, it becomes clear that official certification can never in itself give rise to obligations. The question at issue is whether we should define law as something certified by officials according to a given set of procedural rules, or whether we should reserve law for something which we are prepared to acknowledge as giving rise to obligations in a much wider sense. In the case postulated earlier, in which wicked men have come to political power, we would, if we used the narrower positivist framework, talk about morally bad laws. It must be noticed, however, that in terms of this conception they have authority (in terms of the rules) to enact wicked laws. If we used the terminology of the radical conception, on the other hand, we would refuse to confer the designation 'legal' on regulations unless we could find arguments which provided a democratic reason for such a recognition; and in the case in which wicked rulers have abused their power we would say, 'These politicians have abused their position by using the trappings of law to gain their evil ends.' There would be no question of their having authority to do this, and in so far as they achieved their ends by means of their position of authority, this would be seen as an abuse of trust and as an assumption of power beyond that for which they were authorized.

There is no obvious way in which these two conflicting judgements about the political effects of the various orientations to law can be settled. In favour of my claim that positivism provides a weak defence, I may point to the fact that some theorists self-consciously moved towards a natural-law position after experiences under the Nazis. The effects of tyranny, then, seem to have driven at least some away from the positivist position.[14] It is also clear that those who wish to abuse rights while at the same time pretending to respect the rule of law have been attracted to positivist arguments (as in South Africa and Rhodesia). More important, I offer the following considerations in an attempt to show why the claim that natural law conceptions offer a better defence against political leaders who abuse power is the more plausible.

First, the positivist conception does not allow us to question the legality of what politicians may do, provided their enactments are correctly promulgated in terms of the accepted procedures. This leaves them in a powerful ideological position, for in these circumstances those who are hesitant about challenging the excesses of a government have as their most powerful defence the utilitarian argument for the maintenance of lawful order. Potential disobedients are thus left with a tough choice once courts have ruled, because there can be no further argument about legal duty, and the question 'Shall I break the law?' is posed in a way which marshalls on the side of those who wish to abuse power all the politically important considerations associated with civility.

Second, the natural-law perspective, on the other hand, provides an interpretation of civility and 'respect for law' which allows scope for arguments which appeal to theories of the democratic commitment. Thus, according to this view, in opposing the assumed authority of an evil court one does not *ipso facto* reject the notion of political duty; on the contrary, opposition and even disobedience may in some circumstances become a responsible way for a democrat to behave.

Third, tyrants often use the symbols of legitimacy and authority to provide themselves with an important instrument for social control. What we need to encourage, then, if we wish to provide the best defence, is more public questioning of the basis of authority itself — we need to distinguish law from the trappings of law — and this means that we need to move away from the idea that law can be equated with procedure. If judges were forced to assess cases on their merits, our respect for them would depend, to some extent at least, on the kind of argument they put forward in defence of their findings. A theory which effectively excludes a moral dimension from the purview of the court often confers on it an undeserved dignity. Few people like to raise moral questions when this becomes embarrassing, and most of us are far happier when we are restricted to a technical and neutral framework. If we can keep our dignity without declaring our moral commitments, we are usually happy to do this. We must, therefore, persuade people that their integrity is compromised by the roles they accept in political processes if we hope to provide some defence against tyranny. Liberals who accept the distinction betweeen 'what is legal' and 'what is moral' have often been extraordinarily quick, when the chips were down, to hide behind their conception of legality at the expense of morality. I do not pretend that such people would offer any challenge to the abuse of authority even if they did accept a different theory of law; I do, however, submit that they would not be able to so easily retain a spurious dignity if such a theory were not widely current.

When I say that courts should assess cases on their merits, I do not mean that they should set themselves up as policy-planners, usurping the authority of legislative bodies. Any court which set out to do this would be abusing its authority and would be quickly brought to heel by the other branches of government. But courts do have a special concern where rights are at issue, for it is when moral arguments which appeal to 'justice' are deployed that courts must come into their own. Obviously, most courts could collaborate, after a few purges, with tyrannical political leaders. It should, however, be clear from my discussion that, where this is the case it is better to have a debate about what the law is than to concede respectability to a puppet court. What we should keep in mind is that it is not merely lawyers and judges who must be concerned with the discussion about law and the significance of rival conceptions of democratic civility; journalists, academics and the more courageous politicians must often provide leadership in times of crisis. I have argued that if they are to respond effectively, they would be foolish to show any commitment to the positivists' conception of the rule of law.

Notes

GENERAL INTRODUCTION
1. J. Rawls, *A Theory of Justice* (Oxford, Oxford University Press, 1973); R. Nozick, *Anarchy, State and Utopia* (Oxford, Blackwell, 1974).
2. C. B. Macpherson, *The Political Theory of Possessive Individualism* (Oxford, Clarendon Press, 1962); *The Real World of Democracy* (Oxford, Clarendon Press, 1973); *Democratic Theory* (Oxford, Clarendon Press, 1973); R. Dworkin, *Taking Rights Seriously* (London, Duckworth, 1977).
3. Macpherson, *Possessive Individualism*, pp. 263ff. See my discussion, pp. 128ff *ante*.
4. K. Marx, *Introduction to the Critique of Political Economy* (1857), tr. N. I. Stone (Chicago, 1913), pp. 266–8; quoted by S. Lukes, *Individualism* (Oxford, Blackwell, 1973), pp. 75, 76.
5. Marx's attitude towards 'rights' is stated clearly in his essay 'On the Jewish Question' (1843), which is published in T. B. Bottomore (ed.), *Early Writings* (London, Watts, 1964). He does not change this early opinion. My quotation is from F. Engels, 'Socialism: Utopian and Scientific', in *Selected Works*, Vol. 3 (Moscow, Progress Publishers, 1970), p. 116.
6. Macpherson, *Possessive Individualism*, p. 269.
7. G. W. Mortimore, 'Rational Action' in S. I. Benn & G. W. Mortimore (eds.), *Rationality and the Social Sciences* (London, Routledge & Kegan Paul, 1976), p. 96.
8. K. Popper, 'The Logic of the Social Sciences', in *The Positivist Dispute in German Sociology*, tr. G. Adey and D. Frisby (London, Heinemann, 1976), p. 103.

9. That economists make a lot of simplifying assumptions is well illustrated by Kenneth E. Boulding, in 'Towards the Development of a Cultural Economy', In L. Schneider and C. Boujean (eds), *The Idea of Culture in Social Sciences* (Cambridge, Cambridge University Press, 1973).
10. It is in this sense that Marx has been interpreted as a 'strategy theorist'. See, for example, Talcott Parsons's comment in *The Structure of Social Action* (New York, McGraw-Hill, 1937), p. 492:

Marx, through his doctrine of interests, elevated not only competition but the whole structure of the economic order into a great control mechanism, a compulsive system. This is the essential meaning of Marx's conception of economic determinism. It is not a matter of psychological antirationalism, but of the total consequences of a multitude of rational acts...The peculiar form of compulsion found in the capitalist system are not universal but are limited to its particular 'conditions of production'. Under feudalism exploitation of labour in the capitalist enterprise was not the dominant feature of society and with the advent of socialism it will cease to be...

See also, R. Dahrendorf, *Class and Class Conflict in Industrial Society* (London, Routledge & Kegan Paul, 1959), Pt I, esp. ch. 1; R. Aron, *Main Currents of Sociological Thought* (Harmondsworth, Penguin, 1965), Vol. 1, pp. 136ff.

PART I: Marxism Reconsidered

INTRODUCTION
1. For a description of various conceptions of individualism, especially methodological individualism and ethical individualism, see Lukes, *Individualism*, chs 17 and 18. On methodological individualism, see J. O'Neill (ed.), *Modes of Individualism and Collectivism* (London, Heinemann, 1973); J. Watkins, 'Ideal Types and Historical Explanations', in O'Neill (ed.), *Modes of Individualism*; 'Historical Explanations in the Social Sciences', in O'Neill (ed.), *Modes of Individualism*. Also Watkins's 'Methodological Individualism: A Reply', *Philosophy of Science*, 22, 1955, pp. 58–62; J. Rex, 'Ideal Types and the Comparative Study of Social Structures', in his *Discovering Sociology* (London, Routledge & Kegan Paul, 1973); B. Barry, *Sociologists, Economists and Democracy* (London, Collier-Macmillan, 1970), pp. 13–40; Benn and Mortimore (eds), *Rationality and the Social Sciences*.
2. L. Althusser, *For Marx*, tr. B. Brewster (Harmondsworth, Penguin, 1966). Althusser distinguishes three stages in the development of Marx's thought: a first stage dominated by liberal rationalist humanism, a second stage dominated by the influence of Feuerbach's communalist humanism and a final stage dominated by Marxist materialism. See 'Marxism and Humanism', pp. 221–46.

3. Althusser claims that there is a fundamental shift in Marx's perspective once the theory of historical materialism is developed, which makes it misleading to think that there is any continuity between mature Marxism and the Marx of the early humanist and rationalist periods. Following the historian of science Thomas Kuhn's *The Structure of Scientific Revolutions* (Chicago, University of Chicago, 1962), he claims that Marxism represents a distinctive *paradigm* and must, therefore, be considered conceptually unique, representing a way of seeing history that is radically different from earlier approaches (including that of the early Marx).

Chapter 1: Marx, Holism and Methodological Individualism

1. Lukes, *Individualism*, esp. 125ff.
2. The best attempt to distinguish these assumptions is still that of Parsons, in *The Structure of Social Action*. See also Barry, *Sociologists, Economists and Democracy*; Lukes, *Individualism*; O'Neill (ed.), *Individualism and Collectivism*.
3. On this point see Barry, *Sociologists, Economists and Democracy*, ch. 1.
4. I do not wish to imply that individualist writers necessarily blur the distinction between a response and an action. Many do take trouble to stress the point that human responses are mediated by a conscious sense of purpose, but they endeavour to understand these strategies as appropriate to a specific set of circumstances. It is for this reason that Karl Popper, for example, has argued that the methods of natural science are not necessarily the most appropriate in the social area (the logic of scientific explanation is, of course, the same in both areas for Popper).
5. G. Homans, 'Bringing Man Back In', *American Sociological Review*, 29, 1964, pp. 809–18; *Social Behaviour: Its Elementary Forms* (London, Routledge & Kegan Paul, 1961); *The Nature of Social Science* (New York, McGraw-Hill, 1968).
6. Parsons, *Social Action*, esp., Pt I, pp. 3–122.
7. For useful commentary on Parsons's argument see Barry, *Sociologists, Economists and Democracy* and Percy Cohen, *Modern Social Theory* (London, Heinemann, 1968).
8. D. Hume in F. Watkins (ed), *Theory of Politics* (London, Nelson, 1951), pp. 33–6 (Comprising *A Treatise of Human Nature*, bk III, pt II, sects ii–iv).
9. S. Freud, 'Totem and Taboo', tr. J. Strachey, *Collected Works* (London, Routledge & Kegan Paul, 1950), ch. IV.
10. Freud, *Collected Works*, p. 143.

NOTES   233

11. E. Fromm, *Fear of Freedom* (London, Routledge & Kegan Paul, 1960), p. 9.
12. K. Popper, *The Open Society and its Enemies* (London, Routledge & Kegan Paul, 1966), Vol. 2, p. 98; quoted by Lukes, *Individualism*, p. 114.
13. For an attempt to state Freud's position in a way which avoids the problem, see H. Marcuse, *Eros and Civilization* (London, Routledge & Kegan Paul, 1956), pp. 59–77. For criticism and commentary, see A. MacIntyre, *Marcuse* (London, Fontana, 1970), ch. 4.
14. See the *Economic and Philosophical Manuscripts*, in which Marx describes the alienating effects of 'needs' (especially the need for money) which are made necessary under the capitalist mode of production. The social system is condemned because the 'needs' which are appropriate at that period in history are in conflict with the human essence as Marx conceives of it. The two manuscripts are published in Bottomore (ed), *Early Writings*.
15. Macpherson, *Possessive Individualism*, pp. 263ff.
16. Bottomore (ed), *Early Writings*. Also, K. Marx, *The Poverty of Philosophy* (Moscow, Progress Publishers, 1955).
17. Marx distinguishes between 'essential needs' found in all social systems, 'which only change their form and direction under different conditions' and will, under socialism, be permitted 'to develop normally', and 'false needs', which are entirely the creation of the social system. See 'The German Ideology' in *Selected Works*, Vol 1, 1964, pp. 30ff. For commentary see Patricia Springborg, 'Karl Marx on Human Needs', in Ross Fitzgerald (ed), *Human Needs and Politics* (Rushcutters Bay, N.S.W., Australia, Pergamon, 1977).
18. For a review of the literature see J. Mitchell, *Psychoanalysis and Feminism* (Harmondsworth, Penguin, 1974). Her own position is stated in the Conclusion, 'The Holy Family and Femininity', and provides a good example of the kind of theorizing which I am contrasting with the materialism of Marx. For a materialist response to Freud's views by a feminist, see S. Firestone, *The Dialectic of Sex* (St Albans, Paladin, 1972), pp. 46–72.
19. The best account of Marx's views on human nature are in B. Ollman, *Alienation*, 2nd edn (Cambridge, Cambridge University Press, 1976), pp. 73–126. See also, B. Parekh, 'Marx's Theory of Man', in Parekh (ed), *The Concept of Socialism* (London, Croom-Helm, 1975); C. B. Macpherson, 'Needs and Wants: An Ontological and Historical Problem', in Fitzgerald (ed.), *Human Needs*.
20. See *Hegel's Philosophy of Right*, tr. with notes by T. M. Knox (Oxford, Oxford University Press, 1952): 'On Civil Society', pp. 122ff., 'On the Family', paras 181 and 182, 'On the State' pp. 160ff. For commentary, see S. Avineri, *Hegel's Theory of the Modern State* (London, Cambridge University Press, 1972), esp. pp. 133ff. Hegel's

argument, especially his claims about the significance of moral and religious forces in stabilizing social systems, are similar to those of some of the more conservative modern political sociologists such as S. M. Lipset. See Z. Pelczynski, 'Hegel's Political Philosophy: Its Relevance Today', in Pelczynski (ed.), *Hegel's Political Philosophy* (Cambridge, Cambridge University Press, 1971).
21. T. Hobbes, *Leviathan* (Oxford, Clarendon Press, 1909), pp. 94–8.
22. Hobbes, *Leviathan*, p. 121.
23. Quoted by M. Cranston in his Introduction to J. J. Rousseau *The Social Contract* (Harmondsworth, Penguin, 1968), p. 21.
24. See Cranston, Introduction to Rousseau, *Social Contract*.
25. For an account of Rousseau's assumption see Macpherson, 'Needs and Wants', in Fitzgerald (ed.), *Human Needs*.
26. See Avineri, *Hegel's Theory of the Modern State*, pp. 135ff.
27. See Marx's 'Critique of Hegel's Doctrine of the State' (1843), in *Early Writings* (Harmondsworth, Penguin, 1975). For commentary, see S. Avineri, 'The Hegelian Origins of Marx's Political Thought', in Avineri (ed.), *Marx's Socialism* (New York, Lieber-Atherton, 1973); *The Social and Political Thought of Karl Marx* (Cambridge, Cambridge University Press, 1968), ch. 2.
28. Bottomore (ed.), *Early Writings*.
29. For a recent statement see H. Braverman, *Labour and Monopoly Capital* (New York, Monthly Review Press, 1974).
30. Marx makes this point most forcefully in 'The German Ideology' and 'Critique of the Gotha Programme'; for a typical statement see my quotation p. 48 (from 'The German Ideology'), also p. 238 (from 'The Communist Manifesto').
31. Marx and Engels, 'The German Ideology', in *Selected Works*, Vol. 1, pp. 19ff.
32. R. Harré, *The Principles of Scientific Thinking* (London, Macmillan, 1970), pp. 26, 27.

Chapter 2: Historical Materialism and Consciousness

1. See Ollman, *Alienation*, pp. 6, 7, 8.
2. G. Lukács, 'Class Consciousness', in Lukács, *History and Class Consciousness* (London, Merlin Press, 1971), pp. 46–83.
3. Lukács, 'Class Consciousness', p. 47.
4. For a review of the links between Marxism and classical economic theory, see R. Meek, *Studies in the Labour Theory of Value*, 2nd edn (London, Lawrence & Wishart, 1976); E. Mandel, *The Formation of the Economic Thought of Karl Marx* (New York, Monthly Review Press, 1971); R. Aron, *Main Currents in Sociological Thought*, Vol. 1, esp. pp. 136ff.

5. Dahrendorf, in his *Class and Class Conflict*, talks about 'latent interests' rather than 'objective interests'. Similar views can be found in Robert K. Merton's famous essay 'Latent and Manifest Functions', in his *On Theoretical Sociology: Five Essays, Old and New* (New York, Free Press, 1967), pp. 39–73. Merton's use of the term 'function' rather than 'interest' is deceptive, for in this essay he emerges as a major critic of holistic functionalist theory; his own position is closer to the Reductionism of Malinowski and George Homans than to that of the 'functionalism' of Radcliffe-Brown, Durkheim or Parsons.
6. For Parsons's commentary on Hobbes, see *The Structure of Social Action*, pp. 3–122.
7. This is one way of interpreting Hegel's epigram 'What is rational is actual and what is actual is rational'. For commentary see Avineri, *Hegel's Philosophy of the State*, p. 123.
8. Marx and Engels, 'The German Ideology' in *Selected Works*, Vol. 1, p. 35.
9. M. Olson, *The Logic of Collective Action: Public Goods and the Theory of Groups* (Cambridge, Mass., Harvard University Press, 1965), p. 2.
10. F. Engels, *Anti-Dühring* (London, Lawrence & Wishart, 1943), pp. 26–7; For commentary, see Ollman, *Alienation*, pp. 52–71.
11. For Ricardo's views on 'rent' see his *The Principles of Political Economy and Taxation* (London, Everyman Library, Dent, 1969), pp. 33–47.
12. For a discussion of this contradiction see J. S. Mill, *Principles of Political Economy* (Harmondsworth, Penguin, 1970), Vol. 1, Bk VI, pp. 72–80.
13. This point is made forcefully by Ernest Mandel. See his *An Introduction to Marxist Economic Theory* (New York, Pathfinder Press, 1973), also his more comprehensive *Marxist Economic Theory*, tr B. Pearce (New York, Monthly Review Press, 1968).
14. Lukács, 'Class Consciousness', p. 51. For Marx's own view on the difference between his position and that of classical economists, see *The Poverty of Philosophy*.
15. Lukács, 'Class Consciousness', p. 51.
16. Marx and Engels, 'The Holy Family' (1844), in *Collected Works* (London, Lawrence & Wishart, 1975), Vol. 4, p. 37. This passage is quoted by W. A. Suchting in his article 'Marx, Popper and "Historicism"', *Inquiry*, 3, Autumn 1972, pp. 235–66.
17. The theory of the 'embourgeoisement' of the working class is a popular one, and it is noticeable that most of those who put forward this kind of view take it that their evidence somehow refutes Marxism. As I have shown, this is not the case, for Marx's theory does not focus on the consciousness of the proletariat. For a discussion of research focused on the subjective consciousness of the working class in modern

236 NOTES

capitalist systems, See M. Mann, *Consciousness and Action among the Western Working Class* (London, Macmillan, 1973); D. Kavanagh, *Political Culture* (London, Macmillan, 1972). Barry, in *Sociologists, Economists and Democracy*, questions the methodological assumptions of much of the research in this area.
18. J. Plamenatz, *German Philosophy and Russian Communism* (New York, Harper & Row, 1965), pp. 18–28.
19. Ollman, *Alienation*, pp. 6, 7, 8.
20. Marx, 'The Eighteenth Brumaire of Louis Bonaparte', in *Selected Works*, Vol. 1, pp. 394–487; and 'The Civil War in France', Vol. 2, pp. 178–242.
21. In his widely read 'Methodological Individualism Reconsidered', *British Journal of Sociology*, 19, 1969, pp. 48–70, Steven Lukes writes:

> It is important to see, and it is often forgotten, that to *identify* a piece of behaviour, a set of beliefs, etc. is sometimes to explain it. This may involve seeing it in a new way, picking out hidden structural features. Consider an anthropologist's interpretation of ritual or a sociological study of (say) bureaucracy. Often explanation resides precisely in a successful and sufficiently wide-ranging identification of behaviour or types of behaviour (often in terms of a set of beliefs). (Quotation taken from Alan Ryan (ed.), *The Philosophy of Social Explanation*, Oxford, Oxford University Press, 1973, p. 126)

It is difficult to see why we should consider this kind of identification as properly part of social science. Certainly, it provides an understanding of what it is people are doing at one level and, certainly, sociology as a distinctive science can only begin after competent identifications of the kind that Lukes has in mind have been made. The point is that it is surely reasonable to ask for something more by way of explanation than identification — unless what is being identified is a strategy. A child can identify a bank, but I doubt whether he or she will be able to explain the role of financial institutions in capitalist systems. For excellent commentary on this point, see W. G. Runciman's response to J. Donald Moon, in *Political Theory*, 5, 2, 1977, pp. 183–204.

Lukes's failure to see that 'strategy identifications' are often different from other social descriptions of action — primarily because they require reference to the motives and intentions of individuals — and can, consequently, ground explanations at a level which is different from that achieved when we identify behaviour correctly, merely repeats the mistake made by Peter Winch in his *The Idea of a Social Science and its Relation to Philosophy* (London, Routledge & Kegan Paul, 1962). Thus, 'She is voting' may be a correct description identifying a form of behaviour, but it is informative in a different way from 'She votes to please her husband and father', which may also be a

correct description of the same action. A similar confusion lies behind the arguments of those German theorists (I think particularly of Habermas) who, following Lukács, condemn behavioural sociology for the alleged vice of 'reification'.
22. Popper, *The Open Society*, ch. 14; A. Ryan, *John Stuart Mill* (New York, Panthean Books, 1970) pp. 180–85; O'Neill (ed.), *Modes of Individualism and Collectivism*.
23. Marx and Engels, 'The German Ideology', in *Selected Works*, Vol. 1, p. 19.
24. K. Popper, *The Poverty of Historicism* (London, Routledge & Kegan Paul, 1957), pp. 81, 82.
25. Popper, *The Open Society*, Vol. 2, pp. 187ff.
26. On this point see R. Meek, 'Karl Marx's Economic Method', an appendix to his book *Studies in the Labour Theory of Value* (2nd ed., 1956); also W. A. Suchting, 'Marx, Popper and Historicism'.
27. The 'falsification' of scientific theories is said by Popper to be of central importance; clear proof that a theory is false is, however, not always easy to come by. On the problems here see Imre Lakatos and Alan Musgrove (eds.), *Criticism and the Growth of Knowledge* (Cambridge, Cambridge University Press, 1970). See also P. Feyerabend, *Against Method* (London, New Left Books, 1977).

For a statement by a philosopher who defends a view of scientific method compatible with what I take to be Marx's actual approach, see Harré, *The Principles of Scientific Thinking*.
28. See, in particular, Nelson Polsby, 'How to Study Community Power: The Pluralist Alternative', *Journal of Politics*, 22, August 1960, pp. 474–84.
29. Dahl's views on 'power' and methodology are most accessible in his *Modern Political Analysis*, rev. edn (Englewood Cliffs., N.J., Prentice Hall, 1976); see also his important paper 'The Ruling Elite Model', *American Political Science Review*, 52, 2, 1958, pp. 463–9, from which I have taken the four recommended steps listed in the text. His views on democracy can be found in *Politics, Economics, and Welfare* (New York, Harper, 1953); *A Preface to Democratic Theory* (Chicago, University of Chicago, 1956); *After the Revolution* (New Haven, Conn., Yale University, 1970).
30. Dahl, 'The Ruling Elite Model'.
31. P. Bachrach and M. Baratz, *Power and Poverty* (Oxford, Oxford University Press, 1970), pp. 3–17. Bachrach also has a useful book which reviews utilitarian democratic theory from the point of view of a moral idealist. See his *The Theory of Democratic Elitism* (London, University of London Press, 1969).
32. Bachrach and Baratz, *Power and Poverty*, p. 7.

Chapter 3: Marx's Ethical Individualism and his Conception of Democracy

1. It is not surprising that his contribution has not been greatly admired by commentators. Lucio Colletti (Introduction to *Marx: Early Writings*, Harmondsworth, Penguin, 1975) and Louis Althusser (*For Marx*), to take two sympathetic scholars whose opinions on other issues differ greatly, both concede that Marx's contribution to political philosophy is not the most distinguished or successful part of his work. As for those who are hostile to Marx's revolutionary political perspective, there has been a constant flow of criticism claiming that there is no distinctive Marxist ethic worth discussing and that Marx's was essentially a religious sensibility, articulating a secular doctrine of eschatology. See E. Kamenka, *Marxism and Ethics* (London, Macmillan, 1969); R. Tucker, *Philosophy and Myth in Karl Marx* (Cambridge, Cambridge University Press, 1964).
2. 'The Communist Manifesto', in *The Revolutions of 1848* (Harmondsworth, Penguin, 1973), p. 85.
3. For example:

When the ancient world was in its last throes, the ancient religions were overcome by Christianity. When Christian ideas succumbed in the eighteenth century to rationalist ideas, feudal society fought its death battle with the then revolutionary bourgeoisie. The ideas of religious liberty and freedom of conscience merely gave expression to the sway of free competition within the domain of knowledge. (*The Revolutions of 1848*, p. 85.)

4. See *The Poverty of Philosophy* (1846-7). Also, for general commentary, H. Draper, *Karl Marx's Theory of Revolution* (New York, Monthly Review Press, 1977), Vol. II, pp. 486-9.
5. In approaching the topic this way I follow Steven Lukes, *Individualism*, pp. 125-46; he regards 'freedom' and 'equality' as the core ideas. See his discussion in ch. 20.
6. I discuss these two positions more fully in Part II; see pp. 128-37 above.
7. See J. W. Chapman, 'The Moral Foundations of Political Obligation', in *NOMOS XII* (New York, Atherton Press, 1970), pp. 142-76. Also, C. B. Macpherson in his *The Life and Times of Liberal Democracy* (Oxford, Oxford University Press, 1977), and in 'Do We Need a Theory of the State?', *European Journal of Sociology*, XVIII, 1977, pp. 223-44.
8. Barry makes the distinction between ideal-regarding and want-regarding approaches in his *Political Argument* (London, Routledge & Kegan Paul, 1965). The example about taxing beer to subsidize the theatre is his own. For further discussion see Rawls, *A Theory of*

Justice, pp. 326–7, and B. Barry, *The Liberal Theory of Justice* (Oxford, Oxford University Press, 1973), pp. 20–6.
9. One can be a utilitarian without embracing possessive individualist assumptions. Indeed, the notion that we are essentially the owners of our capacities, and what we acquire through the exercise of these, is much more compatible with deontological ethical commitments (see my discussion pp. 132–34). Most utilitarians indirectly embrace possessive individualism because they hold to the view that the right to own and control property privately is essential for economic efficiency. Thus, they provide a want-regarding justification for recognizing the rights which possessive individualists defend on ideal-regarding grounds.
10. Barry, *The Liberal Theory of Justice*, pp. 21, 22.
11. See Lukes, *Individualism*, p. 48, for discussion of this point.
12. See J. S. Mill, *Utilitarianism* (London, Dent, 1910). Rawls, in his *A Theory of Justice*, p. 426, tries to defend Mill's distinction by referring to what he calls the 'Aristotelian Principle'. For criticism, see Barry, *The Liberal Theory of Justice*, pp. 27–30.
13. T. H. Green, *Lectures on the Principles of Political Obligation* (London, Longman, 1959), p. 207.
14. Green, *Principles of Political Obligation*, p. 221.
15. Both Nozick and Rawls, for example, make use of similar arguments. See my discussion of Nozick. whose arguments are the same as (only more sophisticated than) those of Green, pp. 165–75 above. Rawls is concerned with a slightly different problem, for he wishes to determine how much inequality may be justified (see *A Theory of Justice*, pp. 65–83, where he discusses his 'difference principle').
16. See Hegel's Third Part (pp. 105–223) in the *Philosophy of Right*. For commentary see Avineri, *Hegel's Theory of the Modern State*, pp. 132–75.
17. See especially his commentary on paras 287–97 of Hegel's work in *Early Writings*, pp. 100–16.
18. *Early Writings*, p. 233.
19. The best commentary on Marx's dispute with Bauer (and on his early contributions in the *Rheinische Zeitung*) is to be found in Draper, *Karl Marx's Theory of Revolution*, Vol 1, ch. 8.
20. Quoted by Marx, *Early Writings*, p. 227.
21. Section II of his 'Critique of the Gotha Programme', in *The First International and After* (Harmondsworth, Penguin, 1974), pp. 354–6.
22. In describing Marx in this way I follow Hal Draper, in his *Karl Marx's Theory of Revolution*; see his chapter 'The Democratic Extremist', pp. 31–60.
23. Qualifications of this kind about the way that the 'economic base' influences the 'superstructure' were added by Engels, who wanted to allow for the 'relative independence' of the latter. What he had in mind,

however, is not always clear. Perhaps what he wished to draw attention to was the complexity of the processes at work in social life which make specific prediction impossible (for example, the rent and price of housing in Melbourne will be determined in *the last instance* by the cost of production; meanwhile, many other factors such as the rate of growth of the population, the availability of finance, and the current building regulations will have an immediate effect on the price). If, however, Engels wanted to allow for the relative independence of the 'superstructure', it is difficult to see why this qualification does not constitute an abandonment of historical materialism. (See L. Kolakowski, *Main Currents of Marxism* (Oxford, Oxford University Press, 1978), Vol 1, pp. 335–46). On this point, see also E. P. Thompson's witty discussion of the use that Althusser makes of notions such as 'structure in dominance' and 'overdetermination' in his *The Poverty of Theory* (London, Merlin Press, 1978). He writes (p. 273):

We are introduced to a very great lady, who is not at all to be seen as a slender superstructure sitting on a somewhat large basis, but as a unitary figure, *La Structure à Dominante*. She is a 'totality'...what determines her existence and structures her dominant personality is, in the last instance, 'economic', but since the last instance never arrives, it is courteous very often to overlook this material determination. It is impolite to keep on reminding the great lady that she is determined by her tummy. It is more helpful to characterize her by the contradictions in her temperament, and to examine these in their own right, instead of continually harping on the fact that they originate in a bad disposition.

24. The best discussion of the functions of the state from a Marxist point of view is to be found in E. Mandel, *Late Capitalism* (London, New Left Books, 1976), ch. 15. He writes:

the repressive function of enforcing the rule of the dominant class by coercion (army, police, law, penal system) was the dimension of the state most closely examined in classical Marxism. Later, Lukács and Gramsci laid greater emphasis on its integrative function, which they ascribed essentially to the ideology of the ruling class.

25. See Draper's discussion of Marx's analysis of Bonapartism in *Karl Marx's Theory of Revolution*, Vol 1, pp. 385–417.
26. See *Eighteenth Brumaire of Louis Bonaparte* (1852); *First Draft of the Civil War in France* (1871); and *The Civil War in France 1848–1850* (1871).
27. See Marx's account of the Paris Commune in 'First Draft of the Civil War in France', *First International and After*, pp. 261–63.
28. The phrase that the state will 'wither away' is taken from Engels, *Anti-Dühring*, 3rd English edn. (Moscow, Foreign Language Publishing House, 1962), p. 385. Avineri comments as follows:

NOTES 241

There is a marked difference between the terms Marx and Engels used when discussing the ultimate disappearance of the state under socialism. While Engels in the famous passage in his *Anti-Dühring* speaks about the state 'withering away' (*der Staat wird nicht 'abgeschafft', er stirbt ab*), Marx always refers to the abolition and transcendence (*Aufhebung*) of the state. *Absterben des Staates* and *Aufhebung des Staates* are clearly two different terms deriving from quite different intellectual traditions: while Engels' *Absterben* is a biological simile, Marx's *Aufhebung* is a philosophical term with clear dialectical overtones. (*The Social and Political Thought of Karl Marx*, p. 203)

As can be seen from my discussion, I believe that Avineri exaggerates the differences between Marx and Engels.

29. See Kolakowski's criticisms along these lines in his *Main Currents of Western Marxism*, Vol. III, pp. 528f.
30. See Draper, *Karl Marx's Theory of Revolution*, Vol. I, pp. 239–49.
31. Marx uses this phrase very rarely. The most notable instance occurs in his discussion 'Critique of the Gotha Programme' where he writes (*The First International and After*, p. 355):

Between capitalism and communist society lies a period of revolutionary transformation from one to the other. There is a corresponding period of conflict in the political sphere and in this period the state can only take the form of a revolutionary dictatorship of the Proletariat.

32. It is doubtful (given Marx's view that political life reflects imperatives within civil society) that he ever conceived the possibility of a fully autonomous bureaucratic state of the kind called 'totalitarian' today. Nevertheless, as Draper shows, Marx and Engels did speculate about the state 'swallowing up civil society', and they regarded the emergence of Caesarism in the Roman Empire as a case in point. See Draper's commentary, *Karl Marx's Theory of Revolution*, pp. 465–8.
33. This was the idea underlying the Lassallean *Gotha Programme* of which Marx was so critical. For commentary, see Kolakowski, *Main Currents of Western Marxism*, Vol. 1, pp. 238–44.
34. This view is stressed by the modern revolutionary Ernest Mandel. He writes:

It is not by chance that the labour movement has been at the forefront of the struggle for democratic freedoms in the Nineteenth and Twentieth Centuries. By defending these freedoms, the labour movement at the same time defends the best conditions for its own advance. (*From Class Society to Communism*, London, Ink Links Ltd., 1977, p. 93.)

Kolakowski tells us that Engels wrote an introduction to Marx's *The Class Struggle in France 1848–1850* in which he argued that civil liberties are a crucial weapon in the struggle to achieve socialism; see *Main Currents of Western Marxism*, Vol. I, p. 361.

35. See Draper's commentary on this aspect of Marx's contribution in *Karl Marx's Theory of Revolution*, Vol. 1, pp. 306–8.
36. Kolakowski, *Main Currents of Western Marxism*, 'Epilogue', Vol. III, p. 528.
37. Macpherson comments on J. Habermas's *Legitimation Crisis* in his 'Do We Need a Theory of the State?'.

Chapter 4: Marxism and Utopia

1. R. Dahl and C. Lindblom, *Politics, Economics and Welfare*, p. 273.
2. Bachrach, *Democratic Elitism*; See also, G. Duncan and S. Lukes, 'The New Democracy', *Political Studies*, II, 1963, pp. 156–7; J. Walker, 'A Critique of the Elitist Theory of Democracy', *American Political Science Review*, LX, 1966, pp. 285–95; C. Pateman, *Participation in Democratic Theory* (Cambridge, Cambridge University Press, 1970); H. Kariel, *Frontiers of Democratic Theory* (New York, Random House, 1970). But see Dahl's response in *After the Revolution*, esp. ch. 12; and his reply to Walker in *American Political Science Review*, LX, 1966, pp. 295ff.
3. See particularly Dahl, *After the Revolution*, pp. 80–98 *passim*.
4. Macpherson, *The Life and Times of Liberal Democracy*, pp. 98–108.
5. Marcuse, *Eros and Civilization*; Fromm, *The Fear of Freedom*. For a recent statement and review of the literature, see Mitchell, *Psychoanalysis and Feminism*.
6. See Firestone, *The Dialectic of Sex*.
7. Especially, 'The German Ideology' and 'Critique of the Gotha Programme', in *Selected Works*, Vol. 1 and Vol. 3.
8. Marx and Engels, 'Manifesto of the Communist Party', *The Revolutions of 1848*, pp. 70ff.
9. See Brian Barry's analysis of the 'general good' in 'The Public Interest', in A. Quinton (ed.), *Political Philosophy* (Oxford, Oxford University Press, 1967).
10. See Maurice Cranston's remarks about this connection in his introduction to the Penguin Books edition of J. J. Rousseau, *The Social Contract* (Harmondsworth, 1968). See also, for interesting observations about the connection between Rousseau and Plato, J. Plamenatz, *Man and Society* (London, Longman, 1963), Vol. I, pp. 388–96.
11. J. D. May, 'Locating Democracy', *Politics*, XI, 2 (November) 1976, pp. 165–9. Many of the remarks which follow are taken from my rejoinder to May in the same issue of *Politics*, pp. 170–5.
12. The problems are thought to arise out of the industrial revolution. Those of central concern to democratic theory involve:

NOTES 243

(a) *The need for experts.* So many of the decisions which have to be made involve issues which few of us are actually competent to comprehend. Sometimes the problem is one of background in a relevant scientific discipline, sometimes the difficulty relates to the question of time, and sometimes the difficulty arises because we do not have the necessary information to make rational decisions.
(b) *The problem of bureaucratization.* Planning requires that information be gathered by agencies which advise those in authority. This means that the ordinary citizen is often unaware of when or how decisions are made or even what information is available to officials; they are moreover often deliberately kept ignorant and are left out of the processes of consultation. Furthermore, it is very difficult for them to compete with professional bureaucrats for influence.
(c) *The passivity of citizens.* Political issues for most people are so remote that they take little trouble to keep themselves informed.
13. I. Berlin, *Two Concepts of Liberty* (Oxford, Clarendon Press, 1958).
14. Macpherson, *Possessive Individualism*, pp. 263–4.
15. *Capital* (Harmondsworth, Penguin, 1976), Vol. 1, pp. 758–9, fn. 51. (Quoted by Steven Lukes in his *Individualism*, p. 150.)
16. Kamenka, *Marxism and Ethics*, pp. 11–12.
17. Macpherson, *Democratic Theory*, p. 51.
18. F. Engels, *The Origins of the Family, Private Property and the State* (London, Lawrence & Wishart, 1973) esp. pp. 144–6. For commentary see H. Draper, 'Marx and Engels on Women's Liberation', in Roberta Salper (ed.), *Female Liberation* (New York, Alfred A. Knopf, 1972), pp. 83–108.

Chapter 5: Problems with Marxism as an Ethical Theory

1. The best discussion, although unsympathetic, is E. Kamenka, *The Ethical Foundations of Marxism* (London, Macmillan, 1962); and *Marxism and Ethics*.
2. Kamenka, *Marxism and Ethics*, p. 12.
3. Berlin, *Two Concepts of Liberty*.
4. On this point I am in agreement with Althusser and Kamenka.
5. For liberal theory on the role of groups in political life, see D. Truman, 'The American System in Crisis', *Political Science Quarterly*, December 1959, pp. 481–97; *The Governmental Process* (New York, Alfred A. Knopf, 1955), esp. pp. 501–24; H. W. Ehrmann (ed.), *Interest Groups in Four Continents* (Pittsburg, University of Pittsburg, 1960); V. O. Key, *Political Parties and Pressure Groups*, 5th edn. (New York, Crowell, 1964).

6. J. H. Kautsky (ed.), *Political Change in Underdeveloped Countries: Nationalism and Communism* (New York, Wiley, 1962); *The Political Consequences of Modernization* (New York, Wiley, 1977).
7. Rawls, *A Theory of Justice*, Pt 3, ch. VII.
8. K. Baier, 'Ability, Power and Authority' (paper read at the Australian Philosophy Conference in Canberra, 1974).
9. Berlin, *Two Concepts of Liberty*, p. 15.
10. Macpherson, *Possessive Individualism*, pp. 40–3; *Democratic Theory*, pp. 10–16 and 64–6.
11. Berlin, *Two Concepts of Liberty*, p. 15.
12. Macpherson, *Democratic Theory*, p. 101.
13. Berlin, *Two Concepts of Liberty*, p. 14.
14. Macpherson, *Democratic Theory*, p. 109.
15. Macpherson, *Democratic Theory*, p. 101.

PART II: Radical Individualism

INTRODUCTION
1. C. B. Macpherson, 'Rawls's Models of Man and Society', *Philosophy of Science*, 3, 1973, pp. 341–7.
2. Rawls, *A Theory of Justice*, p. 128.
3. R. Nozick uses the notion of an 'invisible hand mechanism' to great effect in *Anarchy, State and Utopia*, pp. 312–17.
4. Rawls, *A Theory of Justice*, p. 303.
5. Dworkin, *Taking Rights Seriously*, p. 182.
6. Barry, *The Liberal Theory of Justice*, p. 166.
7. Macpherson, *The Life and Times of Liberal Democracy*, pp. 108–15.

Chapter 6: The Point of the Rights Thesis

1. Macpherson, *Possessive Individualism*, pp. 263–4.
2. Nozick, *Anarchy, State and Utopia*, p. 160 (also Pt. II, Sect. II, pp. 183–228).
3. Nozick, *Anarchy, State and Utopia*, p. 160.
4. Nozick, *Anarchy, State and Utopia*, pp. 153–4.
5. Nozick, *Anarchy, State and Utopia*, p. 155.
6. H. L. A. Hart, *Law, Liberty and Morality* (Oxford, Oxford University Press, 1963), pp. 30–4; G. Dworkin, 'Paternalism', in Wasserstrom R. (ed.), *Morality and the Law* (Belmont, California, Wadsworth, 1971).
7. W. Godwin, *Enquiry concerning Political Justice and its Influence on Morals and Happiness*, 2nd edn. (London, 1796).

8. H. L. A. Hart, *The Concept of Law* (Oxford, Oxford University Press, 1961), ch. II.
9. On 'rule utilitarianism' see R. B. Brandt, *Ethical Theory* (New York, Prentice Hall, 1959); K. Baier, *The Moral Point of View* (New York, Cornell University Press, 1958); M. Singer, *Generalization in Ethics* (New York, Knopf, 1961); J. Rawls, 'Two Concepts of Rules', *Philosophical Review*, 64, 1955, pp. 3–32.
10. On 'What if everyone did the same?' see Singer, *Generalization in Ethics*.
11. D. Lyons, *The Forms and Limits of Utilitarianism* (Oxford, Oxford University Press, 1968).
12. J. J. Smart, 'An Outline of a System of Utilitarian Ethics', in J. Smart and B. Williams, *Utilitarianism: For and Against* (Cambridge, Cambridge University Press, 1973), pp. 63–4; for Quinton's views on torture, see *The Listener*, 86, 2 December, 1971, pp. 757–8.
13. P. Singer, 'Review: *Anarchy, State and Utopia*', in *New York Review of Books*, XIII, 3, March 1975, pp. 19–24.
14. Rawls, *A Theory of Justice*, pp. 161–83.
15. Rawls, *A Theory of Justice*, pp. 30–1.
16. Dworkin, *Taking Rights Seriously*, pp. 169–70.
17. Rawls, *A Theory of Justice*, p. 29.
18. Dworkin, *Taking Rights Seriously*, pp. 170–1.
19. H. L. A. Hart, 'Are There Any Natural Rights?', *Philosophical Review*, 64, 1955; reprinted in Quinton (ed.), *Political Philosophy*, pp. 53–67.
20. David Lyons seems to think that this conclusion cannot be avoided. See his 'Rawls versus Utilitarianism', *Journal of Philosophy*, 69, 1972, pp. 535–45.
21. Dworkin, *Taking Rights Seriously*, pp. 93, 94, 99.
22. *De Funis v. Odegaard, 94 S. Ct. 1704 (1974)*. For Dworkin's views on 'positive discrimination', see his discussion in *Taking Rights Seriously*, ch. 9.
23. *Sweatt v. Painter, 339 U. S. 629, 70 S. Ct. 848*.
24. See the response to Dworkin by the liberal Louis B. Schwartz, 'The Bakke Case', *New York Review of Books*, XIV, 21 & 22, January, 1978.
25. Dworkin is not necessarily committed to the view that the medical school's policy of positive discrimination is a desirable one (in the sense that it promotes good social goals at minimum cost to the community). He claims only that, if the school authorities have genuinely reached such a conclusion, then the implementation of the policy does not violate rights. See especially his reply to critics in *New York Review of Books*, XXIV, 21 & 22, January, 1978.

Chapter 7: Rawls's Conception of Justice

1. There are other ways of interpreting Rawls's method. For a very different view and assessment, see Lyons, 'Rawls versus Utilitarianism'. I am following Dworkin's interpretation in *Taking Rights Seriously*, ch. 6.
2. Rawls makes the following remarks about 'rights':

> Justice as fairness has the characteristic marks of a natural rights theory. Not only does it ground fundamental rights on natural attributes and distinguish their bases from social norms, but it assigns rights to persons by principles of equal justice, these principles having a special force against which other values cannot normally prevail. Although specific rights are not absolute the system of equal liberties is absolute practically speaking under favorable conditions. (*A Theory of Justice*, fn. 30, p. 506.)

3. Rawls, *A Theory of Justice*, p. 136.
4. Nozick, *Anarchy, State and Utopia*, p. 160.
5. For Rawls's arguments supporting the maximin strategy in the original position, see *A Theory of Justice*, esp. sect. 26. Such a strategy, Rawls tells us (pp. 152–3), is most appropriate in situations in which there is no good way of calculating the probabilities; gain does not mean very much above a minimum requirement; loss below a minimum is catastrophic. These conditions may be said to apply in societies which have attained a reasonable level of affluence, and Rawls believes that they provide a good reason for supporting his suggested maximin approach. For commentary, see B. Barry, 'On Social Justice', in R. E. Flathman (ed.), *Concepts in Social and Political Philosophy* (New York, Macmillan, 1973).
6. See Rawls, *A Theory of Justice*, p. 62; the full principle is quoted by me on p. 124 above.
7. Barry, 'On Social Justice'. More recently David Lyons, in his 'Rawls versus Utilitarianism', has suggested that Rawls has no good reason for excluding from his original position information about history and sociology which would make it possible for an actuarial estimate to be made of the risks involved in choosing various principles.
8. For an elaboration of this point, see Lyons, 'Rawls versus Utilitarianism'.
9. See Rawls's discussion of the 'best bet' option in *A Theory of Justice*, pp. 165–75.
10. See especially his 'Distributive Justice', in P. Laslett and W. G. Runciman (eds.), *Politics, Philosophy and Society*, 3rd series (Oxford, Blackwell, 1967), pp. 58–82.
11. Rawls, *A Theory of Justice*, p. 169.
12. Rawls, *A Theory of Justice*, pp. 176ff.
13. Rawls, *A Theory of Justice*, ch. VII, sects 70–3.

NOTES 247

14. A similar point is made by Barry in *The Liberal Theory of Justice*, p. 15.
15. Rawls, *A Theory of Justice*, p. 48; on 'reflective equilibrium', see pp. 48–51. Also, Dworkin, *Taking Rights Seriously*, pp. 156–7.
16. Rawls, *A Theory of Justice*, p. 167.

Chapter 8: Rawls and his Critics

1. J. Feinberg, 'Rawls and Intuitionism', in Daniels (ed.), *Reading Rawls*.
2. Nozick, *Anarchy, State and Utopia*, p. 161.
3. Nozick, *Anarchy, State and Utopia*, p. 93.
4. Nozick's use of the idea of 'validating conditions' is similar to that of Howard Warrender in his *The Political Philosophy of Hobbes* (Oxford, Oxford University Press, 1957), pp. 14–7
5. Nozick, *Anarchy, State and Utopia*, p. 178. As this quotation shows, Rawlsian considerations would not be permitted by Nozick, for the worst-off cannot complain that they would be better off under socialism or even under a capitalist system where taxation is used to redistribute wealth. This kind of concession to consequentialism is not tolerable to Nozick.
6. Nozick, *Anarchy, State and Utopia*, pp. 174–82.
7. Wilt Chamberlain, to refer to Nozick's example (*Anarchy, State and Utopia*, p. 161), has a monopoly, or at least a decisive competitive advantage, for nobody can play basketball quite like him. He can, therefore, because he is offering something unique and scarce, demand a return for his efforts which is much higher than that of other players whose offerings are not unique. Does he try that much harder than the others, or contribute that much more towards getting his team a win?
8. Nozick, *Anarchy, State and Utopia*, p. 258.
9. Nozick, *Anarchy, State and Utopia*, p. 259.
10. Nozick, *Anarchy, State and Utopia*, p. 260.
11. Macpherson, *Possessive Individualism*, pp. 197–251.
12. Feinberg, 'Rawls and Intuitionism'; Barry, 'Justice and the Common Good', *Analysis*, 21, 1960/1, pp. 86–90; *Political Argument*, ch. 1.
13. Rawls's views are stated in *A Theory of Justice*, pp. 34–40; the quotation is from p. 39.
14. R. M. Hare, 'Rawls's Theory of Justice', in Daniels (ed.), *Reading Rawls*, p. 84.
15. Dworkin, *Taking Rights Seriously*, pp. 159–68.
16. Dworkin, *Taking Rights Seriously*, pp. 160–2.

248 NOTES

Chapter 9: Approaches to Democratic Theory

1. Nozick, *Anarchy, State and Utopia*, p. 115.
2. For Nozick's discussion of his principle of rectification see *Anarchy, State and Utopia*, pp. 152–3.
3. Nozick, *Anarchy, State and Utopia*, p. 149.
4. Nozick, *Anarchy, State and Utopia*, p. 330.
5. Macpherson, *Possessive Individualism*, pp. 197–222.
6. Brian Barry makes the point that, given Nozick's assumptions about the nature of 'rights', it is not surprising that he finds such difficulty showing how a legitimate state could have come into being. But why should we accept his conception of rights? ('Review of *Anarchy, State and Utopia*', in *Political Theory*, 3, August 1975, pp. 331–6.)
7. We must, of course, note that Nozick indulges in some modelling of his own; see his discussion of Utopia in Pt 3 of *Anarchy, State and Utopia*.
8. Nozick, *Anarchy, State and Utopia*, pp. 121–4.
9. Rawls, *A Theory of Justice*, pp. 274–84.
10. Rawls, *A Theory of Justice*, p. 302.
11. Rawls, *A Theory of Justice*, pp. 62–3.
12. The best discussion of these is to be found in R. Dahl, *Polyarchy* (New Haven, Conn., Yale University, 1971). He lists seven sets of complex conditions favouring the effective functioning of liberal democratic processes (see p. 203) and discusses each of them. I list only the heading he provides: 1. Historical Sequences; 2. The Socioeconomic Order; 3. The Level of Economic Development; 4. Equalities and Inequalities; 5. Subcultural Pluralism; 6. Domination by a Foreign Power; 7. Beliefs of Political Activists.
13. See Dahl, *After the Revolution*, pp. 10–26.
14. R. Miller, 'Rawls and Marxism', *Philosophy and Public Affairs*, 3, 2, 1974, pp. 167–91; also in Daniels (ed.), *Reading Rawls*.
15. Rawls, *A Theory of Justice*, p. 226.
16. Macpherson, *The Life and Times of Liberal Democracy*, pp. 64–9.
17. Macpherson, *Democratic Theory*, pp. 134–6.
18. J. Dunn, 'The Political Philosophy of C. B. Macpherson', *British Journal of Political Science*, 4, 1974, pp. 489–500.
19. Rawls, *A Theory of Justice*, p. 225.
20. Macpherson, *Democratic Theory*, p. 137.

Chapter 10: The Concept of Law

1. I have taken the concept of the *auctor* view of authority from a paper by R. Peters, 'Authority', in Quinton (ed.), *Political Philosophy*, pp. 83–96; see my quotation below, p. 205.

2. Hart, *The Concept of Law*, esp. pp. 76–96.
3. For Hart's discussion of H. Kelsen's *General Theory of Law and the State* (Cambridge, Mass., Harvard University Press, 1949), see 'Kelsen Visited', *University of California Law Review*, 10, 4, 1963, pp. 709–29.
4. Hart, *The Concept of Law*, pp. 198–9.
5. Hart, *The Concept of Law*, p. 113.
6. R. Dworkin, 'Is Law a System of Rules' in *Taking Rights Seriously*, pp. 32ff.
7. Peters, 'Authority', in Quinton (ed.), *Political Philosophy*, p. 94.
8. Hart, *The Concept of Law*, p. 206.
9. Dworkin, *Taking Rights Seriously*, pp. 183–4.

Chapter 11: Disobedience and the Rule of Law

1. See J. Schumpeter, *Capitalism, Socialism and Democracy*, 3rd edn. (London, Allen & Unwin, 1950), pp. 250–83; Dahl, *Polyarchy* and *A Preface to Democratic Theory*; Rawls, *A Theory of Justice*, pp. 356–68.
2. See especially Rawls, *A Theory of Justice*, pp. 350–5; S. Hook, 'Social Protest and Civil Disobedience' in J. Murphy (ed.), *Civil Disobedience and Violence* (Belmont, California, Wadsworth, 1976); C. Cohen, *Civil Disobedience* (New York, Columbia University Press, 1971).
3. Especially Hook, 'Social Protest and Civil Disobedience'.
4. J. Murphy, 'The Vietnam War and the Right of Resistance', in *Civil Disobedience and Violence*. Also Dworkin, *Taking Rights Seriously*, pp. 206–23.
5. B. Russell, 'Civil Disobedience and the Threat of Nuclear Warfare', in H. A. Bedau (ed.), *Civil Disobedience* (New York, Pegasus, 1969), pp. 153–60.
6. In the points which follow I have used Cohen's exposition in his *Civil Disobedience* as a guide.
7. Hook, 'Social Protest and Civil Disobedience'.
8. For liberal views which associate property damage with violence, see Cohen, *Civil Disobedience*; A. Fortas, *Concerning Dissent and Civil Disobedience* (New York, Signet, 1968); Hook, 'Social Protest and Civil Disobedience'. Rawls comes close to saying that there is an association in *A Theory of Justice*, p. 366.
9. Clearly it makes a difference whether a liberal writer adopts a utilitarian justification or recognizes rights as fundamental. In my view, utilitarian writers tend to be disposed to restrict the meaning of nuisance and are more tolerant than those liberals who assume Lockean rights.
10. Hart, *The Concept of Law*, p. 207; also the note on pp. 254–5.

11. See the cases reported in *Trials of the Resistance*, essays by Noam Chomsky, Ronald Ferber, Francine Gray, Florence Howe, Andrew Kopkind, Paul Lauter, Herbert Packer, Emma Rothschild, introduced by Murray Kempton (New York, Vintage Books, for the *New York Review of Books*, 1970).
12. See Cohen, *Civil Disobedience*, pp. 201–7.
13. Hart, *The Concept of Law*, p. 206.
14. See H. L. A. Hart, 'Legal Positivism and the Separation of Law and Morals', in *Harvard Law Review*, 71, 1958, p. 598; and L. Fuller, 'Positivism and Fidelity to Law', *Harvard Law Review*, 71, 1958, p. 630.

Index

I have listed books and articles referred to more than once so that their publication details may be found.

Althusser, Louis 11 f.; *For Marx* 231, 238, 240
Aron, Raymond *Main Currents of Sociological Thought* 231, 234
Authority 199–210
Avineri, Shlomo: *Hegel's Theory of the Modern State* 233, 234, 239; *Social and Political Thought of Karl Marx* 234, 240 f.

Bachrach, Peter 54–6; *Power and Poverty* 237; *The Theory of Democratic Elitism* 237, 242
Baier, Kurt 244, 245
Baratz, Morton 237
Barry, Brian 61 ff., 242, 275; *The Liberal Theory of Justice* 239, 244; *Political Argument* 238; Rawls 125, 150–2; 'On Social Justice' 246, 247, 248; *Sociologists, Economists and Democracy* 231, 232
Bauer, Bruno 69–71

Benn, S. I. *Rationality and the Social Sciences* 230, 231
Bentham, Jeremy 17, 61, 62, 101, 132, 133
Berelson, Bernard 97
Berlin, Isaiah 98, 107; liberty 115; property rights 115–16; *Two Concepts of Liberty* 243, 244
Boulding, Kenneth E. 231
Bottomore, T. B. *Early Writings* 230, 233
Brandt, R. B. 245
Braverman, H. 234

Categorical Imperative 63–4
Chapman, J. W. 238
Civil Disobedience 216–29
Cohen, Carl: *Civil Disobedience* 249
Cohen, Percy 232
Colletti, Lucio 238
Consciousness: class conflict 44–6, 48, 58 f.; Lukács 35–43
Cranston, Maurice 234

Dahl, Robert 98, 194, 242, 248; *After the Revolution* 237; democracy 86–7; *Politics, Economics, and Welfare* 237; power 53–4, 237; 'The Ruling Elite Model' 237; Utopian theory 97
Dahrendorf, Ralph *Class and Class Conflict* 231, 235
Democracy 72–7, 86–9 *passim*, 95–105, 125–7, 183–97 *passim*, 214–16, 242–3 (n. 12)
Draper, Hal 72, 74, 239, 240, 241, 242, 243, *Karl Marx's Theory of Revolution* 238
Dunn, John 248
Dworkin, G. W. 244
Dworkin, Ronald 1, 3, 121, 244, 245, 247, 249; abstract and concrete rights 142 f.; discretion 204–6, 209; intuitionism 177–9; legal positivism 99, 204–8; positive discrimination 143–5; 190; Rawls's egalitarianism 124; rights thesis 137–143; *Taking Rights Seriously* 230; Vietnam War 215.

Economic Fundamentalism 46–9
Ehrmann, H. W. 243
Engels, F. 29, 73, 74, 91, 92, 46, 103, 107, 108, 191, 235, 239, 241, 243; natural rights, 2, 230; withering away of the state 240–1

Feinberg, J. 161, 175; 'Rawls and Intuitionism' 247
Firestone, Shulamuth *The Dialectic of Sex* 233, 242
Freud, S. 19–21, 91, 232
Fromm, Eric 21, 23, 242; *Fear of Freedom*, 233.
Fuller, L. 250

Godwin, William 133, 244

Gotha Programme 70–1
Green, T. H. 60, 65, 121–2, 239; rights 64, 66–7

Hare, R. M. 176, 247
Harré, Rom 33; *The Principles of Scientific Thinking* 234, 237
Hart, H. L. A. 207, 233, 244, 245, 249, 250; legal positivism 199 –202, 208–9, 226; natural right 141, 145, 163–4
Hegel, G. W. F. 37, 60, 64, 65, 239; historicism 49–51; Hobbesian individualism 25–8, 38; Marx's criticisms 67–71; *Philosophy of Right* 233; property 29; Rousseau 28–9
Historical Materialism 32, 34, 43–5; consciousness, 36–9, 240
Historicism 30, 47, 49–51
Hobbes, T. 5, 6, 15, 60–3 *passim*, 101, 186, 199; authority 202 –3; *Leviathan* 234; order and the state 18, 25–8
Homans, George 14, 23, 232
Hook, Sidney 213, 219; 'Social Protest and Civil Disobedience' 249
Humanism 63–7
Hume, David 18, 60, 63, 232

Individualism: ethical 59–65; methodological 13–22, 32–4; possessive 2, 3, 60–1, 101, 128–132, 180–5, 239; radical 137–145; utilitarian 132–7
Intuitionism 156–7, 175–9
Invasive relationships 104, 115, 150, 244 (n. 10)

Justice 124, 163–5, 171–5, 187; fairness 156–60; positive discrimination 143–5

INDEX 253

Kamenka, Eugene 107–9; *Marxism and Ethics* 238, 243
Kant, I. 5, 63–4, 65, 107–9
Kautsky, J. H. 244
Kelsen, Hans 200
Key, V. O. 243
Kolakowski, L. 78; *Main Currents of Western Marxism* 240, 241

Legal Positivism 199–202, 208–11, 212–5, 223–229
Legitimation Crisis 83–4
Liberalism: civil disobedience 214–21; democratic theory 96–100, 213; freedom 111–19; humanism 63–5; law 198–9, 208–11; Lockean tradition 128, 180–5
Liberty 111–19, 187–90
Lindsay, A. D. 60
Locke, John 5, 6, 101, 181, 183
Lukács, George 52, 235; 'Class Consciousness' 234, 35, 46; order 38–9
Lukes, Steven 47, *Individualism* 230, 231, 232, 236, 239, 243
Lyons, David 'Rawls versus Utilitarianism' 245, 246

MacIntyre, A. 233
Macpherson, C. B. 90, 107, 109, 111, 115, 132, 150, 183, 190, 191, 233, 242, 243, 244, 248; Berlin 115–7; democratic theory 95–105, 102, 194–5; *Democratic Theory* 230; 'Do We Need a Theory of the State?' 238, 242; human powers 111–3; *The Life and Times of Liberal Democracy* 238; possessive individualism 2, 128–9; *Possessive Individualism* 230; Rawls 121–2, 244; *Real World of Democracy* 230; rights 125–6; social change 192–3; State, 81–4
Mandel, Ernest 235, 240, 241
Mann, M. 236
Marcuse, H. *Eros and Civilization* 233, 242
Marx, Karl 1, 3, 17, 101 ff.; alienation 30–2, 37; contradictions of capitalism 31, 37 ff.; 40–2; democratic commitment 71–7, 102–5; *Early Writings* 238, 239; *The First International and After* 239; *Gotha Programme* 70 f.; Hegel 25–32, 37, 67–9; historicism 30, 47, 49–51; human needs 24, 233; humanism 11 f., 65–7; individualism 22–5, 30, 32–4, 65–7; objective interests 42–6; political liberties 76–7; political philosophy and ethics 2, 5–6, 102 f., 106–9; *The Poverty of Philosophy* 233; Ricardo 41; *The Revolutions of 1848* 238, 240; romanticism 65–6, 77–8; Rousseau 29–30, 109–10; *Selected Works* 230, 233, 234, 235, 236; the state 67–72, 73–7, 240–1; Young Hegelians 48, 69–71
Marxism, behavioural political science 51–6; capitalist crisis 81–4; economic base/superstructure distinction 46–9; ethics 102 ff., 106–9; freedom 111–119; and Rawls's liberalism 110 f., 189–95; revolutionary transformation 79–81; Utopian theory 93–5
May, J. D. 242
Meek, R. *Studies in the Labour Theory of Value* 234, 237
Mill, J. S. 60–5 *passim*, 90, 134, 235, 239
Mill, James 40

INDEX

Miller, Richard 189 f., 248
Mitchell, Juliet *Psychoanalysis and Feminism* 233, 242
Moon, J. Donald 236
Mortimore, G. W. 4, 230
Murphy, J. 'The Vietnam War and Civil Disobedience' 249

Natural Law 210, 213–4, 223–9, 246
New Left 91
Nozick, Robert 1, 5, 239, 244, 247, 248; *Anarchy, State and Utopia* 230; democratic theory 183–5; entitlement 129–31, 161 ff., 165; fairness 163–5; 171–5; Hart 163 f.; historical and end-state principles 130 f., 140, 161 f.; justice 130; minimal state 181–2; possessive individualism 129–131; Rawls 161–5; rectification 182 f.; theory of value 167–70

Ollman, B. 234, 236, *Alienation* 233
Olson, Mancur 39, 45, 52; *The Logic of Collective Action* 235
O'Neill, J. *Modes of Individualism and Collectivism* 231
Order 17–22, 25–8, 38–9

Parekh, B. 233
Parsons, Talcott 15–22 *passim*, 38, 232; *The Structure of Social Action* 231
Participation: democratic ideal 86–91, 242 (n. 2)
Pateman, C. 242
Paternalism 132 f.
Pelczynski, Z. 234
Peters, Richard 205, 249; 'Authority' 248
Plamenatz, John 46, 236, 242
Plato 91–5 *passim*

Pluralism 51–6, 243 (n. 5)
Polsby, Nelson 237
Popper, Karl 17, 230, 237; *The Open Society and its Enemies* 233; Marx 49–51; situational analysis 4 f.
Power: concept 112–19; political, 51–6, 83–4, 195–7

Quinton, Anthony 136 f.

Rawls, John 1, 3, 6, 109–11 *passim*, 119, 123 ff., 133, 164, 166, 238 f., 239, 244, 245, 246, 247, 248, 249; civil disobedience 217; democratic theory 185–9; deontological approach 138–13; gambling problem 150–60; intuitionism 156 f., 175–9; justice 124, 187; liberty 187–90; maximin strategy 148 ff., 246 (n. 5); original position 6, 109 f., 147 f., 157–60 *passim*; political obligation 213; radical individualism 137–43; reflective equilibrium 157, 176 ff.; rights 246 (n. 2); strains of commitment 153–5; *A Theory of Justice* 230.
Reformism 36 ff., 76 ff.
Rex, John 231
Ricardo, David 40 f., 235
Rights, civil 64, 76 f., 125–7, 187–9, 210; property 29, 37, 60, 64, 66 f., 115 f., 162
Rights Thesis 125–27, 137–45
Rousseau, J. J. 5, 60, 64, 65, 109 f., 146, 234; origins of civil society 27–32 *passim*; Utopian theory 91–5 *passim*
Rule of Law 214–16
Runciman, W. G. 236
Russell, Bertrand 216, 249
Ryan, Alan 237

Schumpeter, Joseph 86, 97, 98, 249
Schwartz, Louis B. 245
Singer, M. 245
Singer, Peter 245
Smart, J. J. C. 136, 245
Social Contract 22, 27, 38 f., Rawls 109 f., 146–50, 158 f., 186
Springborg, Patricia 233
State: Lockean theory 182–3; Marxist theory 67–72, 73–7, 81–4, 240 f. (n. 28); Order 18, 25–8
State of Nature 17–22 passim, 26–9, 38 f.
Strategy Analysis 4–7; consciousness 35–43; marxism 40–6; minimal state 181 f.; Rawls's original position 148–52 passim, 186–9; social order 17 f., 38–9
Suchting, W. A. 'Marx, Popper and Historicism' 235, 237

Thompson, E. P. 240
Totalitarianism 50, 75, 241 (n. 32)
Truman, David 243
Tucker, Robert 238

Utilitarianism: democratic theory 86–7; individualism 61–3, 132 –7; legal theory 199–202, 208 –11 passim; property rights 60; rule utilitarianism 134–6
Utopian Theory 78, 91–5; Marxism 95–105

Violence in Politics, 79–81, 222

Walker, Jack 242
Watkins, F. 232
Watkins, J. W. N. 231
Winch, Peter 236

Young Hegelians 68–71